T0381550

A Legacy of Love

A Legacy of Love

The Story of The Ora & Ann Wolfe Family

By Juanita L. Tryon

iUniverse

iUniverse books may be ordered through booksellers or by contacting:

iUniverse
1663 Liberty Drive
Bloomington, IN 47403
www.iuniverse.com
1-800-Authors (1-800-288-4677)

Because of the dynamic nature of the Internet, any web addresses or links contained in this book may have changed since publication and may no longer be valid. The views expressed in this work are solely those of the author and do not necessarily reflect the views of the publisher, and the publisher hereby disclaims any responsibility for them.

Any people depicted in stock imagery provided by Thinkstock are models, and such images are being used for illustrative purposes only. Certain stock imagery © Thinkstock.

ISBN: 978-1-5320-2881-6 (sc)
ISBN: 978-1-5320-2880-9 (e)

Library of Congress Control Number: 2017911228

Print information available on the last page.

iUniverse rev. date: 07/21/2017

Table of Contents

Section III: Life On The Farm

Section IV: Children's Adult Life Chapters

Section V: The Mature Years

Introduction

I want to tell you a story!

This story will be known as the family history of the very close knit, large and rather boisterous family of seven children – well actually eight but I will explain that later – of Ora and Ann Deckard Wolfe. These seven children were all raised in a coal mining/farming area of Southern Indiana.

The musings and memories of the three children of Ora and Ann still living are recorded here. The three still living in this year of 2016 are Juanita Louise (Nita) now 96 just this summer, Robert Wayne (Bob) who turned 90 just after Christmas last year and Ruth Eleanor who was 83 in January of this year.

Together we have decided to make a concentrated, coordinated effort to put as many of the events of the past generation on paper as well as we can remember and record them. To each of us some events are as if they happened yesterday and some are more of a recollection, rather fuzzy around the edges.

This is not a genealogy book of who begat whom filled with names, dates and places. We all feel that who begat whom is not as interesting as what "whom" did after he/she was begat. Our family had its own genealogist by way of marriage. My husband Floyd's sister, Virginia Rose Kennedy, worked as a genealogist for many years. She traced the records of hundreds of names that came to her through the Vigo County Courthouse in Terre Haute. She had free access to all the County records and traveled to many old cemeteries in that area looking for names and dates.

In fact, many years ago Virginia did most of the genealogy research for the Wolfe Deckard families that are used in this book. Known as Aunt Vee to her nieces and nephew, Susan, Janice and Mike, she loved her work and wrote a poem in 1979 that took second place in a genealogy poetry contest it was entered into.

Grandma's Genealogy

Remember as a little child,
You sat on Grandma's knee
And listened while she told you tales
About the family.

She told about the folks she knew
And those she'd heard about.
So many names, she mentioned,
It was hard to sort them out.

You got them pictured one by one;
You had their names to guide you,
And now you'd give a million
Just to have them here beside you.

Grandma isn't here today;
She gave up on life's game.
Oh! How you wish she'd left a list
Of each and every name.

Dear Friends, pray sit thee down today
And write your family tree.
Make notes of those you know today
And those of memory.

Remember, there may come a day
YOUR grandchild on YOUR knee
He'll look up at you longingly
And say, "Grandma, who are we?"

A great regret in these later years of our lives is that we were not more oriented toward family history in 1970 when Bob, always the family historian with a wonderful recall of former events, drew up an extensive outline (the Outline I used) for this book. In trying to get this project underway, Bob gave a section of his outline to each of his siblings, keeping some for himself of course.

Bob not only gave parts of the outline to Juanita and Ruth (and himself) but he gave it to Dale, Evah, James and Max as well. Everyone thought it was a wonderful idea, but no one took it seriously enough to dig in and get to work on it. No one was dedicated enough then to help Bob get started on this monumental project that was so dear to his heart. At that time we had access to not only the memories of the three of us, but of the four who are now gone.

Thanks to our family newsletter, "The Wolfe Call" that was started in the 1980s and carried on for several years, some memories of those four were written by them and captured and saved in the newsletter. Those writings have been used here.

Certainly now, we realize the folly of our actions – or I should say – of our inactions. What we would give now to sit down, the seven of us and reminisce and record our memories. We all know we have a past but when we are younger, busy and sometimes overwhelmed with life it is only natural to be more concerned with the present and the future than the past. Those we deal with on a daily basis.

Thanks to Bob's persistence and his steadfast desire to see this family history written, during all of these years, he saved a myriad of family information that will now become available for the large extended family to enjoy in this family book.

"The greatest gift you can give your family is a strong family narrative." These are the words of the well-known writer, Bruce Feiler. He has proof to offer in the results of psychological testing that firmly establishes the fact that young people who know their family stories are better able to overcome personal difficulties without long term detrimental effect.

Dr. Paul Nussbaum said it in a different way. In his book, "Save Your Mind", he said "The most valuable asset you have to leave to your younger family members is your family story. Keep your mind active so you can convey it."

Even Ann Landers said in one of her columns a few years back, "The most wonderful gift from a grandparent is an oral history."

It seems good to have our intuitive feelings confirmed. From the earliest family reunions the seven members of the second generation wanted to help the younger family members understand the hardships our parents had needed to overcome in rearing seven children to active, productive citizens during this period in our history. We knew it motivated us – we felt it would motivate our children.

To do this, we used our annual family reunions to tell and demonstrate the family narrative – our story. But in this environment it could only be done piece meal at best. Here the three of us (Juanita, Bob and Ruth), have done our best to describe the lifestyle of the first generation (Ora and Ann) and each of the second generation until they became adults. We have endeavored to do this as fully and as accurately as we can.

Friends close to the family often seem surprised at the closeness of family members and the strength of the family bonds. We believe the teamwork required to have a successful reunion every year for nearly 50 years - and not a year has been missed - is in a large way responsible for this closeness.

It has been difficult to know just where would be the best place to stop for this story. We certainly know the narrative does not stop here. However, we feel certain the third or fourth generation is better equipped to continue the story for accuracy and to more properly describe the difficulties faced by our family in later years.

These difficulties are not the same as the hardships of life on a "hard scrabble" farm during the depression years or earning a living 200 feet underground. It seems that the difficulties, while no easier to overcome, have been more relational including addictions, frequent job changes and those resulting from our changing national culture. This seems a perfect reason to have our family exert increased influence.

We are hopeful that future generations will be more diligent than we have been and capture pertinent information while those who can contribute are available. We have wished so many times we could ask questions of family members who are no longer here.

We have confidence that later generations can further develop this narrative and continue its influence in our family culture. We believe this challenge is worthy of time and effort by third and fourth generation members.

Section I

ORA AND ANN WOLFE – FOUNDING COUPLE

Chapter 1

Courtship Of Ora And Ann

Ora Wolfe and Ann Deckard were both products of hard-working farm people which set their life style for their future years. They both were born and raised in rural Sullivan County, Indiana, in farm homes approximately two miles apart. They attended different churches and different schools so they had not been life-long friends.

The five girls and two boys in the Deckard home, as well as their mother and father, were very active members in the neighborhood Hickory Methodist Church. The siblings all attended Park School, a one-room red brick schoolhouse within easy walking distance, about three-quarters of a mile, from their home.

Ora's family of four boys and one girl and their parents were members of Berea Church of Christ on Indiana State Road 54, about a mile and a half north of their home. They attended Pirtle School in their district.

In one of his notes, Dale, the oldest son of Ora and Ann, remembered that although it was not a topic for much discussion, he asked Dad (Ora) once how he and Mom (Ann) met. Dad told him, "The first time I laid eyes on Ann Deckard was at a special meeting at Hickory Church. I asked her if I could walk her home and she answered that she would be pleased to have me do so."

Church was a social, as well as a religious gathering, and one of the most likely places for young people to meet in the early 1900's. One of the activities for young people at Hickory Church at that time was a Glee Club. A Glee Club is a musical group or choir group, which traditionally specializes in the singing of short songs. Ann and her sisters, who all loved to sing, were members of this singing group. They traveled with the Glee Club performing for various churches, picnics and other outdoor events in the area.

The mode of transportation for the Glee Club was a wagon fitted with four corner posts and a canvas top trimmed all around with fringe. Three teams of decorated horses pulling the open wagon full of beautiful young women, seated for traveling, was an impressive sight. It was not by accident that a picture of the Glee Club on one of these outings showed Ora riding his horse beside the wagon as one of the flag bearers. Ann's brothers were probably among the young men on horseback also.

No doubt a great part of the songs the Glee Club sang were the beautiful old hymns that our generation grew up with and still love to sing today. Nothing speaks to my soul like the old hymns do. Other songs popular in those early days and maybe sung by the Glee Club at picnics or other summer activities were, "Wait Till the Sun Shines Nellie", "Shine on Harvest Moon", "Put on Your Old Gray Bonnet", "Sweet Adeline" and many others we still enjoy at "sing-alongs".

A large part of Ora and Ann's courtship would have included just visiting at Ann's home, meals around the table or outdoor games such as baseball or croquet. We all remember hearing a funny story about one of Ora's visits in Ann's home. Bob, youngest of Ora and Ann's four boys, in particular, remembers hearing it many times and relates it thus:

> *"Ora had gone home from church with Ann's family for Sunday dinner. With Ann's brothers and sisters, Floyd, Tilda, Dulsee and Alice all still at home and maybe Lon or Ina who were married with their spouses, the table must have been full, maybe even a little crowded.*
>
> *Floyd was seated next to Ora. The meal proceeded quietly, for the Dutch farmers were known to be a rather sober lot. Floyd wanted a pickle from a dish on the other side of Ora. Instead of asking for the pickles to be passed, he reached with his fork, stretching over Ora's plate.*
>
> *Feeling this was a bit impolite and no doubt with a young competitive urge, Ora, being more of a free spirit than was customary at this table, intercepted the pickle with his fork, on the way to Floyd's plate.*
>
> *Having made such a commotion and ending up with no pickle was a bit embarrassing to Floyd. Being a bit older and larger than Ora, Floyd was prepared to defend his right to the pickle.*
>
> *By this time, Ann's father, always kind but also rather stern, looked up through his eyebrows and said quietly, "Boys that will be enough." Settle down and eat your dinner!" And that was the end of the subject. Nothing more needed to be said."*

Ann was the fourth of the Deckard children to leave home when she and Ora married in 1910. Lon, Ina and Floyd had all found their mates and married previously.

One by one, that nest was being emptied.

Marriage Of Ora And Ann

Ora and Ann were married September 18, 1910, the day of Ora's twenty-third birthday. Ann was 20 but turned 21 about three months after their wedding. They were wed at the Deckard home place.

It must have been a festive occasion for with two older brothers and an older sister already married there was much to celebrate.

Ann's white wedding gown was, of course floor length and was made of fine taffeta. The short sleeved bodice was decorated with literally dozens of tiny stitched-down pleats from the rounded neckline to the waist. It was worn over a long sleeved under bodice of very fine netting encrusted with stitched- in floral pieces and the high, ruffled collar was held upright and in place with small metal stays.

The full skirt was pleated at the waistline and hung in folds over two or three petticoats. Her tightly corseted fourteen inch waistline was emphasized with a matching ribbon belt with a bow on the side. White silk high-heeled, high top shoes that buttoned up the sides completed the ensemble.

Ora was resplendent in a dark wool suit with a cream colored vest, white shirt with a white celluloid collar and a white ascot tie. His shiny black shoes with high tops buttoned up the sides.

Not much is known about the wedding gifts the newly married couple received. We do know Ann's parents gave them a cow and a calf and we believe the tall wooden churn was a wedding gift from them, too. I also think I remember hearing that Ora's parents gave them bedding including a straw tick filled with straw and a feather bed or feather mattress as we would think of it. All her married life, Ann had a collection of beautiful dishes she cherished and some of them may have been wedding gifts from her sisters and brothers.

The young couple rented a small house a little way west of Scotchtown, on the way to

Sullivan, known as the Dromedary Place. When asked many years later why they moved there, Ann told Bob, "Oh, Dad thought he was going to get rich farming."

However, at age 23 Ora started to work in a coal mine, so that would have been during the first year of their marriage. No doubt a job in the underground mine became available and with a wife and a new baby on the way it seemed more logical to take a job with a regular weekly payday than to plant corn and wait for the farmer's harvest to mature for income.

Coal mining had been active in the United States since Colonial times, but became a major industry in the 1800's with a number of new mineral discoveries causing a series of mining "rushes". Bituminous coal had become one of Indiana's most valuable resources and Shirley Hill Coal Company had opened its Shirley Hill Mines No. 21 & 22 in 1906 and Ora spent his early working years there in the underground tunnels.

Nine months and four days after Ora and Ann's wedding, they became the proud parents of their first child, a boy they named Dale.

By the time their second child, a boy they named George Edward after both grandfathers, George Washington Deckard and Charles Edward Wolfe, was born in 1913, the couple had just bought and moved into a three-room house that was just a long stone's throw from the log home where Ann was born and raised.

With three of her sisters still unmarried and living at home, it must have seemed to Ann to be the best of both worlds. She certainly relished being a new wife and the mother of two healthy, happy baby boys and to have her mother and sisters within walking distance must have seemed like the icing on the cake. Her older sister, Ina, had been married since April of 1907 and she and her husband, Frank Creager lived within walking distance to the east of Ora and Ann.

The new home was three good-sized rooms and was adequate for the small growing family. It was situated on a four and one-half acre plot of land that provided plenty of fertile land for a good big garden, plus plenty of space for chickens to be raised for meat and eggs, cows for milk and butter, a few pigs for meat and horses. The horses pulled the plow to break the ground for gardening as well as pulling the wagon and buggy for chores and travel.

The three room house was built in a T formation with the front room facing the road (the east) and this room was centered between the two other rooms attached in back. A door went through the west side of the living room into the north room which was the bedroom and a single door on the south side of the west wall gave entrance to the kitchen. The north wall of the living room was fitted with another door that opened out to a nice open porch.

From the porch, not only the North/South road in front of the house was in view but the main road running east and west about 500 feet to the north was plainly visible. That was helpful, because, just as we can usually tell whose car is parked across the street or pulling into the drive today, folks then could recognize whose horse or team of horses with buggy, wagon or some mode of transportation, was arriving.

Ora and Ann's home was rather sparsely furnished but included the necessities and that seemed to be enough. A stand-table in the center of the living room held a lamp (when needed), a folding bed and a few chairs furnished the room. Between the two doors that led out into the kitchen and the bedroom was a chimney, so a stove could be set up in the winter. A big round Warm Morning Heating Stove provided warmth in the living room and was taken down and moved out of the house in the summer.

Although Ora and Ann were blessed to be close to Ann's family, they were also fortunate enough to have a few other good neighbors which became lifelong friends. The lane that turned south from the main road and went past their house, continued on for three quarters of a mile and had three more houses before it ended just over a little ditch with a rather rickety bridge and on up a small hill to a dead end where the last house stood.

The closest house south was another three-room house similar to Ora and Ann's. It was used as a rental property, therefore, those neighbors changed frequently. Nora and Earl Long were among the renters and with small children about the same ages as Ora and Ann's it proved to be a good relationship and the two families remained friends for many years, even after the Longs moved away.

Johnny and Ellen Boone lived next door to the rental property. They were older and had lived there for a few years when Ora and Ann bought their place. The Boone's had a beautiful daughter, Alta who became a good friend to Ora and Ann's children although she was older. The Boone house was built on a little grander scale and had a sweeping porch around the front and south side of the house. Ellen was friendly and a good neighbor to Ann.

Different families moved in and out of the house on the hill, but most of them had children who made good playmates and friends for Ora and Ann's children.

Where the lane Ora and Ann lived on, intersected the main county road, a three room house was constructed like Ora and Ann's, except the porch was added to the south side of the house instead of the north side. Rufus and Mattie Brewer bought that house when they moved to Indiana from Virginia and lived there with their four children, Ed, John, Myrtle and Annalou. Their house sat on a 1 ½ acre plot and gave them room for a garden and corn patch, but they were never farmers nor had cattle.

Mattie and Ann were close friends as long as Mattie lived and she lived there until she died as an old woman. The Brewer children were older – more the ages of Ora and Ann – and they all married and moved into homes of their own before most of Ora and Ann's children were born.

Being from Virginia (Virginnie Mattie called it), some people in the neighborhood thought of them as "Hillbillies" but Ann always treated Mattie with dignity and insisted her children do so as well. We honored her with the title Grandma (actually, we called her Granny) and she lived up to the title for we all spent time at her house and she cared for us.

Rufus understood the soil and told Dale the exposed yellow clay hills needed to be protected from the sun - with weeds, hay, straw or any sort of mulch.

Granny kept milk, fresh meat, lunch meat, and butter in the well near the water, as her only refrigeration. In those days all wells did not have pumps and such was Granny's. Bricks, the same as the sidewalls in the well were brought on up out of the well to about waist height. An arbor five or six feet higher than the bricks was built for a grapevine, climbing roses or a climbing floral vine of some kind. This was built over the well for shade which helped to keep the water cool in the summer.

Directly above the well a pulley was attached so a sturdy wooden bucket or even just a heavy zinc bucket attached to a long heavy rope run through the pulley was used to draw water. This bucket was Granny's refrigeration and she pulled it up as she needed milk or butter or something that was in it. If she needed water, she had to pull the bucker up, unload it, lower the bucket and bring up water, pour it into the household bucket, reload the contents and lower it again to the water. It was remarkable how good that cool, clear water tasted.

Later, when Rufus had died and "Uncle" Bill Mosier was courting Mattie, (she had three husbands) Uncle Bill walked across the field from the road past No. 1 coal mine and sometimes stopped and ate with us before he walked on to Mattie's. If we had chicken, Mom often scalded, skinned and fried the feet, he would eat the chicken feet, crunching the bones, right up to the leg. If we were eating popcorn, like on a Sunday afternoon, there was one dish pan for the family and one for Uncle Bill.

Chapter 3

Ora's Genealogy

When talking about his ancestry, Ora always said proudly, "I'm Scotch, Irish, Welsh and Johnny Bull." We all knew that "Johnny Bull" meant English. Being young and unimpressed at that time with family ancestry, I never questioned him about which parent came from which country. I do not remember that any of my siblings did either.

My research shows that "Wolfes" were of English, Dutch, German, Welsh and Irish origin, but I have not been able to determine, with certainly, from which lines our family was descended. The Wolfe family name is thought to be of Norman origin and, as most names did, comes from an early family member who bore some "fancied" resemblance to the wolf, either in appearance or behavior.

Endless spelling variations are a prevailing characteristic of Norman surnames. Old Middle English lacked any spelling rules and medieval scribes generally spelled words the way they sounded to them, so the same person is often referred to by different spellings in different documents. This name has been spelled Wolfe, Wolff, Wolf, Woolf, Wolfe, Wolff, De Wolfe and many more ways.

W O L F E, as our name is spelled, is considered to be the English spelling and they were first found in Cheshire, England where they were descended from Hugh Lupus Wolfe, the Earl of Chester, a subject of King William the Conqueror.

Ora's great, great grandfather, George A. Wolfe, was born in 1782 in Tennessee. Nothing was found about when his family came to Tennessee or from where they had come.

In 1803, George married Rebecca Simpson in Tennessee. It is assumed that they moved shortly after their marriage to Ohio as their first child, Thomas Jefferson Wolfe, was born there in 1804. The rest of their nine children are recorded as being born in Ohio also. George, however, is recorded as having died in 1858 in Warren County, Indiana at the home of a daughter.

Ora's great grandfather, Thomas Jefferson Wolfe, married Eliza A. Messick in 1831. They continued to live in Ohio until about 1840, and then moved to Indiana. Four of their ten children were born in Ohio and the six younger ones were born in Indiana.

John Jefferson Wolfe, Ora's grandfather, was born in 1833 and was the firstborn of Thomas and Eliza. He (John) married Nancy Jane Empson in 1856. We assume they wed in Indiana since that is where the family had moved when John was about eight years old.

Charles Edward Wolfe was Ora's father and the grandfather of my siblings and me. He was the second child of John Jefferson and Nancy Jane's ten children. The oldest child and the youngest were girls with eight boys in between.

On April 16, 1877, John Jefferson and Nancy Jane had twin boys, Ira and Ora. The twins were not strong and healthy. Ira died at the age of four months and Ora died at about 14 months of age. What a heartbreak this must have been for the family…the older children as well as the parents. Charles Edward was 15 years old and his older sister, Eva, was 17.

Charles Edward, second child of John Jefferson and Nancy Jane, was born on April 27, 1864, in Sullivan County, Indiana. On February 8, 1887, when he was 23 years of age, he married Isarelda Elvira Woodward, also of Sullivan County.

Isarelda Elvira's father was Eli Woodward, name pronounced "Woodard" our father would point out to us. He probably came from Virginia to Ohio, following his marriage to Margaret McCormick. Their children, including Elvira's father, were born in Ohio. Eli was the third child and born April 1, 1818.

Isarelda was born into a rather unusual family situation. Her father, Eli, married Eliza Jane Ammerman on October 19, 1837. They had a family of eight children before Eliza Jane died on March 18, 1863 at age 43. On March 17, 1864, Eli married Ruth E. Shipman Pirtle, the widow of George Pirtle. The first of the six children born to this union was Isarelda Elvira. Their fifth child was Clement Woodward, who died at 6 months of age. Not only did Isarelda Elvira have five siblings by her mother, Ruth Shipman Pirtle, but she also had eight half brothers and sisters from her father's first marriage to Eliza Jane Ammerman. She may also have had half brothers and sisters from her mother's previous marriage to George Pirtle, but no record was found of that.

Charles Edward and Isarelda Elvira (our grandparents) were known to family and friends as Ed and Elvira and began their married life in a small home near Sullivan, Indiana, in the Shiloh Church area. Their first child was our father, Ora Clement Wolfe, born on September 18, 1887, in Sullivan County. Although, I never heard it discussed, I believe we can safely assume that he was named after Ed's little brother, Ora, who died at 14 months and Elvira's little brother, Clement, who died at 6 months of age.

This union produced three more boys: Walter William born September 10, 1889, Raymond Earl born on Ora's birthday, September 18, 1891 and Dova Earnest, born August 7, 1893.

The daughter that I'm sure Elvira longed for, was born on November 1, 1895 and named Fay. Her joy was to be short lived, as there was an epidemic of diphtheria not long after Fay was born.

Diphtheria was a disease that was highly contagious and deadly for children. Fay contracted diphtheria and died on October 11, 1887, less than a month before her second birthday.

At that time, there were no effective immunizations or medications to help. Diphtheria was a disease of the upper respiratory system and started with a sore throat, fever and chills. It caused a thick covering to form over the back of the airways and made breathing very difficult. It was called the "strangling angel of children", "throat distemper" and "throat ail". Now there are vaccines and special medicines to fight this disease, so epidemics are unknown. However, current reports I read stated that of those who get diphtheria today, one out of ten actually dies from it.

It was five years before another baby was born to Ed and Elvira, but on July 22, 1900, a baby girl was born and was named May. This event must have brought much joy, especially to Grandma (Elvira). Her baby girl at last.

Bob remembers our Dad saying that his father, Ed, left home for two years when times were hard to "follow the harvest". Dad felt that he just needed to get away from home and Bob has no memories of his saying where these years were spent. I recall Mom saying that he may have just felt the need to get away for a while. Grandma, Elvira, was known to have a sharp tongue and to make her feelings known. This could have been a time of frustration and depression and Grandpa, Ed, having a much milder disposition, may have felt it best to leave for a while. Since there are five years between the birth of Fay and May, this may have been that time. This is speculation but seems to make sense.

Imagine what this must have been like for Grandma to be alone, with small children, in a rural setting for two years. It couldn't have been easy. Consider a young mother with four young boys who need three meals a day; clothing, clean and mended; chores, both indoors and out. There were no doubt cows for milk, cream and butter. Cows must be milked twice a day and the milk strained and kept cool and when the cream came to the top it would need to be removed, saved and churned into butter. There would have been chickens for eggs and meat and they would need to be fed and watered twice a day and the eggs gathered daily. It would have been necessary to grow a garden every summer for potatoes and turnips for winter eating and many other vegetables to eat fresh, but also to can for the winter's food.

Heat in winter would be a challenge as well, as it would have been wood fireplaces which meant wood chopping and ashes to be carried out each day. The cook stove would also have been wood and/or coal fired.

The mode of travel would have been on foot, by horseback or horse and buggy. Horses, of course, need care twice a day also.

I'm sure some of the children could have helped but this would have been a near full time job for a man and wife with some children's help but it seems an incomprehensible task for a woman alone, even with some help from her boys.

It is not known if Grandpa sent money home, but one of the souvenirs from his trip "out west" was the ear of a jack rabbit which he brought back for my Dad, Ora. Dad kept this for years and proudly showed it to his own children and to anyone else he thought might be interested. There was also a pair of brass knuckles which one of Ora's great grandchildren has now.

One of Dad's treasures from his family was a lovely basket that his father had made for him. It was to serve as his lunch pail when he started to school. It was about a three-quart size and made from white ash and no other materials. Grandpa started with the trunk of a dried white ash tree, split it with wedges, and then brought the pieces about 10-12 feet long into the house. On long winter evenings he would rive widths with a small froe into very small strips. These were then soaked in water to make them pliable and then they were woven into a basket. The handle, rim and stays were small white ash branches that were soaked to make them pliable enough to bend and form into the shape of the basket. Bob said, "I always loved this lunch basket and I talked Dad out of it when I returned from the Navy. Unfortunately, I was not committed enough to take proper care of it and it was stolen from Nita's back porch when I was living at her home, in about 1947".

The following story is Bob's memories of Grandma and Grandpa's "house on the hill" and was written by him many years ago. All siblings remember being at this house:

> Although the childhood home of Ora was well known to all his children it was seen as an empty, old-fashioned home on a high hill by his grandchildren.
>
> Being one of the few two-story homes in the vicinity and located on a prominent point on a high plateau, it seemed immense to the grandchildren who visited from small homes and had large families.
>
> This was the third home which Ora's family lived in and they moved there when he was 13 years old. He had previously lived near the Pirtle Schoolhouse in the Shiloh neighborhood and another house near the Sulphur Springs, also in the Shiloh area.
>
> This home was located one and one-half miles west of Uncle Lon Deckard's home on the only road leading off the gravel road from Route 54 near Berea Church to the Aunt Sade corner. This was a dirt road, very picturesque in summer and fall but a rutted nightmare in winter and a quagmire in early spring. It wound through woods, descending to Buttermilk Creek, with the entrance to the farm just before crossing the creek.
>
> The entrance was a classic of the area, having large gateposts with an overhead beam and a real "boughten" metal gate. From the gate, the house was visible through a stand of huge oaks on a "high" hill.

The first set of buildings on the right consisted of a wagon shed and corn crib with a larger shed used as a garage in later years. Further on was a barn in the lowlands on the right and through the barn lot gate stood another wagon and tool shed, with all past automobile license plates nailed to the wall. A well with a pump, a watering trough for livestock and a coconut shell drinking cup for Grandpa and anyone else who could drink the pungent Sulphur water. Grandpa was the only farmer in the area with a Red Poll dairy herd.

To the left on up the hill was the house, smoke house, meat house, outside toilet, chicken house, and garden and calf lot. These were considered the "women folks" responsibilities. There was also a well there for the calves, chickens and Grandma's drinking water.

The house was two story and the downstairs consisted of a good sized living room heated only with a coal fired "grate" (fireplace) in the east end, a large kitchen and a bedroom.

The kitchen is the most remembered room. There was a long table in the center near a south window and a cook stove (wood/coal burning) on the north side. A small table was centered under the west window and contained two water buckets since each grandparent required their own drinking water. A cream separator, a pie safe and the walnut corner cupboard which was painted every few years with yellow brown floor paint to "clean it up a bit".

After Grandma and Grandma sold their farm, this three cornered cupboard spent several years in the kitchen at The Farm home and when Dad built modern built in cabinets for the kitchen there, it moved to the garage where Dad stored tools in it. When Dad moved to Michigan after Mom's death, it was moved to our (Bob and Ginnie's) home. We removed the many coats of paint down to the beautiful walnut wood and it now resides with our older daughter and her husband, Linda and Del Shannon.

One other piece of furniture remembered is the gramophone in the living room.

A stairway off the west end of the living room led to a two room upstairs which was used by four boys, Ora, Raymond, Walter and Ernie, at one time. In later years it was a haven for the grandchildren who found old copies of The Saturday Evening Post with exciting Western stories to while away the time on cold or rainy Sundays or workdays while the adults visited or worked.

The entrance to the house used by the family and friends was from the south porch into the living room, while strangers would knock at the living room door on the north porch. The north porch was always kept clean and neat for sitting in the evening or Sunday afternoons, while the south porch had the clutter of farm tools used in everyday farm life---buckets for garden produce or chicken feed use, half bushel measures, axe, pitchfork, shovel, etc. The north porch provided a good view of the road and gate, while the south view was of the "working" area of the farm.

Visits to the home were of two kinds—those to help with farm activities when many congregated to help in threshing, haying, etc. and Sunday afternoon social visits with the family.

This farm was one of the few in the area that raised wheat on the high plateau on the eastern part of the property. This required binding, shocking, threshing with large crews, dinners at noon for the crew, straw stacks and wheat in two bushel (120 lbs.) bags, cooking the tremendous dinners with two meats or more, lots of vegetables and pies, cakes and fruit for dessert.

The men spent time in friendly banter, talking farming, livestock and outdoor sports, while the young men tried feats of strength. John Wolfe, oldest son of Uncle Raymond, became a hero by lifting a two bushel bag of wheat (120 lbs.) over the sideboard of a wagon with his teeth!!

A straw stack usually stacked in the calf lot, provided shelter for the calves, a slide for the grandchildren and straw for new "straw ticks" for everyone. These were a part of the bedding and used under feather "ticks". They were most welcome after the older straw lost its loft even though it was stirred and fluffed every day. Often the straw would be so high on the first night of use that the small fry would need to stand on a chair or be helped up to get into bed. Alas, it soon shrank as it became matted but the fresh aroma lingered.

Haying time consisted of cutting hay, using a sulky rake for windrowing, sometimes shocking the hay before storing it loose in the big barn loft or stacking it in the field. This farm was one of the few with a buck rake used to carry shocks or windrows to the barn or stack and that saved the time and effort of stacking loose hay on a wagon.

If the hay was put in the loft, a hay fork on a trolley was used. In good years there was extra...usually stacked in the south lowlands. A typical way would be with Bob or Max bringing in the hay with a buck rake, older grandchildren pitching it on the stack. Ora, who was a good craftsman and could shape and "top out" a stack, would be in the command position on top. Sometimes he would put a son on the stack and with much detailed, though largely unintelligible instructions, would teach the boy the skill.

The farm also contained a good amount of woods, part of which Grandad termed his "walnut orchard" and good bottom land along Buttermilk Creek... used for growing grain.

The farm was sold at auction in 1941 after Grandad's age, coupled with the disappointment and financial strain of seven consecutive losses of his corn crop, made it unattractive for him to continue.

Since Grandma and Grandpa Wolfe lived some distance from us, we did not see them very often. Actually it was only about two miles distance, but the mode of transportation, by foot, on horseback or horse and wagon, made it seem quite a long way.

Grandma did not seem to be a very happy person and was known to be sharp spoken and to make known her wishes. Some of that may have been due to the hard life on the farm. I saw her smile occasionally but I do not remember ever hearing her laugh. Also, I do not ever remember her being affectionate to any of us children. I never recall her hugging us or holding any of us on her lap. We were all pretty much in awe of her. I wouldn't say that we were afraid of her for she was not mean to us, but we never felt close to her or felt that any of us were special in any way to her.

We always felt that Grandma favored Aunt May's children and in retrospect, knowing how she must have longed for a daughter and especially after the loss of her first girl baby, it is easier to understand now how that might have been true. Being her only daughter and youngest child, Aunt May probably visited her often and brought her children along which would mean she would have seen them more often and known them better.

Recently, Aunt May's only daughter, Betty, told me the story of Grandma's riding horse, Peekaboo. She said that Grandma used to ride her, side-saddle, and "sail" over the fence on her so that she wouldn't need to get off to open and close the gate. Betty told her that she feared that she would fall off the horse during the jumps and Grandma answered, "I'm not about to fall off that horse. I had my leg wrapped around that saddle horn." Grandma always rode Peekaboo side-saddle.

Grandpa was a very even tempered person. Bob remembered him often with a twinkle in his eye and ready with a pleasant story or joke. In Dale's notes about the Wolfe grandparents he said, "The Wolfe grandparents lived farther away and we never had a close relationship with them as we did with the Deckards. I remember Grandma as rather loud and sharp-spoken. Grandpa was the opposite and he and I had a high regard for each other."

I recall one summer that Evah and I went to stay overnight with Grandma and Grandpa. Mom had called on the old wall mounted telephone and made arrangements. After breakfast Evah and I set out to walk the two miles to their house. Grandma called back when we got there to tell Mom that we were okay.

I believe that I was about 7 or 8 years old and Evah about 11 or 12. It was a strange feeling to be there without Mom and Dad but we enjoyed it. Even helping Grandma do the dishes was fun because her dishes were so different from ours. We were there for lunch and for supper that day. After breakfast the next morning, we folded our night clothes, put them back into the brown paper bag and walked the two miles home.

While we were visiting with Grandma and Grandpa, it was the first time I had seen Grandma use the cream separator and I was fascinated by it. It was a large piece of equipment that stood in the kitchen and was pushed against the wall until Grandma pushed it out to use it. It had a large round, metal bowl on top, two spouts at different levels and a long crank handle. The bottom part was just a stand but was attached and had two metal plates that could be swung out for the receiving buckets to sit on. Grandpa milked the cows and brought the milk into the house. Grandma then would strain it and pour it into the large bowl on top of the separator. The crank was then turned at a good pace and shortly, the milk came out one spout and the cream came out the other. I thought it absolutely amazing and simply could not understand how that big machine (it was taller than I was) knew what was milk and what was cream. I have since learned that it used centrifugal force and when Grandma turned the handle it spun the inside of the bowl and the milk, being heavier, came out one spout and the cream which was lighter came out the other spout. I still find that pretty amazing.

Another thing that Grandma and Grandpa had that we children loved was a gramophone. It played music and on the few occasions we were able to listen to it, it seemed remarkable. It was made of oak wood and stood about four feet high. It was about 24" wide and 24" deep. It had a lid, that, when it was lifted exposed the record and a movable arm with a needle that played the music when it was placed on the record. The record was a cylinder about 4 inches in diameter and 6 inches in length, as I remember it. There was a handle to wind the machine until the spring was tight, then the needle was placed on the cylinder and the music played. If the spring wound down before the song was finished, the cylinder turned very slowly and distorted the words and the music, at which time you must quickly rewind and the song would go back to normal and finish the music.

After the farm was sold at auction in 1941, Grandpa and Grandma moved into a smaller frame house in Sullivan and lived there until Grandpa's death in 1944. Grandpa probably missed the active farm life. He always seemed to love farming and was very successful in his early years. Shortly before his death, Grandpa was found unconscious along the roadside of Highway 54 in Busseron Bottom by a man in an automobile. He was taken to Mary Sherman Hospital in Sullivan and died shortly after. He had not told Grandma he was going anywhere, but she thought that he must have been trying to walk back to the farm.

After Grandpa's death, Grandma moved into a small house in Dugger about two blocks from Aunt May's home. Here it was not hard for Aunt May to get to her house to help her in her old age. Also, Mom and Dad could go into Dugger often to see her and Dad was often in the area alone and stopped to visit with her. The last time I saw Grandma, she was sitting up in bed. I remember her pretty white hair, put up in a bun in the back.

Grandma lived alone in this small house in Dugger for the remainder of her life and died at her home on February 13, 1957, just about two months after her 92nd birthday. She had appointed Dad (Ora) her oldest son, as executor of her estate, so it was his responsibility to see that everything was settled legally and fairly. Her estate was very small but Dad felt honored to be able to fulfill his mother's final wishes.

Chapter 4 ═══════════════════════════════════

Ann's Genealogy

In the early 1700's Ann Deckard's ancestors came from near Metz, Germany (now Lorraine, France) to America by way of New York City and eventually settled in the Southwestern part of the State of Virginia. By about 1830-1832, they had all left Virginia and settled in Monroe County, Indiana. They also spread into the other nearby counties of Lawrence, Brown, Green and Sullivan and some even into the state of Missouri.

Ann's grandfather, John Wesley Deckard, was born on November 26, 1823 in Virginia. Records show that in 1850 he married Mahala Ann Butcher in Bloomington, Indiana. After their marriage they moved from Monroe County to Hamilton Township and thereafter into Cass Township in Sullivan County. There they became the parents of 11 children, Ann's father being the second oldest. The eleven were:

James Adams	born October 24, 1850
George Washington	born March 30, 1852 / d. February 4, 1927 (75 yrs.)
Matilda	born December 21, 1853
William Henry (Burl)	born April 22, 1857 / October 10,1916 (59)
Kizzie Arabelle	born September 26, 1858 d. /May 4, 1886 (28)
John Wesley, Jr,	born March 7, 1861
Daniel Voorhees	born September 26, 1863 / d. August, 1865 (2 yrs.)
Andrew Jackson	born March 31, 1865 d. December 11, 1883 (18)
Martha Marie	born June 26, 1867
Sampson Richard	born August 7, 1869 / d. August 14, 1897 (28)
Mahala Jane	born September 8, 1871 / July 2, 1895 (24)

Records show that John Wesley's father (Ann's great-grandfather) was born in 1781 in Wytheville, Virginia and died in Monroe County, Indiana in 1839. He married Christina Hildenborg on September 16, 1814. Christina's father came to America in 1776 and according to the records he served in the Revolutionary Army as a soldier for the next seven years.

Part of favorite family lore were stories about John Wesley's daughter (Ann's aunt), Martha Marie. Although most of Ann's father's siblings spent their lifetime in or near Sullivan County, Aunt Matt, as she was affectionately known by Ann and her siblings, broke that tradition. Aunt Matt married a lawyer, Frederick Grant Boatright on June 6, 1867 and moved to Cordele, Georgia. Here she raised her two children and lived until her death.

Aunt Matt was privileged to have a more affluent lifestyle than her siblings and when she came to visit her parents "up north" she brought with her a Negro woman to care for her children. In later years, Ann told her own children stories about Aunt Matt's "darkie" maid. At that time, black people were rare in Sullivan County and so the presence of a Negro woman in a stiffly starched uniform created quite a stir. The maid was also charged with keeping the two Boatright children, Bernard and Fredrica, in starched clean clothes. Keeping two young children spotless on an Indiana farm was no small task, especially when summer rains created muddy roads and fields.

Aunt Matt continued to create family history when she was granted Membership No. 195379 in the Daughters of the American Revolution, Fort Early Chapter, at Cordele, Georgia on December 6, 1923.

Ann's father, George Washington Deckard, was born on March 30, 1852, near Sullivan, Indiana. On his 30th birthday, he married Nancy Lucilla Robertson, March 30, 1882 and continued the family tradition as a farmer. He and Nancy Lucilla, called Lute by her husband and friends, became the parents of nine children. Seven of these children lived to rear families of their own in the area.

The children of George Washington and Nancy Lucilla Robertson Deckard were:

Alonzo Edward	born	June 8, 1883
Ina Deckard`	born	November 9, 1884
Kate Ivy	born	April 12, 1886 (died about 1893)
Floyd Benton	born	March 3, 1887
Susie Ann	born	December 25, 1889
Dulsee Jane	born	March 14, 1892
Bertha Murl	born	December 23, 1893
Matilda Lucy	born	December 31, 1895
Maty Alice	born	March 6, 1897

True to the sturdy pioneer stock from which they came, one spring day shortly after they were married, George and Lute pulled a wagon up under a large oak tree, used a tarpaulin to cover the wagon bed to serve as a sleeping room, built a "lean-to" and covered it with brush for a summer kitchen. With two hired men to help, they built a two-room home of logs. Here George started his career as a farmer and he and Lute produced their first child, Alonzo (Lon), the year after they were married. Every one to two years until 1897, a new child was born to this union.

As a successful farmer, George continued to acquire land in the area and when he died he owned more than 500 acres of Sullivan County land. He was well known and respected in the community and was known to invest money in various enterprises. Among his investments was the Mutual Truck Company and it was said that he had loaned money to one man to start an automobile agency. Dale (Ann's oldest child) worked for his grandfather as a youth and said that he remembered hearing his grandfather talk about investing and he listened as it was discussed with people who came to talk with his grandfather.

As children were born into George and Lute's family, the two room log cabin was no longer adequate. So, extra rooms were added. The original log rooms were kept intact and used as usual while the building was in progress. The new rooms were added and the original logs were also enclosed with lumber to match the new additions.

To the north of the log cabin, a large room was added for a kitchen-dining area and a second large room was added to the west side facing the road. This west room was called the parlor and the original room with the fireplace became the sitting room. A nice wide "L" shaped porch was added alongside the new rooms and this space holds many family memories of dinners there in summer. The new north porch off the kitchen served as a dining area in summer and a pass through opening from kitchen to porch was very handy when harvest dinners were served.

When it was time for crops to be harvested, extra "hands" were needed to help the men of the family. Some were hired and some came to lend their hands for payment of return help when their crops were ready. Several neighbors, who might also be relatives, gathered early in the morning, soon after breakfast, and worked from sun up to sundown if necessary. The women of the neighborhood came early as well, to help the woman of the house prepare the harvest dinner to be served at noontime when the men would all troop in from the field tired and hungry. These gatherings were social gatherings as well as work days and the men looked forward to the wonderful food prepared by the ladies and a heavily laden table. The table would have been extended to its full length and filled with platters of fried chicken and usually another meat, maybe meatloaf or roast beef. Large dishes of mashed potatoes, cream gravy, corn (on the cob or cut off and fried), green beans, beets, sliced tomatoes, cucumbers and onions, radishes, and any other produce the garden might be producing at that time.

The lady of the house and her daughters, if she was fortunate enough to have them, were up as early as the men for their responsibility was to see that everything was cooked and on the table when the men came in at noon, expecting the "harvest table". They were never disappointed.

Cakes might have been made the day before needed but pies were made fresh the morning of the day they were to be served. There might be fresh apple or peach, raspberry, plum, maybe even gooseberry pies. Whatever fruit was fresh was used. Cream pies were not forgotten and coconut cream, custard and lemon meringue were favorites. Plenty of iced tea and hot coffee would be served and usually, even fresh hot yeast rolls.

Two or three women would be stationed near the table to keep the food moving and to see that the dishes were refilled when they became empty – or near empty. They could pass the dishes through the opening to the kitchen and receive them back filled with hot food. Always, they were attentive until the men were finished and ready to take a few minutes break before going back to the field.

The women never ate until the men finished and the tables were cleared of the dirty dishes. Then they could refill the serving dishes and set the second table. The women could then eat and visit and have their social time to talk about their families and other neighbors and friends. When they finished, they all stayed until everything was cleaned up and the kitchen was "put to rights" again. It was hard work for everyone but also a festive time to gather and have a social time for all.

Ann had been married about four years and had two children when her Mother was scratched by a cat that she was feeding. It was not thought to be a serious injury, but as the days went by the scratch did not heal and it became infected with blood poisoning. The nearest doctor was in Dugger, which was four miles away. It was winter and it would not have been an easy trip by horse and buggy. It is not known why the doctor did not arrive in time to be of help but unfortunately Lute died on January 12, 1914, at 60 years of age.

Dale, Ann's oldest child, would have been about three and one-half years old at the time of his Grandmother's death and in his notes he records that he remembered seeing her only once. Dale said he remembered her as very sick and that she was out of bed for a very short time. That was probably shortly before her death when Ora and Ann had gone to see her and to see if they could be of help. Nothing is known or recorded about her funeral but she was buried January16, 1914 in Hickory Cemetery.

All the children except Alice were married when their Mother died. Dulsee had just married George Boone on April 13, 1913 and they were living at Dulsee's parents' home at the time. After her Mother's death, Dulsee and her husband stayed on at the Deckard homestead and lived with George. That was the only home they ever had and after his death, Dulsee inherited the house, land and stock.

George, our grandfather, lived another 13 years after the death of his wife. No doubt it was a great help and comfort to have a daughter and her husband in his home. Always a hard worker, he continued farming the land but was in failing health the last two years of his life. He died at age 75 on February 4, 1927.

At that time in history, following a death, the deceased was prepared by the undertaker and kept at home for the one to two days of viewing and visitation, then taken to the church for the funeral. Since he, Grandpa, was so well known in the community, his funereal story was published on the front page of the Sullivan Daily Times on February 7th, the day after his funeral.

This is the account as we have heard it over the years from those relatives who were old enough to have memories of being part of it and from the obituary. The newspaper headline read:

"TRIBUTE PAID TO G. W. DECKARD, PROMINANT CASS TOWNSHIP MAN PASSED AWAY FRIDAY - FUNERAL HELD SUNDAY",

There were a few errors in the obituary, however. He was survived by four, not three, daughters. Matilda Willis was omitted. He was preceded in death by two grandchildren, not three. He was a member of Hickory Church for 40 years, not 14.

The funeral presented a picture long to be remembered. A warm spell and rain had made the roads impassable for automobiles for several days. A grandson, Cecil Willis, had to hitch two horses to the buggy, instead of one, to bring the Rev. H. A. Bailiff from Cass to preside at the ceremony, simply because the roads made travel so difficult. The flower girls rode in a wagon and a horse drawn hearse was used to transport the body.

The county road usually traveled from the Deckard home was deemed impassable, even for the horse drawn hearse, so a less traveled private road on the property was thought to be a more reliable route. Harve Lovall of Dugger, a man with a wide experience as a teamster, volunteered to drive the hearse and arrived in proper livery with top hat, tails and gloves.

Even with all his experience as a driver, Mr. Lovall could not avoid the inevitable. Before he got to the main road, the hearse became mired in the heavy clay and was stuck. Ora, whose home was a short distance away, walked home, harnessed a team of horses and came back to pull the hearse out of the mud. He had the presence of mind to bring two single trees and one double tree which were necessary to hitch his team to the hearse, ahead of the other horses.

With much loud coaxing from the driver, Mr. Lovall, slaps on the rumps of the team hitched to the hearse from the other men who were trying to help get the hearse out of the mud and Ora's urging and guiding his team hitched in front of the other horses, the hearse was finally out of the mud. When they were out to the main road, Ora unhitched his team and took it back to the farm. I can only imagine that Ora (Dad) hurriedly took care of his horses then ran to catch up with one of the many conveyances heading to the church or maybe he just walked the distance, somewhat "the worse for wear".

People came to the funeral in wagons, surreys, buggies, carriages - all sorts of horse drawn conveyances—on horseback and on foot. The church yard was full and in addition, conveyances lined both sides of the road, north and south of the church. The lane east of the church was also filled. According to the funeral director, M. J. Aiken, that was the last time he ever used a horse drawn hearse and he had not used one for several years before. He also said that he believed this to be the largest funeral he had ever had at Hickory Church.

Only one automobile made it to the funeral. Somehow, it seems quite fitting that George Washington Deckard, who never owned an automobile, or seemed to care much for them, was buried in the style in which he lived. He was laid to rest in Hickory Cemetery beside Nancy Lucilla, his beloved wife of 32 years on February 6, 1927.

As years went by it was quite an event each Memorial Day to visit the cemetery and visit the grave sites of any relatives who were buried there. Although only two of Grandma and Grandpa's grandchildren were old enough to have any memory of her since she died in 1914, many of us have a memory of some sort of Grandpa before he passed away in 1927. I was almost six and one-half when Grandpa died and I can just remember what he looked like with his snow white hair and long white beard

Nearly all of George Washington and Nancy Lucilla Deckard's grandchildren visited the grave sites of their grandparents and remembered their beautiful headstone. It was an unusual double stone of rather imposing size with a very nice mottled gray and black glazed finish. It is deeply engraved with their names and the dates of their births and deaths on the front.

On the back of the headstone is an engraving in script, placed there at Grandma's death that reads,

"Budded on earth to bloom in heaven,
Goodbye dear husband and children,
Mourn not for me, it is in vain
To call me to your sight again."

I wish I knew if Grandpa wrote these beautiful words. At least, I feel sure he chose them.

Chapter 5 ═══════════════════════════════

Church History

Being raised in a Christian home, church was always an integral part of Ann's life. Old Hickory Methodist Church was the church of her parents and the church she grew up in. She attended and remained a very active member of Old Hickory as long as she lived.

Ann was the driving force that was responsible for all her children attending church regularly and embracing an active Christian faith. She was known by family, friends and neighbors to be consistent in living out her Christian principles. She accepted people as they were and was never judgmental, but it was plain to see that the Christian faith was her highest priority. Her children learned by example as well as by regular church attendance and were expected to follow the precept that was taught at home as well as at church.

Although Ora's family belonged to the neighboring Berea Church of Christ, Ora never made a Christian commitment until the early 1930's. Until that time he was pretty well known for his "cuss" words and salty language and made frequent use of them with some of his friends or when something went wrong. He was never too particular about whether the children were within hearing distance or not but the children were all well aware from an early age that this was unacceptable language for children and none of them used these words – at least never where Ann could hear them.

Ora did attend church some, even Old Hickory for that is where he met Ann in the early 1900s. From the time he made his commitment to Christ, he cleaned up his language and attended church regularly with his family, sat in the "Amen Corner" (a section on the rostrum where a dozen or so men who did most of the work in the church sat) and became a dedicated worker at Hickory.

Old Hickory Church had its beginnings in 1864 as Union Class Circuit, Second District Methodist Protestant Church with Rev. James Hays as pastor and it became a part of Sullivan Circuit.

This church class was located in Cass Township, Sullivan County and by this time the area had previously weathered a cyclone in 1846 that riddled the community and an epidemic of typhoid fever in1852 that took the lives of nearly all the original settlers.

This was primitive territory and it was said that in 1825 wild game was so plentiful a pioneer could stand in the back door of his log home and shoot venison, bears and turkeys when they wandered out from among the thick surrounding woods.

William and Henry Robertson, brothers, and their families migrated to Indiana from Kentucky in 1860 before the Civil War began in 1861. The war lasted until 1864.

William Robertson and his wife, Hellen Jane, purchased land in Cass Township where they built their home. It is likely they had a "house raising" as this was a common practice at that time. All the people in the community would gather at the building site, enjoy an evening of fun and fellowship and camp out for the night. By morning's first light, everyone would be up and by nightfall the house would be built from the ground to the topmost logs, the roof would be added and the floor of split logs, in place. The women folk would be in charge of food for the group of working men.

Also, customarily in those times, the early settlers felt a pressing need for a church where they could practice their faith, renew their spirits and come together for worship and fellowship on a regular basis. The Robertson's and their family and friends were no exception. The only two churches in the area, Antioch Christian Church and Zion Methodist Church were several miles away and not easily accessible with a horse and buggy or wagon.

So William, Uncle Billy, as many people liked to call him, donated hickory logs and a small log church was built on his property. The exact date this log church was built is not known, but it is on record that the Union Class Circuit Second District Methodist Protestant Church was organized in 1864 by the Reverend James Hays and became part of Sullivan Circuit in1884. This new church known as Union was named Hickory Methodist Protestant Church because it was made of hickory logs.

The land granted for the Church on January 17, 1870 for the sum of $5.00, was described as follows:

"Commencing at the Northwest corner of the East half of the Southwest quarter of Section fifteen (15) in Township seven (7) North of range eight (8) West, Running East (12) twelve rods, thence South (9) nine rods, thence West twelve (12) rods, thence North nine (9) rods to the place of beginning, containing one hundred and eight square rods, the aforesaid.

Conveyance is made on the following condition that the above named land is never to be used for any other purpose only for place of religious

> Worship for the Methodist Union Church and in case the aforesaid condition is broken the land falls back to the grantors."

(Deed Record Book 32 page 205)

Land across the road from the church was donated for a cemetery by Linda Parks, probably around 1874 since that is the earliest date to be found on a tombstone there.

As the years passed, more families moved into the area and as families grew larger, the small, one-room log building no longer seemed adequate. The church saw the need for a larger building and many meetings and much talk ensued before any conclusions were made. After exploring every possibility it was decided that the best and most logical spot for a new building was the place where the log church stood.

Along with an expanded congregation came the need for more parking room for horses and buggies and other conveyances of the day. If the Church was torn down, where would the Congregation meet while the new building was being raised? Both dilemmas were solved when the decision was made to build the new church around the old one, then tear the old logs apart and carry them away.

Lumber for the new church was hauled by horse and wagon from Sullivan by our grandfather George Deckard, (Ann's father), John Goodman and Henry Skinner. This was about a ten mile trip each way and according to the story, on the way back with their wagon load; the men rested their horses and ate lunch at Mr. Goodman's home at the Exline Corner. They then proceeded on to the building site where water was being hauled for the church foundation by other members of the congregation.

The plan to build the new church around the old one proved to be a good plan. Services were held as usual in the log church and the story goes that, not a meeting was missed. When the new building was near completion, the old logs were torn down and carried out the front door of the new building and the new church floor was laid.

This new floor must have been one of the most appreciated parts of the new church for it replaced the dirt floor in the original building. According to a cousin, Cecil Willis, his Aunt Matt (Martha) Willis told him the old dirt floor was "nasty, nasty". Not only was it hard to keep presentable, but many of the men who chewed tobacco spit tobacco juice on the floor.

Before the new church, five pastors had succeeded Rev. Hays during the years in the log church: Rev. James T. Harrison was the residing pastor while the church was being built. He passed away April 24, 1893, before the building was completed and was buried in Hickory Cemetery. His funeral was held in the new church following its completion.

Will (Uncle Billy) and Hellen had six children and they all attended Hickory. Personally, we know, and are privy to quite a bit of information about three of them. Nancy Lucilla, called

Lute by family and friends, married George W. Deckard in 1882 and was Ann's Mother. Lute was the Mother of nine children, seven who lived to adulthood and had families of their own.

The Deckards' third child, Kate Ivy, born April 12, 1886 died in childhood at seven years of age in 1893. December 23 that same year, Bertha Myrl was born, but died in infancy one year and five months later. The other seven were Alonzo (Lon), Ina, Floyd, Ann, Dulsee, Matilda (Tilda) and Alice. All, except one, married and had children before their mother died on January 14, 1914 from blood poisoning that was the result of being scratched by a cat.

Alice was the only unmarried child at this time. Dulsee had married just a few months previous to their mother's death and she and her husband, George Boone, stayed on at the family home and remained there for the rest of their lives. They farmed the property and at her father's death, Dulsee inherited the house, land and stock.

Ann's Uncle Bob Robertson was the son of Uncle Billy and Hellen, who lived the longest of any of their six children. At 101 years of age he was still living alone in a small country home taking care of himself. He died before his 102nd birthday. Uncle Bob was probably known more personally by our family than any of Ann's uncles. His wife, Aunt Cora, passed away several years before he did and Uncle Bob enjoyed visiting his nieces and nephews. I remember him visiting in our home many times, however I don't recall him ever staying overnight. It may have been because our small home was overflowing with growing children.

Probably the most well-known of the children of Uncle Billy and Hellen was John. His middle name was Fudd and he was affectionately called Uncle John Fudd. He had a passion for music and possessed a good singing voice. From the early 1900s he was the main song leader at Hickory until his death.

Uncle John Fudd organized the Hickory Glee Club which traveled to other churches in the area and sang in competition. Transportation for the Glee Club was a wagon pulled by three matched teams of decorated horses. The wagon was fitted with a full top trimmed with fringe and chairs so the members could sit while they traveled. Often the singers would just stand in the wagon and perform at picnics or other outdoor activities.

In 1908 the Hickory Glee Club won the first prize of $25.00 singing in competition at Coalmont, a neighboring small town. In 1909, while singing in competition at Morris Chapel, one of the churches in Cass Township, the stage broke and according to reports of people who were there, under the stern direction of Uncle John, the singers kept right on singing – never missing a note.

Old Hickory Methodist Church flourished as the coal mining industry grew and more people moved into the area. The one room building was often filled to capacity and sometimes overflowed with people, mostly young men, standing outside listening at the open windows.

Ora and Ann's children all grew up in this church and attended it regularly. We each made our profession of faith as we became old enough to understand what it meant and to make the decision for ourselves. Mom always insisted that was a decision we had to make for ourselves. It was important to her and she wanted us to understand what it meant.

As long as Shirley Hill Mine was flourishing, the Pond there was used for Hickory Church baptizing's. There was a little beach where the water was shallow enough to walk out into for a ways, and made an ideal place for this purpose. A baptizing was always planned for a Sunday afternoon when the weather was warm and of course a large group from the church attended.

What I remember most about the baptizing's was the people gathered around singing, "Shall we gather at the river, where bright angel feet have trod, with its crystal tide forever, flowing by the throne of God." The refrain was, "Yes, we'll gather at the river, the beautiful, the beautiful river. Gather with the saints at the river, that flows by the throne of God." I still love that old hymn.

In our home, no one ever questioned whether we would go to church on Sunday or to Prayer Meeting on Thursday evening, it was just expected. Besides, we knew we would see friends there because most of our cousins and some of our school classmates went to Hickory.

Hickory was on a circuit with two other Methodist churches in the area and one pastor, sent by the Methodist Conference, served all three churches. Therefore, the pastor regularly preached two Sunday morning sermons and one Sunday evening sermon, each at a different church. A schedule that was mutually agreeable to all three congregations was agreed upon. Sometimes the preaching was before Sunday school at Hickory, sometimes after, but there was Sunday school every Sunday and we considered it as important as the sermon. Church service usually started at 9:30 a.m. with Sunday school immediately following and lasted until 11:30 a.m. We were almost always at home by noon.

There was no break between the services. If the preaching service was first at our church, when it was over, the minister walked down the aisle and out the front door during the closing hymn, to his second service. The Sunday School Superintendent took his place behind the pulpit and announced the first song for the next session. When the music was over and announcements were made, the leader said, "Classes will take their places and the teachers take charge." At that time the congregation moved into the assigned places for the classes and several Sunday school classes proceeded - all at the same time in the same room.

The veins of coal in the area mines eventually were worked out and the mines closed. By the 1930s there was a shortage of jobs in the area and instead of new families moving in, young people looking for work were moving away. Sometimes this meant whole families moving with them. This took a great toll on membership and attendance at Old Hickory.

Although strip mines replaced the underground mines several years later, nothing ever replaced the jobs lost by the closings of the underground mines. Huge, monstrous machines were used to strip away the earth and expose the coal underneath it. Taking the place of many men, other large machines dug the coal out of the ground and dumped it into trucks called gondolas to be hauled away.

When Peabody Coal Company bought the property Hickory Church stood on, the church was moved to property then owned by Peabody, to a different location in the neighborhood. The church was moved a few miles closer to The Farm to the spot where Uncle Floyd's house had stood. It was considered to be a safer location because of the work the strip mine was doing.

The Hickory Cemetery was left in its original location and is maintained in good condition by a Cemetery Fund which was started several years ago by Howard McClelland who was born and raised less than one-half mile from Hickory Church. Howard made the first donation then contacted people he knew would be interested in helping take care of the cemetery and an on-going fund was set up that will continue to be funded.

The Wolfe children of Ora and Ann all moved away after they graduated from high school. Some went to college, some to jobs and three of the four boys were drafted into World War II. None ever returned home to live on The Farm. They all, however, returned home as often as they could for short visits or longer vacations. Our trips home seemed totally incomplete if we were not able to attend a church service at Old Hickory Church where we could see family and friends and sing the old familiar hymns we all loved so much.

Old Hickory United Methodist Church still stands, although it has been moved to a nearby location by Peabody Coal Company. A church service is held every Sunday sometimes with less than a dozen members in attendance. The name was changed in 1968 when the Methodist Church and the Evangelical United Brethern Church merged and the name United Methodist was adopted by both congregations.

Hickory Church served five generations of our family and the nostalgic attachment and profound impact it made still runs deep in our hearts and lives. When we stop and think about those days when the membership overflowed this small church's doors, we can be thankful for the commitment our Mother (Ann) made – and kept - to her faith as long as she lived.

Section II

FAMILY EXPANSION
AND ACTIVITY

Chapter 6 ══════════════════════

The Family's Early Years

Ann and Ora's eight children were all born in the house they bought that adjoined Ann's family's property except Dale, the oldest. Dale was born at the small house they rented immediately following their marriage, known as the Dromedary Place. They didn't live there very long and by the time George Edward was born, they were in the house the children were all raised in.

Children born to Ora and Ann were:

Dale Dennis	b. 21 June 1911	d. 19 August 1993
George Edward	b. 1913	d. 1918
Evah Lucille	b. 22 October 1916	d. 28 March 2003
James Lowell	b. 5 October 1918	d. 29 July 2001
Juanita Louise	b. 20 August 1920	
Max Ora	b. 23 April 1923	d. 4 October 2004
Robert Wayne	b. 30 December 1925	
Ruth Eleanor	b. 23 January 1933	

Dale was born just nine months and four days after Ora and Ann – Dad and Mom – were married. By the time he was two years old a little brother, George Edward, named after both of his grandfathers, was born. Evah, born in 1916, was followed two years later by James on October 5, 1918. James was still a nursing baby in long dresses when the three older children came down with scarlet fever. It was common in those days for all babies, both male and female, to wear long dresses for the first year.

Scarlet fever is a highly contagious disease marked by high fever, a red sore throat and a red rash all over the face, arms, legs and body, affecting mainly children. The house was put under immediate quarantine – no one could enter or leave - except for the breadwinner. I believe Dad was allowed to go to work and the doctor did come and go during that time. There was no special medication available back then for scarlet fever.

An exception was also made for Grandma Wolfe (Elvira), who came and helped out. I expect Grandma, being an adult, was not likely to become infected. Mom told how neighbors and family members brought food and left it by the door, to be brought in after they were gone.

All three children were deathly ill, and George Edward's little body could not fight hard enough to recover. He succumbed to scarlet fever at the age of five and the heart broken parents still had two other very sick children to worry about. Due to the quarantine there could not be a proper funeral so the little casket was pulled up to the living room window and family, friends and neighbors filed by the window for a last look and to show their respect. Church friends and family members prepared the grave at Hickory Cemetery and little brother, George Edward, was laid to rest.

As long as I can remember, we just knew George Edward as "Brother". He had been gone for a couple of years when I was born and when Mom talked to us about him, she called him "Brother". It was several years before I could realize and understand what a tragedy that was for a family. When we did say his name, it was always George Edward not George.

The only picture I can remember of George Edward – Brother – was one of Dale, George Edward and Evah. There were no dates on the picture, but Evah looked to be between eighteen months and two years old. I have often wondered if Mom had a premonition that she needed to have a picture of just the three of them. It is not known whether James was born yet or not when the picture was taken, but he was only a few months old during the scarlet fever epidemic. James was born October 5, 1918 and Brother died in 1918, so it seems James must have been about two months old when Brother died.

Evah never had any recollection of what Brother was like for her small body was so ravished by her illness that Mom and Dad thought they would lose her too. She, of course, pulled through, but had some bad side effects. She had been walking at the time, but her body was so traumatized, she lost that ability and had to learn how to walk again. The high fever also caused all of her hair to fall out, but the new hair came in curly.

In contrast to Evah's hair, my hair was always "as straight as a string" with not even the semblance of a curl. By the time I had enough hair to work with, Mom would curl our hair for church or special occasions. In the absence of curlers of any kind, she put our hair up on rags. That meant tearing narrow stripes of material, something clean and soft, like an old sheet, about an inch or so wide, wrapping the hair around the center of the strip and tying the ends together to hold the hair in place. Evah's hair always came out with beautiful curls, while mine, although it might be curly for a short while, it was always hanging loose and far from pretty by the time I got back home.

At one time, Mom got a curling iron to see if that would work better on my straight hair. The curling iron was held much like a pair of small tongs, with a rod and clamp that was heated on the stove, but that didn't work either. So Mom gave up trying to get my hair to curl. She cut it short with bangs and told me how pretty and perfect it looked! Always the diplomat, she had a way of making everything seem alright.

Dale was seven years old when Brother died, but he could remember very little about the scarlet fever, or even about Brother. He was so sick and in bed when Brother died, he could only remember them bringing the little casket to his bed side and he could barely rise up enough to look at him.

I remember Granny Brewer/Mosier, our nearest neighbor to the north, talking about George Edward. She always talked about how smart he was and what a sweet disposition he had. The remark I remember so well was "he was just too smart for this world". I heard her say that many times. She was like a grandmother to him, as she was to all of us children.

By the time James was born the United States had entered World War I. Dad was 30 years old at the time and had four children so he was not drafted into the service.

Shortly before James was two years old I, Juanita, was born. I'm sure Aunt Dulsee and maybe Aunt Tilda were with Mom at home that day to help the doctor with the delivery and to take care of the two small children, Evah and James, as Dad had to work. But when he came in that evening he brought Mom a gift – a set of cups and saucers. They were very plain, ordinary cups and saucers. Large cups with cupped saucers you could pour hot coffee into, and then blow on it to cool it to drinking temperature. They were of good, sturdy material, glazed white. No trim, nothing fancy, just good, sturdy everyday cups and saucers, meant to be useful. Dad was the only member of the family who drank coffee regularly, but the cups and saucers were used daily. In winter we kids would sometimes have hot cocoa in them or if we were sick we might have hot tea, often sassafras tea and toast.

In lieu of a measuring cup, which Mom never owned until the later years of her marriage, she used one of these cups for a one cup measure. The last cup and saucer of that set still sits on a shelf in my kitchen and I recently decided to see how accurate Mom's measurements were. I took a one cup measuring cup, filled it to the brim with water and poured it into the teacup. It measured one cup exactly!

Max, next in line, was born close to three years after I was, due to the fact that Mom had a miscarriage. I was never aware of this until later in life because those subjects were never discussed, especially around children.

About two and a half years after Max, Bob was born, a few short days after Christmas. Mom must have been working on overload at that time, taking care of five other children and getting ready for Christmas too. Of course Dale was 14 and Evah, 9, so they probably both were a big help to her. And, resourceful as she was, Mom could probably think of things I could do at five years of age. We were all taught to work and be responsible at an early age.

I'm not sure how old Bob was when the accident happened, but he was badly burned on his face and hands when he was but a few months old. I think he was probably about three months old – give or take a little. He was born at the end of December and it happened while the weather was still cold enough to have a hot fire in the Warm Morning heating stove.

The stove, which heated the living room in the three room house, stood on the west side of the living room and the long stove pipe fit into the chimney between the bedroom and kitchen doors. The stove itself was a tall cylinder of thin steel about four feet high and 24 inches in diameter. It stood about eight to ten inches above the floor on four wide legs and the fire pit at the bottom was flanged at the top with a heavy rim trim of decorative silver colored shiny metal that served not only as a decoration but it kept anyone from getting too close to the hot stove bowl. A matching decorative ring encircled the top of the cylinder and the stove pipe was attached to a decorative rounded top.

On this chilly morning, the fire in the heating stove was hot and Bob, in the high chair, the same chair we all had used, had been pulled close to the stove for warmth, but not close enough to reach the stove. Dad had gone to work, Mom was in the kitchen getting Dale, Evah and James off to school and Max and I were in the warm living room with the baby.

Max, at almost three years old, was cavorting around, making Bob laugh. He would step up on the rungs of the high chair and back down, up and down, maybe said "boo' and they both thought this was great fun. Suddenly when Max stepped up or down – nobody knows exactly how it happened - the high chair turned over and threw Bob onto the hot surface of the stove. Of course he tried to push away with his little hands and naturally started screaming. Mom came running and pulled the high chair upright and got him out, but his hands and face were badly burned. He was crying so hard and in such pain that he rubbed his feet together so hard his little shoes came off.

I don't know whether Mom was able to call Dad at work or whether she called a neighbor who went and got Dad, but he came home and brought some of the pink Vitamin E oil that was used at the mine when a miner got burned.

I remember Mom and Dad taking strips of clean cloth, soaking them in the oil and completely covering the burns with them. I'm sure Mom didn't get much sleep for several nights, for she kept the cloths saturated, day and night, with the oil. She was vigilant and in constant prayer for Bob's healing. With much prayer from family, friends and neighbors and help from a loving God, the oil worked its miracle. Bob's burns healed perfectly in record time and not a scar was left on his face or hands. By the time he was six months old there was no indication that he had ever been burned.

Things were going along nicely for the family of eight, including six growing children, all about two to two and one half years apart in age. But by the time Bob was nearly four years old the Great Depression of 1929 reared its ugly head. The stock market crashed on October 24, 1929, causing much devastation in the United States, affecting the whole world. The Depression lasted for ten years and caused worldwide havoc. Banks failed, credit collapsed, prices in world trade collapsed.

People who had bought gold and invested in stocks were in shock when one night they were rich and the next morning they were wiped out. Many who had invested heavily lost everything. Some committed suicide by jumping out of windows of tall buildings, some by gunshot or in some other way.

When President Herbert Hoover's term ended in 1932, Franklin D. Roosevelt (FDR) had been elected president by a landslide. He took office in 1933 and by that time - the height of the Depression - unemployment in the United States had risen from 3% to 24 %. Wages for those who still had jobs dropped 42%. Many farmers lost their farms and, at the same time, years of erosion and a drought caused the "Dust Bowl" in the Midwest and no crops could be raised.

Many of these farmers and other unemployed, ended up living as homeless "hobos" or in shantytowns called Hooverville, named after President Hoover. Hoover, of course was blamed for the condition the country was in.

The nation needed immediate relief and when Roosevelt took the helm as President, relief recovery and reform became his goals. Roosevelt pledged to help "the forgotten man at the bottom of the economic pyramid". Thus, Roosevelt's "New Deal" was spawned.

The concept that became the New Deal had been discussed in earlier years but with no effect. The term "New Deal" was coined during Franklin Roosevelt's presidential nomination acceptance speech, when he said, "I pledge you, I pledge myself, to a new deal for the American people." Roosevelt summarized the New Deal as "a use of the authority of government in an organized form of self-help for all classes and groups and sections of our country".

One of the most far reaching programs of the New Deal was the CCC – the Civilian Conservation Corps – which put three million young people between the ages of 18 and 25 to work. Another ambitious New Deal program was the WPA – Works Progress Administration – and it created jobs for 8,500,000 jobless people.

Between 1935 and 1941, billions of dollars were spent on reforestation, flood control, rural electrification, water works, sewage plants, school buildings, slum clearance, student scholarships and other programs.

It was good that people had jobs. They were working for their government money. No one had to feel that they were getting a "handout". They could put in a full day's work for a full day's pay. This was good for their self-esteem and the country benefited greatly with millions of miles of new roads, new state parks and forests, new school buildings, student scholarships, etc.

Of course these programs all had to be funded somehow and they were financed through new taxes. Federal taxes tripled, but the most important source of taxes was a new excise tax. Excise tax was levied on dozens of everyday items, candy, chewing gum, margarine, soft drinks, alcoholic beverages, cigarettes, matches and many other items. This meant it was substantially financed by the middle class.

Although on the surface, the New Deal was seen as a near perfect program, it was a matter of the seen and the unseen. The New Deal harmed millions of poor people. It channeled money away from the South, the poorest region in the United States. The largest share of the spending and loan programs went to political swing states in the West and East where income was 60% higher than in the South.

Money spent on New Deal projects came from the taxpayer who, because of the high taxes, had less money to spend on food, clothing, etc. Taxes on payrolls made it more expensive for employers to hire people, which discouraged hiring. Some of the programs destroyed jobs because of higher taxes forcing small businesses to close. Some programs forced wages above market level making it more expensive to hire – black people alone were reported to have lost some 500,000 jobs.

Ruth was born just before FDR took office in 1933. Bob had just turned seven. I, myself, find it hard to believe that at twelve, I didn't understand much about what was going on at home. Pregnancy and childbirth were subjects that were pretty much taboo in those times and certainly not talked about in the presence of children. I do remember being in the bedroom with Mom and when she raised her arms to take off her Sunday dress, I thought her stomach looked very large.

Personally, I remember almost nothing about Ruth's birth. What I do remember distinctly is that on Christmas Eve, before Ruth was born in January, I woke up in the night and Evah was not in bed with me. As I lay wondering where she could be, I saw light from a crack in the bedroom door and could hear soft whispering. I stole quietly out of bed and peeked through the crack where the door was ajar and saw Evah and Mom putting gifts under the Christmas tree. And that was the first time I was **really sure** who Santa Claus was! I was 12 years old!!

Bob remembers the day Ruth was born because on his way home from school, Uncle Floyd, Mom's brother who lived about midway between our house and the school, intercepted him on his way home, invited him to come inside and visit awhile. After a half hour or so, Uncle Floyd told him he could go on home and when he got there, Aunt Dulsee (and maybe Granny Brewer) was there and he had a new baby sister. I suspect the doctor may still have been at the house when school was out and Uncle Floyd kept Bob until he saw the doctor's car go back past his house.

A name for this new "wonder" baby was a high priority. Granny Brewer, who came daily to see the baby or help out where she could, said she had a beautiful name picked out – Bonetta Aretta. None of us cared much for that name, but I knew I had the perfect name. I was reading a book series named, "The Five Little Peppers and How They Grew". The youngest child in the story was named Serfronia and called Phronsie for short. I was enamored with the Pepper family; especially the baby girl and I wanted my little sister to be just like her. Mom just laughed, but she had plans of her own.

President Roosevelt's wife's name was Eleanor and Mom had a high regard for her. I expect the name Ruth came from the Bible and seemed to fit perfectly with the name Eleanor. So this new baby was named Ruth Eleanor. When she began to talk at an early age, we kids all loved to ask her what her name was for she answered Fifi Annanor. I still sometimes call her Fifi in jest.

Baby Ruth, with six older siblings, was the apple of everyone's eye – all her brothers and sisters adored her and pretty much catered to her every whim.

During the summer of 1932, Mom and Dad had decided to add more rooms to the three room house that was overflowing with six growing children. I now suspect the greatest motivation for this remodeling, was that a new baby would be arriving the next January. Where in the world did these six growing children all sleep in this three room house? None of us can remember for sure but we have fun speculating. Where did we keep all of our clothes?? There was not one clothes closet in the house. In the first place, one thing I know for sure, we didn't have a LOT of clothes. Mom and Dad didn't have an abundance of clothes either. We had enough – or we thought we did.

I don't remember anyone every crabbing about not having anything to wear. The boys all wore bib overalls during the week and Evah and I had dresses. There were school clothes, everyday clothes and Sunday clothes. Each boy only needed two pair of overalls, for Mom washed every week, winter and summer, rain or shine, and each boy wore a pair of overalls for a whole week. Even then, that meant five pair of overalls in the wash each week. Evah and I had more than two dresses each, for Mom sewed for us and yard goods were relatively inexpensive.

Every day after school, everyone changed from school clothes into everyday clothes for we all had chores to do. Nobody ever wore overalls or school clothes to church on Sunday. Each boy had a little Sunday suit, shirt and tie from a very early age and we girls always had Sunday dresses as well.

The bedroom had a good sized dresser in it with three large drawers and every inside door had a large nail in back, high up, and clothes that couldn't be folded were hung on a hanger on the nails. Mom was a good housekeeper and clothing could not be thrown around or left hanging on a chair. There just was not room for that.

Mom and Dad had bought the brown three room house just south of our property that adjoined it. One of the motivations for buying that home was that it was a rental property, and a succession of neighbors had lived there since Mom and Dad had lived in their home – some good – some not so good.

The last family to live in the brown house before Mom and Dad bought it was not the best of neighbors. Mom and Dad always suspected them of bootlegging, for at night they could often see them out with a lantern, digging in the chicken lot. That was confirmed when Dad put some hogs in that lot after they bought the place. Max, Bob and James were tending the hogs down there one day and found some brown bottles the hogs had rooted up. Sure enough Dad said it was the old neighbor's home brew and he thought he would open a bottle just to see what it was.

Well, it didn't turn out to be so funny. When he pulled the cap off, it spewed its smelly contents half way across the room onto Mom's lace curtains. Mom didn't think that was funny at all!! Home brew on her curtains!!

Although Dale was away at work during the week – he had just got his first job working on a pipeline in Princeton, some 50 or 60 miles away, he might be home on some weekends. The house was still too small, especially with a new baby on the way. Dad and Mom had bought the brown house and Dad had plans to use it to expand our home. So, around the first of July, after the corn crop was laid by – which meant it was too tall to plow anymore and at the final plowing the soil was thrown up around the new corn plants – Dad was ready to start to work on his project.

With James (14), Max (8), Bob (6) and Dale (21), to help when he was home, plus the help of a few neighbors and relatives, the work began. Dad's plan was to use the one room of the brown house that had siding on three sides for a room over the cellar, and to use the lumber in the other two rooms to build three smaller rooms onto our house. Dad was a good craftsman, adept at using almost any kind of tool. He was always resourceful and could do almost anything that needed to be done. He had the vision to see a job through to its completion and this job was no different. Dad had the plan firmly in his head. There was no doubt about who was in charge and who directed the crew.

Bob remembers that Dad took a chalk line and starting at the ridge of the roof, made a line on the roof, down one side of the house, across the floor, up the other side of the house, back across the other side of the roof to the ridge, meeting at the starting point. A chalk line is a strong twisted line (or string) with some resiliency that is covered with a heavy coat of blue powdered chalk. A heavy metal "plumb" (weight) is fastened to the bottom of the string to hold it in place. A second person holds tight to the "plumb" and the string is snapped with the fingers, leaving a straight blue line. After the chalk lines were snapped, with a regular hand saw, Dad sawed down these chalk lines and the house was in sections.

The room that was sided on three sides was kept intact. This room was placed over the cellar Dad had dug to the size of the room. It was called the Smokehouse and was used as outside storage. A trap door was cut through the floor to the right of the front door and over the steps that went down into the cellar. This trap door, made heavy with the re-enforcements necessary so it could be walked on, had to be lifted each time milk, canned goods, baskets of potatoes, apples or other produce were carried up or down, which was twice a day, every day, for milk alone. Of course, every time it was opened, it had to be closed with the same heavy round metal handle. Closing the cellar door was impressed heavily on everyone big enough to be sent to the cellar, for fear someone would fall through the opening.

With saw, hammer and nail puller the other two rooms were divided into large sections of roof, walls and floor. These were loaded onto a hay rack and hauled up to the house where they were taken apart and used as lumber to build the two small bedrooms, with a nice closet between them and a new kitchen.

Bob said, "This was a remarkable feat for a man with no formal carpenter training, with just the help of his sons and a few neighbors and friends." "A feat that was not taught in my engineering school", Bob laughed.

As usual, all family members joined in and worked as needed. Bob said, "At six years of age I was not considered to be a "full hand" but I'm sure Jim at thirteen and Max at eight gave a much better account of themselves. I specifically recall being issued my own little chipping hammer and was assigned the task of cleaning the mortar from the bricks of the old chimney so they could be used to build the new chimney in the new kitchen."

"Uncle Bill" Mosier, Granny Brewer-Mosier's second husband, helped with the finishing carpentry work and Uncle Cornie Willis did the plastering. He was the closest thing to a trained craftsman that worked on the remodeling job. His real job was doing this sort of work, as well as refinishing floors and doing other inside work. I believe Mom and Dad paid him something for the work he did. I also believe Uncle George came some and helped, for free, and probably a few other neighbors did, too.

What a miracle and a blessing this must have seemed to Mom. It was more room than she had had in her 22 years of married life. For the first time, she and Dad had their own bedroom. The other new little bedroom was the boy's room and James, Max and Bob slept in one bed. Dale was away, except on weekends, from the time of the expansion. Evah and I had the big bedroom to ourselves and felt quite privileged. Baby Ruth slept with Mom and Dad until she was two or three years old.

Although it was several years before those white plastered walls had any wallpaper on them, I never heard Mom complain. She was one to make do and put her priorities in place. It was more years than that before the woodwork was all finished around the doors. When Mom did put new wallpaper on, she brought it all the way to the edge of the door jambs and the big crack that was eventually covered by the woodwork was hardly noticeable.

The wood/coal cook stove was moved into the new kitchen along with the kitchen cabinet. Dad with his gift of ingenuity, found a drawer that had been discarded somewhere on a trash pile, brought it home and built a lovely little kitchen table around it. It was a work table for Mom in the new kitchen.

The drawer had a design on the front (the two drawer pulls were shaped like upside down sea shells), but the rest of the table was very plain. Each leg was cut from, probably, a two by two piece of lumber but slanted smaller at the bottom. The table top was lumber Dad sawed to length from a tree trunk, and then hewed it out himself. It was thick lumber, one and one half to two inches thick and its defining mark was a beautiful dark knot about two inches in diameter in the upper left corner. The table had no finish at all, just the lovely bare wood sanded smooth and worn slick with use over the years.

That table was given to one of Evah and Bill's sons, Stephen, a few years before the house was closed up for good. It now is used as a desk in his and his wife, Marlene's, bedroom. I did put two coats of good varnish on the table top after Mom was gone and Dad moved to Michigan. Even though we moved the table into the kitchen every winter, the summer weather was hard on it without someone there to take care of things.

The new kitchen had a back door to the west and a front door to the east that opened onto a little screened-in porch. This was a lovely place to sit in the heat of the summer and catch a breeze that came around the corner of the house. It was also Mom's favorite place to sit in the early summer mornings and write her endless notes and letters. As long as I can remember, Mom wrote weekly to all her children that were away from home. Sometimes just a brief note – a penny postcard maybe – but she wrote. I lived in Terre Haute, only 25 miles away, but I still got letters and notes occasionally. I got more phone calls because they were inexpensive.

After the remodeling, the old kitchen became the dining room and still held the big square, hardwood table that Mom and Dad went to housekeeping with. The dining room chairs were as old as the table but they had not held up as well. When Evah was a senior in high school, which would have been shortly after the house remodeling, she bought six new chairs for the dining room.

Evah didn't have a job, but Mom gave her money to buy a senior class ring at school and without asking permission or telling anyone – not even me – she ordered new chairs out of the Sears and Roebuck catalogue and used her ring money to pay for them. What a surprise for all of us. Mom liked the chairs, of course, but was not pleased that Evah had used her ring money for them. After Mom was gone, we all agreed that Evah should have the chairs. She took them home to Michigan and used them in her kitchen for some time.

Also, in the dining room was the glass doored safe where Mom kept her beautiful, old dishes. These beautiful dishes were divided among her children when Mom died in 1967. Each child got something of them, but we three girls got the lion's share. The boys got more things of Dad's. Now antiques, we all love those old dishes. To me, mine are the most cherished things in my home.

Another of Dad's projects of ingenuity was procuring and placing concrete walks from the back kitchen door to the chicken house, the outhouse and the coal shed. This was about 1935 or 1936. The daily treks to and from these outbuildings kept the grass worn off the paths and they were either dusty during the dry spells or muddy when it rained. Six active children and two adults could bring a lot of dust, dirt or mud into the house and walks of some kind were badly needed. Possibly with a little nudge from Mom, Dad stretched his imagination and came up with a plan.

Since Bob was directly involved in this project of Dad's, his remembrance, as well as his knowledge of the different steps in Dad's master plan and the hard work it took to bring it to fruition, are much better than mine. His words are used here as he describes the laying of the sidewalks at the farm thus:

"Shirley Hill Mines #22 and #23, approximately one mile directly north of the house, had been shut down for some time and the "iron had been pulled". Since the mine property had been abandoned, what was left lying around was considered "available".

Shirley Hill mines had a good "wash house". After a few years of un-use, weeds and tall grass had taken over the mine property and about all that remained of the wash house was the floor, a large, solid concrete slab about four inches thick.

Under Dad's directions, the boys were again mustered and his new project began. Basically, a cold cut chisel – a very large heavy chisel with a long handle – and a sledge hammer were all the tools required. Chipping a groove about one inch deep in the brittle concrete would cause it to break – pretty much where desired. This large slab was cut into pieces of varying sizes, mostly about two to two and one half feet wide and six feet long. The largest of all the pieces was about five feet wide and six feet long and was to be placed as a stoop outside the back kitchen door.

Each piece was dragged by our team of horses from the mine site to the house and put in place. Under Dad's direction the boys were taught how to properly rig chains to cause the front end of the concrete slabs to rise off the ground when being pulled, so no sled was needed.

While I was old enough to swing a sledge for relief stints, the older boys could do it better and I was usually relegated to holding the cold cut chisel. Often I would drive the team home since I had had plenty of experience with a team at that age. I was probably nine or 10 years old then.

As I look back now, it is easy to believe with proper management and planning, sidewalks could have been poured long before this time, since Dad certainly knew the art of mixing concrete. However, what is not possible to picture now are the specific items that kept rising to the top of the priority list for the time and money available.

Reflection makes us all thankful for the conveniences of our modern lives. Life on our farm in the 1930's provided very little money, cheap family labor and a man of the house who was clever and resourceful enough to make much with the little that was available.

Chapter 7

More Early Years

Due to the number of coal mines around us which provided jobs, the area was quite heavily populated. Not only were there three more houses on our road, but up by Park School, a little settlement of homes was called Stringtown. On the east/west run of the road, there were six houses, all in the span of less than a quarter of a mile.

On the north/south road past the school house was the Macaulay house and two other houses on the east side of the road just several yards apart. On the west side of the road was a woods and property owned by Grandpa Deckard.

Memories of these woods bring back the memory of a song Mom sang to us when we were small. It was entitled "Babes in the Woods" and must have been popular in the 1900s for Mrs. Macaulay sang it to the Macaulay children too. Jeanette, the older of the two Macaulay girls whom Dale married in 1937, said that when her mother sang it to them she always thought that the woods across the road were the woods where the little children were buried. These are the words to the song.

"BABES IN THE WOODS"

My dears don't you know, how a long time ago,
Two poor little children whose names I don't know,
Were carried away on a bright summer's day,
And lost in the woods as I've heard people say.

And when it was night, so sad was their plight,
The sun it went down and the moon gave no light,
They sobbed and they sighed and they bitterly cried,

And the poor little things, they laid down and died.

And when they were dead, the robins so red,
Brought strawberry leaves and over them spread,
And all the day long they sang them this song,
Poor babes in the woods, poor babes in the woods.

We all loved to hear Mom sing this sad little song and I don't believe it damaged our psyches in any way. I would be inclined to think it just made us more sympathetic. However, I never sang it to my children or to my grandchildren, for by that time, it was thought to be inappropriate for children.

Farm boys as well as farm girls became ingenious at finding ways to entertain themselves and Bob and Max, about two years apart in age, were good at this.

One quiet Sunday summer afternoon, when they were looking for something to do, Bob and Max found an old wheelbarrow bed and one of them got the idea right away that they could make a boat out of it and it would be fun to see who could stay afloat the longest on the stock pond.

The wheelbarrow bed had long since been separated from its wheel and the handles and two of the holes where the bolts had been were torn larger than they should be, but a good big daub of mud would close them up. So the competition began and the boys were amazed at how long they could stay afloat. Of course, it would eventually sink. Just a couple of cycles and they had the water in the pond muddied up until it was unfit for the stock to drink.

Just about that time, Dad walked by and he failed to see any humor in the situation. He instantly recognized that the horses and cows would not drink this water. Dad said in a stern voice that the boys knew meant business, "You know the cattle are not going to drink that water so you boys get down to the spring and fill the watering trough so they can drink." Max, being the older of the two, sent Bob on down to the spring while he got their "boat" out of the water.

Fortunately, the spring was almost full of water. So just with a two and one half gallon bucket with a bail handle, Bob got down on his knees to dip the water out. He moved the cover which was just an assortment of boards, off and started dipping water out and carrying it to the watering trough. Dipping water out faster than the vein of water was bringing it into the spring caused a drop in the water level and he had to keep reaching farther down to get to the water.

Bob told me, "I should have gone back to the barn or to the tool shed and got a piece of rope to tie onto the bail handle but I thought that would waste time. I wasn't concerned until the board I was leaning on slipped out from under my hand and fell into the water, taking me with it."

"I distinctly remember," said Bob as he retold the story to me "reaching the bottom of the spring (about eleven feet down), making a U-turn and starting my accent. Quickly I bumped my head on a two by twelve inch by four foot board that had fallen with me into the water. The surface seemed very crowded but I was able to get past it. Being barefoot, my toes helped me grip the bricks on the side of the spring and I climbed out."

"Ever mindful," Bob continued, "that the cattle were drinking from the trough and that they may want more than I had been able to dip and carry over, they might try to drink directly from the spring and fall in. I rounded them up and started driving them to the barn."

Bob said as he approached the barn, Jim came out and could see the dripping wet kid brother. He alerted the family and since everyone was happy to see him wet but alive, he felt great. Dad and Jim finished watering the stock and with Mom's help, Bob got to change into dry clothes

Remember, I told you how good Max and Bob were at finding ways to entertain themselves? Well, sometimes they didn't even have to look - sometimes it just seemed to drop from the sky, unannounced and I'm sure it didn't always seem like entertainment to them. However, in retrospect, I think even they can see some humor in this next little story.

It was a hot Sunday morning when Dad stuck his head in the back door and yelled, "Bob, Max get out here and get Johnny's Boone's hog out of our corn patch."

It was during the "dog days" of summer – the second or third week of August - when Indiana is as hot as blue blazes. When they got outside Dad told them, "You can't get a hog to go back the way he came, so you'll have to drive him up through the barn lot, out the gate and out to the road to Johnny's barn lot."

This story has been repeated many times so the details are vivid in our memories. It was 1934 or 1935. The boys had their Sunday morning chores done and were trying to get ready for church at 9:30 a.m. These instructions were not very welcome, but the corn needed to be saved.

The south property line on our place was Johnny Boone's north property line. The line was divided evenly and often repaired together as a neighborly gesture. A good woven wire fence had been installed but where a ditch intersected the fence, it was hard to make the fence "hog tight". The ditch was on Johnny's side of the fence, therefore it was his responsibility.

The hog was found and the boys thought this would be easy. They knew how to get the gate open, run the hog along the fence through the gate and down the road to Johnny's house and it would be done. The weather was hot and getting hotter but the job was proceeding exactly as planned. After all, these farm boys knew how to get a hog out of the corn patch and back home.

Max and Bob were anxious to get the job done, so they maybe drove the hog a little hard, for just as they got the hog ready to exit our barn lot – but still on our property – this inconsiderate hog, weighing about 200 pounds, laid down by the fence post and died!

The boys didn't know just what to do, but they did know they had to tell Dad. They also knew Dad didn't always take an unexpected event of this magnitude lightly. However, Dad was a realist and was quick to assess the situation.

"Bob get my sticking knife," Dad said. He had a special knife to reach the juggler vein and he knew the blood needed to be emptied immediately. Dad said, "Max go tell Johnny we have a hog to butcher and we need some help." Bob heaved a sigh of relief – at least this time he drew the easy job.

Dad knew we were responsible and were obligated to pay damages for the hog, but in the midst of the great depression, we couldn't afford to waste food.

Butchering is no easy task, even when planned ahead. Preparation had to be accelerated. A platform, waist high for scraping the hair off the hog, water heated in the cast iron kettle and a scalding barrel tilted against the platform while the water was heating were all necessary. A block and tackle was mounted in the walnut tree and a "gamble stick" was prepared for hoisting the hog for splitting and cooling. The hog was then wrestled onto the platform.

Once the hog is bled (and he didn't die in the most convenient place), he must be gotten to the platform. Boiling water is dipped and carried to the barrel which is leaning against the platform and chocked securely for 200 pounds of weight could cause the barrel to tip and scald anyone close to it.

Dad never had a thermometer, but seemed to know if the water was too hot so a pail of cold water was kept nearby for if the water was too hot it would "set" the hair. The "gamble stick" was wedged under the ham strings (the Achilles tendons) of the hind legs to grip and slosh the front end of the hog in and out of the barrel a few times, and then a hay bale hook was used under the jaw to slosh the rear end up and down. Dad is pulling the hair all during this phase to see when the hair will "slip".

Once the hair is just right, the three boys with corn knives as scrapers went to work scraping the hair off the skin all over the hog's body. Dad and Johnny worked on the shanks and feet. Everyone worked as fast as possible for the skin must be free of hair or nearly so, and the carcass hanging with the entrails out in a wash tub and the carcass washed down with cold water from the well before anyone could stop for lunch.

The women had plenty to do, for fresh meat will not keep in the heat. Hams and shoulders were sugar cured or salted down. Side meat was cleaned, cut into chunks, and covered with brine in a ten gallon stone jar but much needed to be canned. Ribs, backbone, and sausage needed to be canned and fat needed to be cut and rendered into lard within a couple of days before it spoiled. The cellar at about 65 degrees was the coldest place available.

Church had to be given over to the necessity of saving the hog. It was a long full day for everyone involved. It is not known what payment was agreed on by Dad and Johnny, but they would have easily agreed on the weight. Hogs "on the hoof" were quoted every day on the radio and in the Sullivan Daily Times newspaper.

In any case, Johnny's hog was in our corn patch and Johnny helped with the butchering.

(Personally, I thought Johnny's hog was the one in the wrong.) The relationship never seemed to suffer any between the two men or the families.

Around 1930 or so, Winfred Robertson, whose home was right on the corner where the road turned south and went past the church, put up a glazed block building next to his house, about the size of a garage and put in a little grocery store. It was stocked with a supply of staples such as flour, sugar, salt, bread, milk, etc. and was a handy place to get to if you ran out of something and could not get into town right away.

He had devoted a small space in his glass showcase to an assortment of penny candies. Sticks of hard candy, single chocolates, etc. were a penny a piece. Any one of us could spend quite a long time walking up and down in front of the showcase deciding how to spend three or four pennies. If there were more than one of us, it took longer for we all helped each other spend the pennies.

The road turned south at Winfred's store and continued south to a substantial settlement and went past Hickory Church and Cemetery to the crossroads. John Lackey lived there in the only two story house in the area. Bob traveled the countryside to deliver the Grit Newspaper and his memories of the area and the people who lived in the area are still vivid. I asked Bob about some of the neighbors.

Bob said the early automobiles in the community were owned by Lex Robinson, a Maxwell; Uncle Frank Creager had a Maxwell and Uncle Floyd Deckard had a Dodge. These were all 1915 to 1917 models."

Dad's first automobile was a 490 Chevrolet bought in 1920. The 490 name came from the fact that it was $490 new. Dad paid $125 for it used. It would run approximately 30 to 35 miles per hour. They would frequently take the back seat out, go to the watermelon patch in Oaktown and bring it back filled with watermelons and muskmelons. Dad was pumping in the mine at night and took time off for family shopping on Saturday.

Mom never learned to drive. I'm not sure why, but I think she just didn't have any desire to. She was not an adventurous person and was very content with what she had. She also had more children than any of her sisters and it would have been more of a challenge to take three or four children out in the car than just with one or two. It was several years before cars were closed enough to be safe for small children to ride in the back seat without an adult to watch them.

Aunt Dulsee did learn to drive and Mom could ride to church with her in later years for special meetings but when we children were all small, she always thought she had plenty to do at home. Dad could go to town on the weekends to take her shopping and once a week was often enough to get groceries if you planned ahead and she was a good planner.

Another way Dad tried to make some extra income was by raising dogs. He owned a Horace Lytle book on birddog training. He bought a high priced setter dog or two, and trained and traded several dogs. I heard him say many times he would always take off the first ten days of bird (quail) season and shoot a box of shells a day – an unheard of expense!

Also the best season Dad ever had was the season he knocked down 96 quail and only lost one! This was due to "a little six month old setter "bitch" that distinguished odors so well she "would point one bird while retrieving another one in her mouth".

As I got better at my math I could figure 10 x 25 divided by 96 was about two and a half shells per bird – and that over good dogs! However, Dad could always out shoot his sons!

No doubt Mom enjoyed some extras too during these years, but would have been as frugal as ever. Her main emphasis was always on family and church.

One family story about this time was that Mom was caring for the three children with Dale the oldest about six years old. He was with her in the kitchen and was fussy. To keep him happy she gave him a $10.00 gold coin to play with thinking she could watch him. After a while he started doing something else and, of course, the coin was GONE. Search as she would – no coin could be found. Months later, after many wipings of the table covering, a ring appeared on the oilcloth, showing where he had slipped the coin between the table covering and the table top. The mystery was solved and the coin was found.

Bob remembered Happy Carr and told me this about him. "One friend of Dad's was an especially colorful fellow. John Lovel (Happy) Carr was a sandy haired Irishman with a cheery smile and a propensity to tell wild tales. He had served in World War I and regaled us all with his "war stories". He told how he avoided K.P. duty – how he drank water with green scum one-half inch thick on it – how he stole his father-in-law's knife – how he caught and rode wild cattle – and on and on."

Bob continued, "Happy owned a race car and Dad served as his mechanic for a share of the profits - profits which never materialized. He was also fond of saying, "My stomach is just like a wire basket – it will hold anything I throw in it." Later he became a diabetic and had to carefully watch what he ate and balance any error with insulin or sugar laced orange juice."

After sitting and thinking for a while Bob went on, "I learned one thing from Happy that became a part of my permanent being. He lived with his wife, Hazel, and a nephew (as a foster child), Forest Stuthard, about one-half miles west of Aunt Dulsee's property. While living he treated them very shabbily – like dirt I always thought."

"After his wife's death Happy went all over the countryside telling everyone what a wonderful women Hazel (pronounced Hagel) was," Bob remembered.

"Although I could not have been more than eight or ten" Bob said, "I vowed then I'd always judge a man by how he treated his wife while she was alive! I have found that to be a good measure of a man."

A woman by the name of Peg Davis would visit in our area. Peg would often walk down the lane to visit with Mom, even though it was a mile or more to our house. It was obvious she liked Mom and Mom was always nice to her. Even though they were different in almost every way, Mom always treated her with respect. She was loud, uncouth, talked constantly and smoked an old fashioned clay pipe, which she held with paper wrapped around it so the bowl would not burn her fingers.

This difference in the two never bothered me like it did Bob. Maybe because, even though I was five years older, I had not read the Zane Grey and other western books that talked about bar maids and prostitutes. He knew more about that life then I did.

I think Bob suspected more about Peg than he knew, and that's why it bothered him. When I asked him why it bothered him so much, he said, "I just could not figure out this relationship between two people so unalike. I continually questioned Mom about Peg Davis until I reluctantly got this story:"

> *"You know, Bob, she was one of them girls that lived above the saloon. (Even at that time I had read my Zane Grey books and recognized the vivid description of the barmaid/prostitute in the book Western Union). None of the women in the area would have anything to do with her and she had no way to go anywhere to buy anything. I could leave the kids with Ma (meaning her mother), hitch the horse to the buggy and go to town. She asked to go with me. I talked it over with Ma who said, "Ann, your fortune is made (meaning you are married and established), so treat her as you would like to be treated."*

Bob said, "So Mom would take Peg to Sullivan on occasion. It was obvious to me that Peg was forever grateful. I've thought so many times – how like Mom to do what she felt was right and let the chips fall where they may."

There was another woman that came to visit Mom on occasion who was very unlike her. I'm not sure she lived over the saloon like Peg did but I think she may have, for she was not in the neighborhood very long.

I can't even remember her real name for we just called her (when she wasn't around) Miss Why-why. If she would be there for a meal, she always wanted to do something to help and Mom would let her peel the potatoes. She peeled such thick peelings Mom thought she might run out of potatoes. Mom always made nice thin peelings and taught Evah and me to do likewise.

Miss Why-why stuttered when she talked. She would say "wh, wh, wh, wh, why" before she could start a sentence and when Mom didn't think we were peeling the potatoes thin enough, she would call us Miss Why-why. Right away we would all try to peel thinner peelings and we would have a little laugh.

I believe that was another instance where Mom treated someone with respect who probably was more used to being laughed at.

I never remember hearing my Mother speak sharp or mean to anyone – nor gossip and talk about people with her friends or her sisters.

Section III

LIFE ON THE FARM

Chapter 8

Bob's Memories

Whenever I would read anything Bob had written about Dad's mining days, I would realize how little I knew about mining and about what Dad actually did in the mines. I lived all my early life with Dad working in the coal mines but never once realized how little I understood about what his job entailed. No big deal was ever made about how dangerous his job was - it was just Dad's job. Today, it is terrifying when I know and understand the danger he was in every day at his job!

I never even wondered why the boys were able to walk over to Shirley Hill and take a hot shower and Evah and I couldn't. In retrospect, I am surprised, even a little shocked, that we didn't raise a fuss or beg to go with them. Now that I am old I begin to wonder about it. Surely Evah didn't wonder about it either or we would have talked about it. Maybe we were just happy to have the boys out of the way when we were taking our baths in the No. 3 washtub on Saturday afternoon. Or maybe because we had never had a warm shower we didn't realize how pleasant it could be.

As I read some of the things Bob wrote about the wash house, the cages that Dad and all the other miners used and where the hot water for the showers came from, a host of other questions came to my mind. So I asked Bob for more and more details about these things. I finally just sent him a long list of questions and some of his replies follow.

Dad's fishing in Shirley Hill Pond was such a huge part of our lives; I can't imagine how we would have gotten along without it. Of course, he fished at other places too, as Bob will tell you, but it was the mine pond that he could walk to any evening after work or on the weekends and catch a good mess of fish. There was no "catch and release" for Dad. Thank heavens! We all loved fried Bass and Blue Gills, especially the Blue Gills and they were always available. Dad fished for the real love of fishing, but he also fished with a purpose - always with a purpose. That purpose was food for our table!

Dad never seemed to tire of catching those fish, bringing them home and cleaning them.

Just as well, Mom never seemed to tire of cooking those fish and we children certainly never tired of eating them. Mom was a master at frying fish. I don't remember her ever cooking any of the fish Dad brought her any way except frying them in a small amount of shortening. Dad never fileted or boned the fish he caught and we were all taught early on to watch for the bones and debone them ourselves as we ate them.

Dad scaled the fish, cut the heads off, split them down the middle (the belly) and took the entrails out and washed them good before he brought them into the kitchen to Mom. She took over then, checked them for scales and cut them into serving size pieces. She always left the tails on and when the tails were washed good and turned in cornmeal before they were fried, as all our fish were, they were nice and crispy and we all loved a piece with the tail on.

I finally made a collection of Bob's stories and am presenting most of them together. Bob's memories of the mines in our area, especially Shirley Hill, and Dad's mining days, as well as his fishing, especially in the mine pond, are recorded here, pretty much just as he wrote them.

Unlike many of Dad's generation, his father did not take him into the coal mines at a very early age. He was 19 or 20 when he first started working in the mines. His first job was at No. 1 in 1907. After marriage he moved to Shirley Hill to be closer to home.

I feel confident Dad started in the bottom (meaning underground in deep well mines) since all young men would have started there. I've talked with Dad much about this early work.

The mines near the Farm were generally known by company names with numbers.

Directly south of our home (about a mile or so) was No. 1 mine. I do not remember the mine working or exactly where the shaft was but I knew the gob pile and have hunted the 200-plus-acre property much.

Directly north (approximately one mile) was Shirley Hill No. 22 and No. 23. These shafts were side by side but were different mines because they were sunk at different times. More importantly, they went into different veins (or seams) of coal, therefore, were totally separate. No. 22 was first into No. 5 vein and No. 23 was into No. 6 vein.

I recall this mine in its final days when the iron was being "pulled". Chester Arthur drove a mule pulling the small railroad cars in which the iron was hauled to the regular railroad and was taken to be used again.

"Pulling iron" was the term for removing the railroad tracks, tipple parts and metal frames of various types – in the days when material was expensive and labor was cheap.

I also recall that the blacksmith shop was working (smith being the old name for metal worker and the type metal – gold, silver, black iron was used to identify the craft). And, of course, the wash house was the last building to shut down and I, with older brothers and/or Dad, would use it for a hot shower on occasion.

In addition No. 10 was about two miles east of Shirley Hill (two and one half -miles from home) and No. 12 & No. 17 about one and one-half miles north of Shirley Hill. I recall those mines only as silent.

An important need for all shaft mines was water, so a mine pond was always dug. This was a reservoir for boiler and wash house water. The boilers were vital to produce steam for the steam operated hoisting engines that raised the cages (open elevators) up and down with men and coal, or anything else that was needed.

The shaft mines all functioned much the same. A deep shaft was sunk to the coal (80 to 150 feet in our area – my recollection) and framed up with heavy timbers to about 12 feet by 24 feet divided so two 12 foot square cages could pass – one up and one down, used as counterweights.

Then a "bottom" was formed consisting of a main underground open area as a staging place for full and empty coal cars waiting to be hoisted up or run back out to the "rooms" empty.

From the bottom, "entries" or main tunnels were developed (by removing the coal) into general main line thoroughfares with runways coming off those. From the runways, rooms were cut. All this was done, just by removing the coal. Some coal would be left standing to help support the "top". Wooden mine props (like fence posts) were used to shore up the top also.

The bottom, entries and runways often had some dirt and gob (slag) removed to make them tall enough for a mule (small horse) to be used to pull the "trip" (a group of small cars pulled together). These mules were often, in the early days, kept underground for months at a time and worked with such a low top until the tops of their ears would become worn off. In later years, regulations forced companies to give them one day off per week above ground.

The rooms, of course, were where the men worked along the side of the entries and runways. There was a very intricate numbering system so you could keep track of this. A pair of men (buddies) was assigned a room as their work place and responsibility. Dad and his buddy were assigned three in the south entry.

Since men were paid $3.00 for a day's work and 40 cents per ton for coal, with gob (dirt, rocks, slag, etc.) loaded free, no one would remove more than the coal if it could possibly be avoided. Two men could load 18 to 25 tons per day. Some veins of coal were thicker than others but all varied somewhat. This could mean working in an area with three or four feet of height from floor to roof. Shirley Hill was better than most with the west main entry running to six feet, average about four feet eight inches.

A day's work would consist of going to the mine shaft, meeting your buddy, going down on the cage, sometimes pulling your own trip, finding your tools (picks and shovels) breaking up the coal into reasonable sizes, loading the cars, and pulling them to the bottom. Loading was usually done from kneeling positions (what powerful forearms that made).

Lunch was sandwiches in the middle compartment, pie in the top compartment and water carried in the bottom compartment (that fit together sort of like a double boiler) of an aluminum cylindrical "miners bucket". All this in a pitch black area lit only by a carbide lamp on each man's cap. These lamps gave a smaller light than a two cell flash light and oftentimes coal dust was smeared on the reflector so it would not shine in your "buddy's" eyes. Like lightening bugs!! Can you imagine all this with water dripping everywhere and a minimum of air circulation, more to prevent explosive gas from forming than for miner's comfort?

Then before you left for the day, you or your buddy had to take hand augers and drill several one and one-half inch diameter holes about three feet deep into the face of the wall of coal and tamp in black powder plus a 20 foot long fuse. Later dynamite was used – pushed into the hole with a "huddle".

Since no blasting could be done with miners working, someone (a trusted, experienced miner – Dad did this often) was paid extra to act as a "Shot fire". His job was to stay down after all the other men had gone out, start at the very back of the runway being worked and light the fuses the workers had charged. He was responsible to count the fuses he had lighted and count the number of blasts that occurred. When you think of the things that could go wrong so a shot would not fire – defective fuse, fuse not properly inserted into the powder, powder wet, rock fall that pulled the fuse out, etc. – it is easy to see the possible problems.

Visualize the fear that would grip a man (Shot fire) if only 18 of 20 shots fired. You couldn't risk a group of miners coming in and having a sputtering fuse rekindle so you MUST go back to find out why!!. This job was for men of iron courage!!

Of course, as John L. Lewis and the United Mine Workers Union gained power (starting about 1906) they bargained for day wages, not pay per ton. This made it necessary for the coal companies to improve the efficiency of the work force. This encouraged specialized jobs to be developed and electricity was brought into the mines.

One of the things I did not understand as a child was the tough work this was and the close bonds it built. I could never understand the close relationship between Dad and Dora Simms. They didn't see each other often – quite an age difference and different social levels for Dora went into management. But there was always warmth between them that I couldn't understand.

I know they were buddies at Shirley Hill No. 23, working much as described above for many years. I can now see how that would build a bond like "war buddies" or blood brothers. If you ran out of water, carbide, had a rock fall, or was adding timber to prop up the ceiling for protection from a slate fall you would feel full dependence on your buddy!!

The community was quite diverse and built around farming and related industry.

Each mine of any significance had a good Wash House where miners could shower after a day in the mines. This was of utmost importance since none of the homes in our area had bath rooms – or even running water.

A Wash House was built large enough to accommodate the number of miners who worked the mine. It was simple in construction, made of concrete and corrugated sheet steel, with a place to shower in one corner.

The remainder of the building included rough benches and personal storage baskets for all working miners. These baskets were approximately two feet in diameter, with six inch high expanded metal sides. Each basket had four to six hooks welded outside the metal sides. These were used, in lieu of lockers, for they offered much better drying for the long underwear, shirts, overalls, etc., commonly worn by miners underground. The clothing they wore would soon become black with coal dust and were always wet from sweat and dripping water from the slate and earth overhead. This was inevitable in the underground mines.

Attached to the ceiling of the wash house with a pulley and a rope to allow hoisting, these baskets were approximately 18 to 20 feet above the floor. Miners came to work, placed their wallets and other personal items into the baskets, changed to their underground garb, hung street clothes on the hooks and hoisted them up. They took their dinner buckets with them into the mine. When the shift was finished they would reverse the process, dress in street clothes after showering, hang wet, dirty clothes on the hooks and hoist them up to dry overnight. Any miner found with a basket lowered that was not his own, was "roughly" dealt with – not quite a lynching, but it was considered a very serious offence.

Only a few of these baskets were in use when the men (and boys) of our family would occasionally go, as a group, sometimes headed by Dale, and walk across the field for a "hot shower". This was much better than a bath in the pond and many times better than a No. 3 wash tub in the kitchen in the winter or the smokehouse in the summer.

It was very important to turn cold water on first and off last since the heating was added with "live" steam being throttled into the cold water stream. As the youngest of the group I was properly impressed and NEVER attempted to adjust the water.

The wash house I'm familiar with would have been used by Shirley Hill No. 23 miners since No. 22 had been closed before my time. Actually No. 23 is only remembered as a reduced crew with Chester Arthur, Top Boss, salvaging the steel from the tipple and closing the mine – called "pulling the iron." No doubt it was used by miners in both No. 22 and No. 23.

It was located on the north side of the cluster of buildings needed around the mine - the boiler house, the blacksmith shop, storage buildings and an engine house where the Engineer lived with the steam engines and operated the cables that lifted the cages (elevators) up and down. These cages hoisted up the coal, the men, the mules, the equipment, gob or anything that went either up or down in the shaft. Each shaft was approximately 12 feet x 24 feet divided in half so that, each cage (there were two) was approximately 12 feet x 12 feet. While one was up being loaded, the other was down to be loaded or unloaded.

The wash house needed to be located for easy access for the miners, for water from the pond and steam from the boiler house for heating. It was on a nice level section that was convenient for their work.

The above ground focal point of the shaft mines (deep well mines) was the Tipple. It was located directly over the shafts which were always divided into two separate shafts for separate cages. Everything going in or out of the "bottom", be it men, coal, gob or equipment, went by way of the cages. The Tipple was of fabricated steel construction much like the frame of a building – but had little or no "skin" on it, it was just a framework.

There had to be two pulleys – one directly over the center of each cage. They must be tall enough so that coal could be sorted and cleaned and fed into rail cars by gravity. My guess is these would vary from 40 to 60 feet high. They had to be located with respect to the engine house where steam engines operated drums of cables to lift the cages up and down – one up and one down. These were the domain of the engineer who had mastered the use of levers to control the operation.

It may be of interest to some to know that in addition to the tipple and the cluster of buildings, each mine needed a pond and a gob pile. The pond was needed for boiler feed since all hoisting of the cages was by steam engines and it was mandatory to have a reliable source of power. Therefore, a substantial pond was always built. In the case of Shirley Hill I would guess the pond covered 30 or more acres in its early years.

Shirley Hill's pond was located on the north side of the cluster of buildings needed around the mine – the boiler house, the blacksmith shop, storage buildings and an engine house where the engineer lived with the steam engines and operated the cables that lifted the cages up and down.

Later, in the 30's and early 40's after the fires had burned out the red shale was used for surface on country roads in lieu of gravel. The lane past the farm and down to Johnny Boone's turnaround for the school bus was surfaced with about twelve inches of this material.

Other buildings needed were clustered around this central system as was convenient.

We used the pond for fishing, swimming and sometimes in winter for ice skating. Fishing was a major use for us. Most farmers were not fishermen or hunters but because of Ora's interest our family was an exception.

Swimming and bathing were limited to men and boys since there were no toilet facilities or even a place to change clothes so we normally swam or bathed without benefit of bathing suits. Bathing, after a hot day in the August hay fields was a real rejuvenator but just a bar of soap and a towel was all that was needed, it was mostly all business.

A "gob pile" is an integral part of any coal mining operation. Gob is the term used for all waste coming from the "bottom" of the mine. This would be rock, clay, slate, etc. Of course some coal was always mixed with this since these seams are formed by natural eruptions and are not smoothly divided. This gob was loaded into the small rail cars (approximately 6 feet wide and 8 feet long) that ran on the small track. These cars were called a "trip". The coal trip was sent one direction with coal for cleaning and the gob trip went to the waste pile.

Miners needed a smooth and solid slate "roof" to prop up for safety reasons. When I knew the gob pile, it would have been approximately 150 to 200 feet long and 60 to 80 feet high. The coal ignited by spontaneous combustion so there were always ten to twelve small fires burning around and on the gob pile. This caused our Mother to worry about the possibility of an empty space below the crust that would break through and trap us. While hunting on a cold winter day though, it was a good place to get warm for there were always some coals and little fires that had rolled down near the earth where we could warm in safety.

The largest settlement of miners in our area was Jericho, about one mile north of Park School. The Company Store there was so called because it was owned and operated by the coal company. Ostensibly, this was to help the miners but it also kept some of them in debt. They (or their wives) could draw advance pay for a price. I don't know that the company ever paid in script or chits, (notes good only at the company store) but many companies did in the early days. There must have been twenty or so homes in this area.

(Note by Nita – Flicker was a slang word for drawing a part of one's pay in advance, something Mom and Dad did not believe in or practice. I remember hearing Mom tell about wives who stopped by the mine office so often during the week that there was little left on payday. Mom thought this was a sign of poor management.)

In addition, in an open field opposite the store and slightly south were twenty or more "company houses" of the cheapest possible construction. These were rented to semi-transient miners with families. They were mostly just two rooms end to end, called "shot-gun" houses.

Single miners would often rent a room – two or three to a bed – and get "board" at a local farmer's place. In addition the Company ran a miners train out from Linton, stopping at Dugger to pick up "commuters" to work the mines.

As always wherever groups of men assemble, liquor, gambling and prostitution came. The "saloon" was also at Jericho and accommodated all of this activity. Not unlike the movies of the old west but perhaps with less style than was shown in the movies.

With this area settled by those from the "Old Country", largely British, they brought the English law which allowed the "serfs" of the feudal system "rights" to travel on other people's land – by foot. This right is still vigorously protected in Britain and most European countries where walking is a part of life – often called "wandering".

There were extensive miner's paths throughout the countryside, often with stiles over fences. A stile is a set of steps on both sides of the fence where there is no gate or other way to cross for some distance. Miners would walk together, single file, when leaving the mine and walk a main path, peeling off in order when they came to their private lane.

There was a miner's path down past the Deckard graveyard which was a mile and one half to Grandad Wolfe's house. Walkers on it were Harry McCarty, Murray Chambers, Dide Neal, and Wash Deckard. The miner's train ran out from Linton, stopping to pick up miners from the city who would come out to work at the Shirley Hill mine. Dad was a check weigh man which was a very responsible position. He was also the first secretary to the mine workers union.

The German and Dutch were most likely farmers. The English, Scots and Welsh were of mining stock in the "old country" and carried that on here.

One Hungarian, Jimmy Pickelnesky, called "Jimmy Pick" or "Hunky" with no offence intended or taken, was a coal miner. He could hold a 20 pound sledgehammer at arm's length and with his wrist lower it and kiss the face of it. Young bucks who tried their prowess at this were "kissed" in the teeth by steel!

One Frenchman, Mr. Andre, lived in the area just south of the church and seemed to be well accepted – although not very active in the community. Two stories were told about him, one I believed and one I didn't.

The first story was that he left his fowl hanging on the clothes line by the tail feathers without cleaning until it dropped – it was then properly aged.

This I believe because on an early trip to England one fall in the late 1960's, I ordered wild grouse at one of the finest hotels. They had done exactly the same aging process, rendering the meat too strong for my taste. The age mark (dark meat) was clearly visible about three-eighths to one-half-inch into the meat from the inside out.

The other story was a regularly told joke which I do not believe! Frenchie cooked some rabbit stew and gave a taste to his neighbor who marveled at how good it was. When asked, Frenchie admitted that he mixed it. The recipe? It was 50/50 one horse to one rabbit.

During World War I (1917-1919) Dad, with four children, was not called (drafted). With John L. Lewis, the head of the mine workers union, in firm charge, men in short supply, the day labor rates had been made universal for any large companies.

This, of course, meant that to improve efficiency they would have to improve methods. This resulted in electricity being brought into the mines. The "trip" (a shuttle that carried the miners like a cable car) was pulled with a motor run by a "motorman" – mules were retired. Dad was one of the early motormen. The motorman could also run the cutting machines that would, like a big chain saw, undercut the face of the coal to improve the efficiency of the blasting.

Electricity which was first in the coal mines was direct current (DC) and could not be transformed for long distance transmission. Soon, however, alternating current (AC) voltage was extended to cities around and electrical skills were in demand.

Since the cutting machines were run by DC overhead trolley wires the miners did their own wiring, hence, Dad became an electrician. He became quite proficient in this skill. International Correspondence School was growing by leaps and bounds and self-teaching books were everywhere. Dad was an avid reader and took advantage of the self-help books.

During this time (I'm not sure just when) Dad got caught underground in a minor slate fall. I *was never able to learn just how bad it was but he lost his two upper incisors. They were replaced with two gold teeth – about the only jewelry a man could wear back then!*

Regardless of "how bad", it was undoubtedly one of the most terrifying experiences one can imagine – miles underground, poor air, pitch black and never knowing whether this was a small rock or the start of an avalanche, it had to be frightening!!

What better motivation to learn the skills required for a "job on top"! About this time Dad graduated to a fireman whose responsibility was to generate steam for the hoisting engineer to operate the cages and to maintain the boilers, boiler room, etc.

He took great pride in the knowledge and skill required and the responsibility. Late in Work War I and for two to three years after, wages were $7.50 per day and often Dad needed to work a double shift – when someone didn't come in, day off, etc. He would bank the boiler, walk home, and eat a quick bite while Mom fixed him another lunch, then go back for another eight hours. This earned him the unheard of rate of $15.00 a day.

This was a hard life for a miner, also a hard life for a miner's wife. In a remote location, alone at night she would often hear noises and see the clothesline post "walk". What kept her from becoming immobilized with fear was that her children needed her protection. I don't really know that she was ever in real physical danger. I am certain she would have given a good accounting of herself had danger threatened her children.

The dangers of no communication, medical attention or fellowship were accepted. Is it any wonder that the "old Dromedary" place could not compare to one within walking distance of the "home place" and a community of known church friends and relatives?

While the men and boys swam in the Shirley Hill pond and on a hot summer evening would bathe there and occasionally ice skate in winter, fishing was very important to our family.

Dad (Ora) was a good fisherman, read the magazines and applied what he learned with success. He was certainly limited by lack of money when I came upon the scene.

My first recollection of Dad fishing was in the very early 1930's when often on Sunday morning he would plan a day of fishing. I would sometimes accompany him although Mom (Ann) made it clear that she would prefer I attend church with the rest of the family. Dad had no rod or cane pole but would go along the railroad track and cut a live "sapling" (tall thin tree about the size of a fishing pole) and add his own line with hook and bobber.

The first order of business was a very small pole equipped with a small hook to catch some minnows for bait – usually silver-sides but small catfish minnows were also considered good bait. Usually the method was to walk out in the water to waist high, lob the minnow out perhaps 20 additional feet and let the poles float but keep them close and wait for bass action. Usually this was on the points from Uncle Floyd's meadow and often produced three or four nice bass – enough for a family meal.

Then, True Temper, a manufacturer of steel rods came upon the scene. These rods were heavy stiff clumsy things but cheap. First came bait casting rods. They would carry a three-fourth or one ounce plug some distance and often stop with a "backlash", a messy tangle that had to be untangled before you could proceed. The standard bait was a large "red head" – broom handle size, about four inches long, plug with a white body and red head. No one knows what the bass thought it was but it fooled a lot of them.

One well known and accepted story of the time: Lester (Rip) Deckard, a cousin who was Jim's age, when he was 11 or 12 years old, mustered enough money to buy a steel casting rod complete with reel, line and red head from Sears and Roebuck mail order catalogue. It came, he assembled it and walked down to Shirley Hill pond, No. 2 point, made one cast, caught a bass 12 or 14 inches long, placed the rod over his shoulder and walked back home with the fish dangling from a hook on the red head. He was proud of his catch and a family hero!

Dad, of course, ever the inventor and craftsman made some plugs of his own design adjusting their shapes and mountings to affect their action. One I recall was whittled out of cedar shaped much like a Lazy Ike. Its reputation was so good that some friends would drive some distance to borrow it. I recall Uncle Ernie, Dad's youngest brother, returning it after getting it caught on a stump, tearing the end treble hook out. Of course, Dad repaired it but his repair never matched the original.

Next, True-Temper Rods had eight-foot telescoping rods in hardware stores at low prices. Dad bought one, and he, and later I, learned to fly cast with this. It had terrible action compared to anything else but was the best we had.

This started him upon a new hobby of Fly Tying.

Early on Dad bought hooks at hardware stores, small little corks for top waters from drug stores and regular sewing thread for the tie. He learned to use acetone to dissolve various colors of colloid to make heads, eyes and to seal the tie.

Mostly Dad made cork bodied floaters or plain hackle flies. He never learned to add tails and wings. However, he never worked with a vice, hackle pliers or the other dozens of accoutrements that I and good tiers (of which I am not) use – and need. The standard feathers were neck and saddle feathers from red, black or barred rock chickens. This made catching bass a real production and catching bluegills (which were much more plentiful) a real fun activity. Many, many great meals of bass and bluegills were a result of this skill of tying flies and fishing.

I recall one trip Dad and a couple of other men (none of his boys) made to Bonair No.1 mine pond about 1935-37. That pond was large with about 15 acres of wade able water with a sandy bottom – ideal for bluegill spawning. By this time he may have had a better rod or had learned to use a leader with multiple flies. On this Bonair trip he used a leader with five flies.

Dad came home with great stories and a gunny sack with fifty good sized blue gills in it. The men folk immediately started to clean the fish and the womenfolk moved with their preparation. All fifty fish were fried making huge platters full. It was our custom to cook all fish that were caught as quickly as possible and we usually just ate until they were gone. Remember we had no refrigeration at that time so even if some were left it was easier to store fried fish than raw ones. Besides there were probably eight hungry mouths that all loved fish, to feed.

I learned Dad's method of fly tying but never did it as well as he did.

Sometime around this time, Dad took the three boys (James, Max and Bob (me), to Hud Woodward's Hardware Store in Dugger. We each selected a cane pole 18 to 20 feet long. This was our best equipment until after World War II.

After 1947, when all the Wolfe boys had returned from Military service, we joined the rest of the world with fiberglass rods in various stages as the technology developed. By that time The Farm was surrounded with stripper pits left when coal mining was stripping over-burden (earth and shale) down to the coal, the coal was removed and a pit was left. While most of the pits did not have toxic water, the sides were so straight with water too deep for ideal fish reproduction. However, there were always some places for spawning and they soon became good bass fishing pits.

So many pits, so few fishermen then and some of the pits were quite remote with poor access for strangers. One was west of The Farm and somewhat south of the gravel east/west road past Granny Mosier's place. Dad had made a road accessible with his home-made tractor. He had built a ladder down to a flat surface by the water's edge. With his trailer hitch he could take visiting family members to his private spot and usually catch a few bass.

My last fishing trip with Dad was the summer of 1978 when he was 90 years old. The Phillips family and our family had fished and vacationed together often because of our common interest and the compatible age of our children.

Knowing that Dad had never caught a trout even though he had read so much about their willingness to take flies we thought we would make that possible for him. Due to a story in Outdoor Magazine, referring to great fishing in Pennsylvania, Potter County and Kettle Creek to be exact, the trip to take Dad was planned. We were camping and Dad insisted on sleeping in the open – fortunately the weather was good during our four-day stay. We chose a campsite near the creek but the terrain to get to it was rough through some wooded area. By the time we got to the creek, Dad was bushed and had lost interest in further activity. Now at 90 years of age myself, I understand.

I always thought I should have planned that trip better. I did save Dad's fishing license at 90 years old and we all greatly admired him for his effort.

This vignette will omit the farm work such as haying, corn production, etc., that has been covered elsewhere in this work. Mother was her "father's daughter" in her attachment to the land, love of farm life and competence in the work of a farm wife – caring for milk products, garden care and husbandry of the chicken flock.

Dad had lived in the environment and was competent in various aspects but had no love for the land or for farm life as such. At least he didn't love the land as Mother did or as most farmers do. In addition, the thirty acres attached to the home place was good farm land but not enough to support a family unless very specialized farming methods were used. The thirty acres one mile away was only about fifty percent tillable and it was poor soil with hardpan underneath.

For both practical and personal reasons, Dad needed to work "off the farm" for cash to support the family. The coal mines were the obvious places to work with six mines within walking distance of home. These were deep shaft mines and the heavy earthmoving equipment needed to remove up to fifty to ninety feet of earth (over burden) for strip mines was not yet available. This work in the deep shaft mines was unpleasant, dirty, wet and hazardous work.

Sometime before my memory, Dad had experienced a slate fall (rock from the roof falling) that knocked two front teeth out. He was lucky as this often resulted in death for the involved miner. This was a well-established fact for originally as the teeth were replaced, they were replaced with two gold teeth. It was common in the 1920 and 30's and treated as a jewel. Later as it lost popularity, Dad's gold teeth were replaced with teeth of natural color.

I have always greatly admired Dad for the fact that he usually had one of the very few highly skilled jobs at a shaft mine. I know he worked in the bottom (underground – the least desirable jobs) for several years. Perhaps the slate fall was a motivation (it would be for me) and at some point he decided to learn the skills of a Fireman to operate a steam boiler. A steam engine was used to raise and lower the cage elevators. Everything that went into or came out of the mines was on the cages. Profit resulted in getting the coal out and most of all, miners used the cages to come and go. Any disruption in the engine performance was considered an immediate tragedy. Imagine being stranded ninety to one-hundred-fifty feet below the surface of the earth!!

The Fireman was under the supervision of the Hoisting Engineer and was generally ignored by the regular mine supervision. That suited Dad, as it would any of us, and besides he was needed when any work was done so his work was more regular.

I was told by Dad that he learned the skill from studying a correspondence course by Audel and no doubt had help from the Hoisting Engineer or a Lead Fireman. I know there were several years during the Great Depression when Dad did not work at the mine. From my personal memory, as the economy ramped up, perhaps around 1938 and Templeton Coal Company reopened No. 17 mine, renaming it John A after the senior Templeton, Dad was the Lead Fireman. That meant day shift (7 a.m. to 3 p.m.), and supervising those on the 3 to 11 and 11 to 7 shifts. He was also responsible, under the Hoisting Engineer, for proper maintenance, care and operation of the coal fired, fire-tube boilers. Not bad for a man with only an eighth grade education.

My respect for this grew as I studied "Steam Power Stations" by Gaffert in the engineering curriculum at Illinois Institute of Technology (IIT). I, also, was responsible for supervising Firemen in the Terre Haute, Indiana, Flemington, New Jersey, and Cartersville, Georgia plants in my various capacities in my engineering jobs.

Dad was not meant to be an entrepreneur as he was much too spontaneous and not given to *carefully planning the future. However, when times were hard he tried several jobs. I will discuss those with which I have seen physical evidence or have personal knowledge of.*

For years there were a few pictures of Dad with rabbits. It was said that the plan was to raise purebred rabbits for sale.

Another way Dad tried to make some extra income was by raising dogs. He owned a Horace Lytle book on birddog training. He bought a high priced setter dog or two, and trained and traded several dogs. I heard him say many times he would always take off the first ten days of bird (quail) season and shoot a box of shells a day – an unheard of expense!

Also the best season Dad ever had was the season he knocked down 96 quail and only lost one! This was due to "a little six month old setter "bitch" that distinguished odors so well she "would point one bird while retrieving another one in her mouth".

As I got better at my math I could figure 10 x 25 divided by 96 was about two and a half shells per bird – and that over good dogs! However, Dad could always out shoot his sons!

He later had plans for pure bred chickens and there were trays approximately eighteen inches square and two inches deep of perforated, galvanized metal that were part of a stack on a rack for growing sprouted oats. This was to provide greens for the chickens. Pure bred chickens needed special care.

(Note by Nita: I remember a funny story Mom used to tell about Dad's special chickens. Happy Carr and Dad were the best of friends but Happy was a big jokester. He got a big kick out of Dad's special rabbits, special dogs and now, special chickens. So he went into town to the hatchery and bought a few Rhode Island Red chickens – just the regular kind anyone could buy. Happy boxed them up as though they were from Dad's specialty company. He met the mail carrier a few miles before he got to our house and talked him into delivering the chickens to Dad.

The chickens came and Dad was proud of them!! Of course, Happy got there shortly after the mailman came. Dad showed off his chickens and told Hap all about them. Dad proceeded to tell all his friends and feed them their special food. Finally the "real" chickens came and "the jig was up". Happy had to confess and they all had a good laugh.)

These three odd jobs were before my time but Dad freely discussed them when asked about the evidence.

I recall this about the large shed on the west end of the barn (the early barn near our house). Above the sliding door the words "Strictly Cash" were scrawled with black paint. This, then, became Dad's auto repair business. He had studied from books and worked briefly as a mechanic in a garage in Sullivan. I recall his brother, Uncle Ernie, bringing his car a few times for repair and never paying for the work done. I don't believe this lasted very long. Dad was a better mechanic than he was a business man.

Following that, Dad worked for a while as a telephone line repairman. I know he had the climbing spurs around for a while – this was before the days of "cherry pickers" for repairman to work from. I'm sure that doing repairs with climbing spurs was very strenuous work. I don't know how long this job lasted or the reason for Dad discontinuing it.

The last odd job I recall Dad having was selling "Can't Slam Door Closers". These seemed to be good door closers. They each had a "catch" about twelve inches before the door closed completely which "caught," (stopped briefly) and caused the door to close softly instead of closing with a bang. However, they were very rough looking with all mechanism, springs and cams exposed. I was surprised to see one of these on a door twenty to twenty-five years ago. I expect they are still being made.

I recall Dad having two other real jobs. One was Fireman at Templeton's John A Mine located on Route 54 at the old No. 12 and No. 17 site and one at a stripper mine. Dad worked at the John A Mine in my high school days and afterward until the mine closed. After we returned from military service, Dad worked at a strip mine in the Pleasantville, Indiana, area. I'm not sure at which mine.

Fortunately his miner's retirement pension was sufficient for Mom and Dad's living. Their life needs and wants were simple. This was augmented with the sale of the farm property with the sales contract allowing them to remain living there for their lifetime.

Chapter 9 ══════════════════════════════════

Development Years

When I look back now and remember what life was like on the farm when we kids were all growing up, it's hard to even remember how hard some of it must have been. Mom and Dad, nor any of us kids either for that matter, ever complained. Of course, it was all we, or they, had ever known and it probably seemed better to them than when they were growing up.

As children, we had no electricity, no running water, no indoor toilet, no central heat, no air conditioning, nor so many things that seem so normal today. Our light for reading or studying at night was a coal oil (kerosene) lamp in the center of the table and if anyone needed something that was in another room, Mom carried the lamp so it could be found, then the lamp was carried back and put in place.

Every drop of water we drank or used was carried into the house from the tall iron pump with the long pump handle beside the front kitchen door. We only used one water bucket and it sat in the kitchen. It was about a two and one-half gallon bucket, usually enamelware, with one long handled dipper for drinking, to dip water for cooking or washing up.

We all drank from the same dipper and water was never wasted. If you got more in the dipper than you could drink, you did NOT pour it back into the bucket. You could put it in the teakettle (where it would be boiled) or in the reservoir that was attached to the side of the stove where the water was always hot to warm and was used for washing up but was never used for drinking or cooking. You didn't throw it out. If it did get contaminated in some way it was poured into a bucket (called a slop bucket) that sat outside the back door and was carried to water the chickens or pigs when the bucket was full.

The toilet was way out by the chicken house and summer or winter, rain or shine, sleet or snow you walked the distance. No one was ever allowed to use the indoor chamber pot unless they were sick. Toilet paper was a page torn from last year's Sears and Roebuck or Montgomery Ward catalogue. Every catalogue had a few slick sheets for special items or advertising on them but most of the sheets were of softer paper and could be crumpled a few times to make them usable.

We had never heard of central heating in those years. All of our heat in the winter was provided by the Warm Morning heating stove and the Home Comfort kitchen range. The bedrooms had no heat at all and in the dead of winter believe me, they were cold. We always had a feather bed to snuggle into and on the coldest nights Mom would hold a small blanket up real close to the stove and get it good and warm. We would run and jump into bed and she would wrap our feet, two or even three children in one bed, and we would sleep warm as toast.

Yes, it was cold without central heat and just the opposite in the summer without air conditioning. The fuzzy cotton blankets used on the beds in the winter were replaced by white bleached muslin sheets and that helped some but when it got so hot we couldn't sleep even with every window and door open we might bring our pillows and lay on the cool linoleum floor in the dining room or by the door on the carpet in the living room.

Winter and summer, Dad was always the first person out of bed in the morning about 4:30 a.m. In winter you could hear him shaking down the ashes in the stove and breaking up the coals, firing up the heating stove so the house would be warm when we all got up. The fire was never allowed to die out in the heating stove all winter long. When Dad went to bed at night he banked the fire, which meant that he covered the existing fire that had died down some in the evening with lots of small pieces of coal which was called slack, closed the draft at the bottom and the fire just smoldered all night and formed a nice crust. When he shook the ashes down into the ash pan, opened the bottom door draft, broke the crust and stirred up the fire it would burst into flames and with a few pieces of fresh coal, the room would soon be warm. Of course, the ashes had to be taken out every day but that was usually a boy's job.

Then, snow or sleet, rain or shine, Dad was off to the barn with milk pails in hand to milk the cows and tend to the livestock. There were two horses and one or two pigs to feed and the two or more cows ate while the milking progressed. The chickens could wait till later, which Mom usually took care of. Often in winter, ice had to be cut in the pond and the ice block removed so the animals could drink.

Some forty-five or so minutes later Dad would return to the house, chores done and about three gallons of milk in hand. By this time Mom had built up the fire in the kitchen stove, made Dad's lunch and had breakfast ready or nearly ready. Breakfast consisted of homemade baking powder biscuits, eggs, ham or bacon from our own butchered hogs and always cream gravy. All supplemented by homemade butter and jelly, milk, sometimes peanut butter, coffee for Dad and milk for the kids. Always coffee for Dad although neither Mom nor anyone else in the family ever drank it, Mom made fresh percolated coffee every morning for Dad. That was the only meal when he drank coffee.

Dad's shift at the mine was 7 a.m. to 3 p.m. He was off to work at 6 a.m. about the time the kids got up. In winter we grabbed our clothes and hurried out by the stove to dress in the warmth. Breakfast was ready and we ate before we did our morning chores. We were always hungry and there was never a problem getting everyone to the table. The boys had outside chores feeding the chickens, cleaning stalls, finishing the barn work and sometimes shoveling snow.

On wash day, nearly always Monday, the iron kettle was placed on its metal stand, water carried from the pump to fill it and a fire built under the kettle. In bad weather the water was carried into the house to fill the reservoir and a couple of buckets full on the stove. In the meantime Evah and I would clear the table and wash up the breakfast dishes. We then helped Mom finish up the school lunches if we had time.

In elementary school we all had to walk the quarter mile to Park School. In the higher grades when we went into Dugger to Junior High or High School we had to be ready when the school bus came. For a few years we walked to the corner by Granny's house but later the bus came down our lane.

After the school kids were out of the house for the day, Mom began her day of work. I'm sure the thought of going back to bed for a nap was never an option. It never entered her mind. The milk Dad had carried in had to be strained, in case some hairs from the cow or pieces of straw had gotten into it, then carried to the cellar, chickens fed (if the boys hadn't fed them) and eggs gathered, plus a myriad of chores and work of a farm wife.

Milk that was a few days old was carried up from the cellar when the new day's milk was carried down. Then it was skimmed of its cream, which was saved to make butter. If it had soured to a clabber, the milk was used to make cottage cheese or just fed to the chickens or pigs. Mom made the most delicious cottage cheese I ever ate by slicing through two or three gallon crocks of clabbered milk, pouring it into a dishpan and setting it toward the back of the kitchen stove to heat slowly. The clabber separated into curds and whey and was poured into the big round strainer that fit over a gallon crock. By the time the whey had all drained into the crock, the curds were cool enough to be broken up into small pieces.

Mom used her fingers to break them into small curds, then poured the curds into a dish, seasoned them with salt and pepper and put good fresh sweet cream over them and it was cottage cheese fit for a king. The whey went into the "slop" bucket to be fed to the chickens or pigs.

On Monday, the weekly wash was the top priority for Mom. Before electricity, weekly washing meant bringing into the house (or under a tree in the summer) two large zinc wash tubs, one for hot water, the washboard and soap and one for the rinse water. The dirty clothes were pressed into the hot water to soak for a while then pulled up piece by piece onto the washboard, rubbed with the big bar of Fels Naptha laundry soap and scrubbed until they were clean. They were wrung by hand and rinsed through the tub of clean water, wrung again by hand and thrown into the laundry basket to be hung with clothespins onto an outdoor clothesline in summer. On rainy days or in the deep of winter, Mom rigged up drying lines by placing long pieces of one inch by two inch lumber between two chairs on three sides of the heating stove and hung the clothes over them to dry. She could use all three sides of the stove and get them all dry that way.

About 1938, after electricity arrived Mom and Dad bought a square tub Maytag washing machine with a wringer. This was kept in the smoke house for we still had to have an extra tub of water for rinse water. The Maytag would wash until you stopped it, nothing automatic, then each piece of clothing was picked out by hand and put through the wringer. The wringer was two rolls of hard rubber held tightly together, one on top of the other, with a mechanism and a hand crank that had to be turned to push the clothes through. It could be turned on its metal pin so the clothing rinsed by hand in the rinse tub could be run through the wringer and they dropped down into the clothes basket. All clothes were washed in the one tub of water starting with the whites and usually only one tub of rinse water. A far cry from the automatic washers of today but still a wonderful blessing!

Ironing on Tuesday was a long tiring job. All washable clothing was made of cotton, no wash and wear, and everything except underwear and socks were ironed. However, I expect the rather full black sateen bloomers with elastic around the waist and the legs worn by the girls were ironed.

Before electricity flatirons had to be heated on the cook stove so a hot fire had to be maintained in it. We had three sizes of irons – one large one for the heavier clothing like overalls, two medium sized and one small iron to get into pleats and gathers. These were put on the stove early for they were three, maybe four inches thick and took a while to heat up. One handle fit all sizes and was a half circle of round smooth wood so it wouldn't get hot. A piece of iron across the open side of the handle was fitted with a latch with a little wooden button on top. You held the handle, pulled the button with your two front fingers, opened the latch and attached it to the top of the iron. The iron was carried to the ironing board, ironed with as long as it was hot enough, carried back to the stove and exchanged for a hot iron. Early in the morning, or the night before, the clean clothes were sprinkled with water, rolled up and placed neatly together in the laundry basket to dampen just enough to iron all the wrinkles out nicely. All the irons were shaped like a rather flat oval and pointed on each end. Overalls were harder to iron than dresses, shirts, tablecloths, etc., but Mom insisted they get the same attention as anything else.

On other days there was the sewing and the interminable mending to be done. A tear here, a rip there, a button off, a seam or hem out all had to be repaired as soon as possible. Mom was a good seamstress. She could make that Singer treadle machine fly and she also made a tiny, beautiful hand stitch.

Mom made many of our clothes especially dresses for the girls. Yard goods were inexpensive, about ten cents a yard for material for a school dress and she could use a pattern several times by adjusting its size and changing the trim. She liked to fancy up the dresses she made for us with hand embroidery, lace, rick-rack or something special. I remember a navy wool winter dress she had bought for Evah and she bought some navy wool and made me one just like it. She put the same little embroidered red flowers and red satin edging on mine and it was a very good match. She made all our pillow cases. I have the last pair she embroidered and I still love to look at them.

The black bloomers (underpants) that Evah and I wore were also made by Mom. They were made of black sateen, very full and gathered at the waist with elastic. The legs were also gathered with elastic and could be worn just below the knee or pulled above the knee which caused them to sort of "bloom" out. Of course we always wore long cotton stockings that came well above the knee and were held up with garters.

I don't remember that Mom ever tried to make overalls for the boys. Good, rugged material was needed for overalls and as they wore out, usually at the knees first, she was adept at patching them. She kept the worn out pairs and used the good parts of them for patches. She made a mighty neat patch. They didn't look like new but the patches added miles of wear to the overalls. Also Mom made some cotton chambray shirts for the boys and Bob remembers her making him a night cap to wear to bed. He had a cow lick in the crown of his head and thought it would lay down better if he slept in a cap. Thanks to the ever thoughtful Evah, Bob has one of the little blue chambray shirts Mom made for him. She tailored it with lovely felled seams and handmade buttonholes. It is a true prize. His story of the shirt follows, as told by Bob:

The Handmade Shirt

"Bob, I have a present for you." was my sister's unexpected comment as we sat around the table enjoying our after dinner coffee. This was Evah and Bill's first evening with us having driven from Michigan to New Jersey for a visit circa 1973.

Being a close family of seven children we visited siblings at every opportunity. The 500 mile trip seemed worth the effort each time any of us had a break in our schedule. A gift was not essential although most often a household gift was presented to Ginnie. I could tell from Evah's inflection that this was special.

A small flat box was presented unwrapped and contained a faded blue work shirt much too small for me.

Seeing the puzzled look on my face she explained. "This is your shirt made for you by our Mother when you were seven or eight years old. On a visit to The Farm in our early marriage while helping Mom clear out and discard some of the accumulation of no longer useful items, I found this. It was in such good condition I couldn't discard it. I kept it, for in those early years the 1950s, you were moving so much. I must admit, I really enjoyed looking at it occasionally for it is the last of her hand made clothing."

We then discussed how much sewing our Mother did of necessity to clothe her husband and family; dresses, blouses and skirts for the girls; mostly work shirts from blue cotton chambray for the boys. The treadle Singer sewing machine was kept busy even though much of the work was just with needle, thread and thimble.

I personally recall the winter I was five years old, standing between the sewing machine and the wall with my Mother peddling away as she sewed something for the family.

Shirt measures: Neck 10 ½" Sleeve – shoulder to cuff 18" Tail – collar down back 25"

The details of this shirt are remarkable for it was not made for display or for show just to clothe her child. It is complete with a double front placket, trimmed pocket, a collar with a full neck band, neat handmade buttonholes, full cuffs with a turned gusset and all seams double stitched.

The shirt though not badly worn has two torn holes. I maintain that older brothers did it although they look much like holes made by getting too close to a barbed wire fence.

By Bob Wolfe, Jan. 14, 2011

And Mom's baking… never ending baking. There was hot bread of some kind every day winter and summer, sometimes more than once. Besides the hot breakfast biscuits, there was always hot corn bread with soup beans or root vegetables that seemed to call for it and greens, picked fresh from the pasture, the fields or sometime along the roadside, screamed for cornbread baked in an iron skillet. All the light bread, as we called yeast bread to distinguish it from the others, was made by Mom. Her large black bread pan held three loaves and she filled and baked the loaves at least twice, maybe three times a week.

When we got home from school we were always hungry. If we were lucky enough to get home about the time the bread came out of the oven and you could tell that by the aroma before you got into the house, a special treat would be a slice of warm bread slathered with home churned butter and maybe homemade apple butter. Other days there were usually apples or sometimes pears from the Kiefer tree by the hen house. These pears were as hard as rocks until about December when they softened (stored in bushel baskets in the cellar) to a mellow, juicy flavor though they kept a somewhat granular texture.

After a snack there were always evening chores. We resisted changing our clothes, but it rarely, if ever, worked. We were expected to change out of our school clothes into everyday clothes to do chores. Our clothes were never washed after just one wearing. That saved on laundry and besides we didn't have enough clothes to wear something different every day. The evening milking was done by Dad until the boys were old enough to do it properly for it was important to empty the cow's bags and utters so they could fill again for morning.

There was always kindling and wood for the boys to carry in to fill the wood box by the side of the kitchen stove under the reservoir and coal buckets to fill and carry in for both stoves in the winter. We girls usually gathered the eggs in the evening and helped Mom with supper.

Supper, the evening meal and all meals were family style. There were always potatoes fixed some way. That was a staple and plenty had been dug, cleaned of the major dirt and carried to the cellar to last through the winter. There would be at least two or three other vegetables from the bounty in the cellar (or the garden in the summer) that included canned green beans, corn, tomatoes, pickles, a variety of relishes and root vegetables like turnips or parsnips in baskets in the cellar. Of course there had to be bread of some kind at every meal. If the bread wasn't on the table when we sat down to eat, Dad's first words would be "Where's the bread?"

After supper was homework time around the dining room table with light from the one kerosene lamp. This lamp gave a faint yellow glow for about six feet in every direction but that didn't detract from the learning experience. We didn't each have homework every evening but with six children in the family, it was a sure bet that someone would have some homework. Of course there was some horse play but homework was taken seriously. If sibling help wasn't sufficient, Mom was always there to help with any subject, especially spelling. She kept after us about spelling and if anyone was having trouble, practice carried over into the next morning orally while we were dressing, at the breakfast table and until we went out the door to school.

If homework was finished quickly and there was time, we would play Riddles, Hully-Gully, Checkers or read poetry. We all loved for Mom to read to us and the poem "Kentucky Belle" was a favorite of everyone.

Friday evening was no homework and Saturday and Sunday evenings were special times. We all enjoyed a big bowl of apples just eaten out of hand, cracking nuts, popping corn or occasionally making cookies or candy. Pulling taffy was great fun and Mom would make a big batch so everyone could get in the act.

There were always lots of black walnuts and hickory nuts gathered in fall and a big bowl full of them provided fun and good snacking. Mom had a special brick and a neat little tack hammer she used to crack the nuts and we each had our own nut picker – a new horseshoe nail that had a good sharp tip performed as well as any picker that could be bought.

Popcorn was popped by the dishpan full. We all loved popcorn and a bowl full wouldn't do the trick. With this size group practical rules developed. The person who volunteered, or was drafted to pop, could taste or eat a few grains but no one else was allowed to be in the kitchen during the popping. Fair play demanded everyone start eating at the same time.

By 8:30 or 9:00 p.m. at the very latest it was off to bed for everyone; morning came early. In the winter the bedrooms were cold but with three boys in one double bed and two girls in another they warmed up fast. During the cold weather when there was no heat in the bedrooms except what seeped under the closed door Mom would hold a cotton blanket next to the stove until it got really hot. Then Evah and I would run and jump into bed and Mom would wrap the warm blanket around our feet, binding them together and we would sleep snug as a bug in a rug all night long. I'm sure she did this for the boys too. She was not one to play favorites.

Life as a child in the country on the farm was good. Our lives revolved around family, church and school. In retrospect we had very little in the way of material things but our "wants" were few and our "needs" were met. Being a part of a large family certainly had its advantages. We were never lonesome. There was always something to do and somebody to do it with. Bored?... we didn't know the word.

I am amazed now when I think back at the freedom we had to wander and run about at will. There was hardly a hint of danger from strangers or in the fields and woods that were so familiar to us. However we did not go to people's houses and go inside without Mom's permission.

Evah and I made a new playhouse every summer. We would take old pieces of rope or string – whatever we could find – and make rooms by roping off sections between the trees. For the kitchen, we needed no more than a flat piece of wood on a box for a table, an orange crate on end for a kitchen cabinet and a large cardboard box we could draw a cooktop on with crayons. Broken dishes of any kind and old pots and pans that had sprung a leak or were not fit to be used in the house anymore were saved for our playhouse.

If worst came to worst and we couldn't find enough old things at home, we could run back to a big ditch that bordered our property and see what another family might have thrown away. With no formal trash pickup, every family was responsible to get rid of the old castoffs and the ditch was used for that purpose. If we were lucky, we might find an old broken chair or some other sort of broken household items we could drag up to our playhouse. Sometimes we could coax our brothers into the playhouse but as a rule they had things of more interest to them to do.

The boys played Marbles a lot. They had a big bag of marbles they shared for it took more than one person to make an interesting game of marbles. They drew a big circle and poured all the marbles, except the taws, into the center of the ring. Each player had his own taw, which was a large shooter marble, and whoever could hold his taw between his thumb and forefinger and shoot the most marbles out of the ring was the winner. I was never too good at this game so I didn't bother the boys much about marbles.

A lot of time could be spent by the boys just roaming the fields with their bean flippers and shooting at anything such as old tin cans, telephone lines or anything else that came into view. However, after you killed a bird, you lost the desire to shoot at birds, so inanimate objects were the best targets.

I particularly liked to go exploring with the boys if they would let me. One afternoon when they decided I could go with them we were back in the woods where wild grapevines grew up in some of the trees. The boys had discovered that since there was a small hole running through the center of the grapevine, if you cut a small dry piece of vine you could light it with a match and smoke it sort of like a cigarette. I don't remember who had the matches for they were certainly taboo but somebody had matches, and we spent a great deal of time finding and cutting dry vines into cigarette size. We didn't have much luck lighting and smoking them but we kept trying.

After being gone so long when we got back to the house Mom said in a rather sharp tone "Where in the world have you kids been for so long?" We hadn't anticipated that question nor were we aware we had been gone a long time. Before anyone else could come up with a good answer, Bob, the youngest one of the bunch, five or six years old at the time, quickly spoke up and said, "Well.....we haven't been smoking grapevines!!" That was a dead giveaway and we were all in "hot water". I expect Mom was smiling on the inside but if she was, we never saw it. She continued with a stern little tongue lashing.

I was always a tomboy. I loved to wear the boys' overalls and play their games when they would let me. Mom used to say that I was happiest wearing a pair of the boy's overalls with a bean flipper (slingshot) and a pocket full of rocks. We always made our own bean flippers and I could make one about as good as the boys could. We found a nice green tree limb about an inch in diameter with a nice strong fork. We took a pocket knife and cut both sides of the fork four or five inches long and the handle about six inches long.

Then you went to the garage and found an old inner tube (Dad always saved them) and cut a long, thin strip of rubber about an inch wide and fifteen or twenty inches long, punched a little slit in each end and stretched the little holes over a notch you had cut on the ends of both prongs of the fork. Now with a few nice smooth little rocks you picked up in the gravel driveway, you were in business.

The boys usually fancied theirs up by cutting the piece of rubber in the center, inserting a small piece of leather to hold the rock with, but I didn't always have time for that engineering feat and it would work without it. Maybe not as accurately, but it worked!

I remember one time in particular when I would have been better off if I had stayed in the house with Evah and Mom. It was after a nice, long summer rain and the sun had come out bright. The boys, with me tagging along, had gone down to the cattle pond close to the barn where the cows were fed and milked. The rain had softened the ground going down to the pond until it was a muddy mess, the kind that squeezes up between your toes. We were always all barefoot in the summer and the boys were skating down the little incline that went down to the little dam around the pond and of course, I joined right in. I didn't see a small piece of glass hidden by the mud, skated right over it and made a big cut on the bottom of my foot.

Of course I started howling and my brothers came running to see what the problem was. They found the piece of glass, and then helped me, dripping with blood, to the house where Mom took over. She always seemed to know just what to do so she cleaned the cut out good, saturated it with one of her magic potions (probably turpentine mixed with sugar) and bound it up tight.

The boys didn't have any trouble with me tagging along for a few days, until my foot healed and could be walked on. I don't remember that Mom saved the piece of glass, and laid it up on the kitchen safe so my foot would heal but if anyone stepped on a rusty nail, (which happened frequently) she always cleaned the wound out good, saturated it with her turpentine and sugar potion then she always laid the nail on the top of the kitchen safe, the highest place in the house, until the wound healed.

We teased Mom in later years about greasing the rusty nail and saving it and she just laughed and said she didn't know how much it helped but she knew it didn't hurt anything. This method always worked in our family. I don't remember anyone needing the doctor for anything as simple as a rusty nail or a cut of any kind.

Mom also knew how to get rid of a cold in short order too. The first question she asked if it was a cold was, "How are your bowels?" If they weren't good, the first order of business was what she called a physic – we would be more apt to say "a laxative" today. Then she got out the Vicks Salve, put a good chunk of it in a tablespoon and held it over the blaze in the lamp until it got hot. After you took a few big sniffs of that, she rubbed it all over your chest and covered your whole chest with a warm flannel rag she kept for that purpose. If you were getting a sore throat, she rewarmed the Vicks and rubbed your neck good and wrapped another flannel rag around it, warmed a small blanket and wrapped your feet in it as she put you to bed. You would definitely be better by morning!

Church was always important in our lives. Mom had gone to Old Hickory Church all her life and it was a good solid Methodist Protestant Church where the Bible was preached emphatically. When we were kids most families in our area attended it. Though it was only one large room, Sunday school classes were assigned different sections and we all knew where our class belonged. There was room for all.

Special events for the youth included a weekly meeting on Sunday evening called Christian Endeavor, later changed to MYF (Methodist Youth Fellowship). To answer roll call each member was required to say (or read if you hadn't memorized one) a Bible verse of choice. Sometimes one of the boys who didn't have a memory verse thought it was quite clever to say this verse: John 11:3, "Jesus wept." That usually brought a little chuckle from the young members and a slight smile to the faces of the adults present.

During the summer months the young people gathered at different homes usually on Saturday for recreation; such as an evening of games often with a big bonfire and wiener roast. In winter a favorite activity for the group would be to meet in a home for an indoor evening of games and a taffy-pull, making popcorn balls or some such fun activity.

Special programs for certain holidays like Christmas and Easter were put on by the youth of the church. An adult or a committee was in charge and any child who wanted to, could participate. A play might be chosen by whoever was in charge; roles would be assigned then and several evenings of practice were scheduled. Those who did not have a part in the play would be given poems to memorize and recite and those who could carry a tune might be asked to sing.

An adult, probably Uncle Cornie, had strung a heavy wire from one side of the building to the other where the rostrum began and that was used to hang sheets on in the summer or blankets in winter for curtains. That separated the actors from the audience and the curtains could be opened and closed. After putting this wire up and taking it down for some years someone had the idea to just leave it up since it was used two or three times a year. That did save work but we wondered if it might give the impression to visitors that the purpose of the wire was to hold the walls up.

Children's Day in June was always celebrated with a program and included lots of practice sessions. Since it was always warm weather it was much quicker from our house to run through the fields, "as the crow flies", to the church and back home. There were a few fences to deal with; some of barbed wire, but the savings in time was worth the effort.

Our family was always active in whatever was going on at the church. Often it was an aunt or uncle or on older cousin in charge of the program. Therefore, we found it not only extra work but fun to participate. Mom would always help us memorize a play part or a recitation and insisted that we devote enough time to it to learn it thoroughly.

Dale and Evah could be counted on to learn their parts if they were given a part in the play. Bob was always a fast learner and was good at recitations. James, with the guitar he taught himself to play, played and I sang sometimes at our Sunday evening meetings. Our cousin, Thelma, Uncle Cornie and Aunt Tilda's only daughter, was the only one in our group who played piano and she talked me into singing solos while she did the accompaniment.

The best thing about singing solos was that I had to go to Uncle Cornie and Aunt Tilda's house on Sunday afternoons to learn a new song and practice. She, being the only girl in a small family of four children and six years older than I was, had makeup and toiletries we didn't have at home. She wouldn't let me wear the makeup but I could always use her Jergens Hand Lotion and that was enough for me.

Actually Thelma was the only person who attended Hickory regularly that played piano. She started at an early age as the pianist for the church and continued with that until she was married and left home. I am not sure which came first Thelma or the piano but she is the only one who played piano all those years.

Park School where every one of us started our formal education began as a one-room brick building. Mom spent all of her school days in that one room but Dale and possibly Evah are the only children in our family to attend there. Our neighborhood had grown much larger as coal mining and farming progressed and the need for a larger school became very evident.

The school property was about five acres and a much larger frame building divided into two big rooms, each larger than the one room building, was erected. This new building was placed much farther back away from the north/south and east/west roads, leaving plenty of room for a spacious playground. Both rooms were filled to capacity with children in grades one through eight. Four grades to a room and one teacher in each room seemed adequate but could not have been easy for the teachers. Not only did each teacher teach all subjects to four grades, they also served as janitors, built fires and swept floors every day.

The first thing before any classes began, the whole room did something together. We always – yes always every day – recited the Pledge of Allegiance and each room had its own American Flag at the front of the room. Usually a good morning song was sung. One I remember was *"Good morning to you, good morning to you, we're all in our places with sunshiny faces and that is the way to start a good day."*

We learned and sang the patriotic songs such as *"America the Beautiful"*, *"My Country 'tis of Thee"* and *"It's a Grand Old Flag"*. Other songs we sang from our Little Golden Song Books were *"The Old Oaken Bucket*, *"Way down upon the Swanee River"*, *"Old Black Joe"* and one entitled *"Juanita"*. It had several verses and the chorus was *"Nita! Juanita! Ask thy soul if we should part! Nita! Juanita! Lean thou on my heart"*. The teacher would then often read a story or sometimes start a book that would hold us spellbound by reading only a chapter a day. That kept us interested even if the lessons seemed dull and we were anxious to get back to school the next day to hear the next chapter.

Three grades of six to eight students each would be studying while a lesson was being taught to another grade. When that lesson was finished the teacher would make an assignment, put the class to work and go on to the next. Each room carried a full curriculum of reading, writing, arithmetic, geography, English and hygiene. A great deal of outside preparation must have been necessary for a teacher to prepare a lesson for that many subjects each day. I suppose lesson plans were kept and used from year to year maybe with a few changes. Still in those days teachers earned a teaching degree in two years at Indiana State Normal College now Indiana State University in Terre Haute, Indiana.

One teacher who taught at Park School with her two year degree from Indiana State Normal was Margaret "Maggie" Wilson. She lived with her family across the road from the school house on the east/west road that went past the school. Maggie was a cousin of Jeanette Macaulay, who later married our oldest brother Dale. The Macaulay house was next door to the schoolhouse on the north/south road. Mr. Macaulay built a stile over his fence behind the school so his children wouldn't have to walk on the road to get to school. A stile had wooden steps up to the top of the fence and steps down the other side of the fence, so a person could cross a fence at that point. Stiles were common throughout the countryside.

Maggie graduated from Indiana State Teachers College (now Indiana State University) in

Terre Haute with her two-year degree and soon after, she taught at Park School. She was the teacher in first through fourth grades in the new two room building. Knowing our family, it was she who thought Bob was "a smart little boy" and was qualified to start school at five years of age instead of six, which was the norm. After presenting her reasons to Mom, Mom finally agreed to let him begin since he would be six by the end of December.

Maggie spent several years at Park School where she was not only the teacher for four grades but was also responsible for building the fires all winter to keep her room warm and for keeping the floors swept and the room in presentable condition. Fortunately she lived near the school for the room had to be warm by the time the students arrived. No doubt she enlisted her brothers to help with the fire building. The fires could be banked at night so stirring them up and adding new fuel during the week was not too burdensome, but on weekends the fire went out and had to be built anew every Monday. Any student, boy or girl, was happy to stay after school long enough to dust the erasers and help wash the blackboards. In fact, it was considered a privilege by students and their parents to be chosen as a teacher's helper.

When Maggie started to teach, married women could not teach school. She and her husband, Harry Hendrickson, who was also a teacher, were married secretly for a few years until that rule was lifted. Mr. Hendrickson was my 8th grade teacher at Park School. After she left home and was married most of her family and new friends called her Margaret. Having known her since childhood, as I told her a few years ago, I could only think of her as Maggie. She said, "Go ahead and call me Maggie, I like it." A remarkable woman with a 40 year teaching career Maggie passed away March 8, 2014, at the age of 106; she would have been 107 on May 12.

Five of the seven Wolfe children spent first through eighth grades at Park School. Bob was bused to the Junior High School in Dugger for his 6th, 7th and 8th grades. By the time Ruth started to school in 1939 the two room frame building was beginning to deteriorate. Enrollment was down since the coal mines were not flourishing as they had been in the late 1920s and early 1930s. There were questions and much discussion about whether to repair the building or close it down. The decision was made to close Park School and Ruth was bused to a small one room building in Dugger for her 5th and 6th grades, then to the Junior High for 7th and 8th. She spent all four years at Union High School as each of her siblings had done and graduated from there. She received her gold watch and Bible as each of her siblings had.

It was never even considered that because we went to a county school and studied with multiple grades in the same room that our education was inferior or impaired in any way. Our test scores were all comparable to those of students in any other school environment. Dale, Bob and Ruth went on to college and had no problems getting admitted.

Chapter 10

Special Days

Throughout the years we kids were in school, school always started after Labor Day, so Thanksgiving was the first holiday of the school year. That meant Thursday and Friday off and a nice long weekend. Of course, chores and farm work were the same on holidays as any other day, which never changed.

If there was still corn in the fields, and there usually was, Thanksgiving weekend meant corn husking. Corn was usually shucked while it was still standing in rows, with the horses pulling the wagon without a driver. The horses would go down the same row they were started on, responding to giddy-up and whoa.

The wagon was equipped with a high backboard. The men of the family all helped, with the youngest nearest the wagon for the ears of corn were thrown into the wagon as they were shucked, some hitting the backboard. Each shucker had a shucking peg, a small tool made of rather light but very strong metal with an open handle that could be grasped tightly and a sharp, slightly curved hook on the front end to help peel the shucks back. The ear of dry corn was broken off and the shucks were left hanging on the stalk. Each man normally handled two rows at a time. This was a cold, everlasting task but the wagon did fill up about two times each day, as a rule.

Thanksgiving dinner was special, although during the early years it never included turkey. We didn't raise turkeys - nor did anyone else we knew. Turkey would have had to be purchased and we had our own chickens. So Mom would kill a nice big fat hen and boil it so there would be plenty of delicious broth. She would then put the whole boiled chicken in a roasting pan and surround it with her homemade dressing, made with some of the broth and put it in the oven to brown nicely. . The rest of the broth was saved for her delicious homemade egg noodles that we loved to put over our mashed potatoes. The usual multitude of vegetables from a bountiful harvest would be followed by berry, peach or apple pies, cake, often angel food, and maybe banana pudding.

During this holiday the boys and Dad usually found some time to go hunting, mostly for rabbits. There were stories about quail hunting but Dad didn't always have bird dogs and shotgun shells could cost as much as $1.00 for a box of 25. Usually rabbits were plentiful and with Rip (Lester) and Ben (Benton) Deckard, Uncle Floyd's boys just across the way, plenty of nice rabbits were brought home. When the rabbits were fried up we liked them about as well as chicken and it was a nice change. Throughout the heavily Democratic Sullivan County, rabbits were sometimes known as "Hoover Hogs" because during President Hoover's Republican administration, times were hard and they were a staple.

With Thanksgiving over, before we knew it the Christmas Season was upon us.

Our Christmas dinner was much like Thanksgiving dinner but with a few added extras. Mom often made a pretty cranberry-apple gelatin salad and a plate of the prettiest little cinnamon apples with white enters. She would peel and core a dozen or so small apples such as Jonathon or some kind that would hold its shape when cooked, then make a red syrup of water and red hots (cinnamon drops), add the peeled and cored apples and simmer them until they could be pierced easily with a toothpick. She turned them as they cooked so they would be a nice even red. When they had cooled, she filled the centers with a mixture of cream cheese and finely chopped nuts. They were so good.

Christmas gifts for each other were usually little things we could make with something we had on hand. As we got older we bought small gifts for each other. Bob remembers the gifts he bought the first year he had money to spend. He spent 10 cents on each of his siblings and bought supporters for Dad's Sunday socks. They were 19 cents for the pair. He bought Mom a new apron in the form of one yard of gingham and she made the apron herself. The gingham cost 10 cents by the yard.

We didn't always have a Christmas tree but the house was always decorated pretty. Mom was always clever about making something out of nothing or very little and she made Christmas special. She took strips of red and green crepe paper and folded them together in a way that when they were let out, they made a chain of intermittent red and green squares. These were strung from each corner of the room at the ceiling to the center, fastened to the ceiling and she bought two big red tissue paper bells about the size of a dinner plate and hung these, one in each room, from the center of the ceiling. Red and green roping was stretched across the top of each doorway and window, hung down on each side and was looped back up.

The first Christmas tree I remember was a bare limb of good size from an oak tree. Dad helped us figure out a way to make it stand and we trimmed the smaller braches to give it a nice shape. We enjoyed stringing popcorn and making chains with white paper and crayons to decorate it. No lights, of course, but with Mom's help we found enough pine cones and other little baubles to make it look pretty. Mom put a white sheet around the bottom to look like snow and it made a nice place to put our little gifts and for Santa to put his gifts.

Santa was always faithful. He never missed us and we were as happy with the gifts we got as any family who may have received much more costly gifts than we did. Usually there was one special gift for each child, plus smaller gifts like stockings and underwear, but always something we needed. I remember the year Evah and I got a doll and doll buggy, one of each, to share between us. Another time I remember getting a two piece sweater set for me, when I was in high school. Bob remembers a pocket knife and mittens. Part of our Christmas under the tree from Santa was always oranges. They were rare and a special treat. Santa also brought stick candy in one pound packages usually spearmint or peppermint, lemon, horehound and cream which was white with a red center all the way through. It was vanilla flavored. The cream candy was always my favorite. We also got a big bag of peanuts in the shell. These were all shared.

One Christmas Eve, when we were all quite small, Santa came personally to our house. He knocked on the door and when the door was opened he stepped inside all dressed in his Santa suit and hat, with his long white beard. He said "Ho Ho Ho" and rolled oranges and apples across the floor to us, said more "Ho Ho Hos", gave a few deep belly laughs and left us all wide eyed. Years later we learned this was Johnny Boone, our nearest neighbor to the south.

Our Christmas dinner was always at noon and sometime in the afternoon we would go down to Grandma and Grandpa Wolfe's house. Mom always had a small gift of some kind for each of them. I don't ever remember going for Christmas dinner but we would visit for a while. Grandma would have a pair of socks for Dad and we kids always got a piece of stick candy to take home with us. We never stayed very long and that was fine with us. We were anxious to get back home to our own Christmas.

Good Friday was another school holiday and we were home for that day, also. Our folks knew it's meaning, but it was not observed as a religious holiday. Bob remembers that Good Friday was the day potatoes needed to be planted to have early ones. We just used potatoes that were still in the cellar if they were suitable for planting. If there was not enough Dad would have gone to town sometime before Good Friday and bought seed potatoes. To prepare the potatoes for planting the eyes needed to be cut out and anyone old enough to use a knife was put to work.

If the potatoes had sprouted and in the dark damp cellar, the sprouts were broken off and two eyes were cut out with a large chunk of potato left on to help the plant get started. We were taught, "Two eyes to a piece, two pieces to a hill."

Dad would take the horses hitched to the plow and make furrows about six inches deep and 24 inches apart all through the potato patch. One person walked down the row dropping two chunks (eyes) about every 24 inches and a second person followed with a hoe and pulled a big heap of dirt over each hill and tamped it down. Red Early Triumph was the earliest kind but

White Irish Cobblers were the best keepers. The potato patch was of a good size, roughly 20 feet by 30 feet for potatoes were a staple to be harvested in the fall and stored for winter long food.

Mom also graveled potatoes occasionally for specific dishes. To gravel potatoes meant to carefully dig into the side of the potato hill when the potatoes were about the size of an English walnut or a little smaller and gently detach a few from the root without disturbing the other small potatoes, taking only a few from any hill. The soil was carefully put back and patted into place. These little new potatoes when scrubbed clean and cooked with the skins on with fresh, new green peas from the garden and were made into Creamed Peas and New Potatoes. It was a dish fit for a King.

Easter following Good Friday was a religious holiday we faithfully observed. Church was important on Easter Sunday to celebrate the resurrection of Jesus Christ. For Easter we often had new clothes, including new white shoes for the girls. That was the first day white shoes could be worn, just as Labor Day was the last day for them to be worn. White shoes were never worn before Easter or after Labor Day.

Very early on Easter Sunday everyone, from the biggest to the littlest child, was up long before breakfast to see if the Easter Bunny had found all the nests we had built here and there in the yard. Saturday evening we had great fun, led by the older sibling, checking out neat places to build nests. When a perfect spot was found hidden away somewhere in the corner or by the fence or maybe underneath a rose bush, we pulled grass and used small pieces of paper or other material to fashion a little nest. The Easter Bunny was very clever and seldom missed a nest even though we thought they were well hidden.

Eggs, signifying new life, were a big part of Easter. Breakfast on this day was never oatmeal or pancakes, but always eggs - as many as we could eat. This was always accompanied by cream gravy and hot biscuits. Sometimes we might have a contest to see who could eat the most eggs. The boys always won these contests; two or three was usually the max for Evah and me. For Easter dinner, Mom always made lots of deviled eggs and again - all we could eat. We each tried to outdo the others.

Being so much younger than the rest of us kids, Ruth's memories of the holidays are somewhat different than ours. When she was born, Dale was away from home and gradually the other children moved out of the house for college or jobs or to serve in World War II. Ruth's memories centered around holidays made special by siblings returning for those special days. Some of Ruth's special memories were noted in an article she wrote several years ago for our family newsletter, "The Wolfe Call". Those memories follow here:

>*What fun to remember at the holiday time of year and at no time was coming home more special for both those away and for those at home - looking forward to the prospect of the "homecoming".*

I cannot remember a time when ALL the children were living at home together since I believe Dale may have been at Purdue when I was born. I only remember certain incidents that were very early and part of those do deal with homecomings and the special preparations we (Mother) made for them. These memories still affect my feelings quite strongly especially at holiday time. I still get a sort of empty feeling if we do not have someone "coming home" for a special day. If it is just "we four and no more", it doesn't seem like enough people and there is not that certain excitement of anticipation of the "arrival"; reminds me again of Edgar A. Guest's poem "The Old Fashioned Thanksgiving".

For those away, any holiday was a time to turn the heart and the car toward home, and especially if there was an extra day involved. The memories get a little jumbled about where everyone was, I tend to get the years mixed together. Seems that Dale and Jeanette were always in Flint, Evah and Jim are there too and Nita in Terre Haute...then Nita and Floyd in Terre Haute... and Bob and I at home.

Before any homecoming, there was much excitement, electricity in the air, the conversation and preparations were all in anticipation of the arrival of the dear ones. Mother would clean and of course I would help in varying degrees as to my age and we would begin to plan the food. Note that I said plan, for there were only limited food preparations that Mother was willing to make ahead. I remember years later while I was preparing the holiday dinner and told her I was making stuffed baked potatoes about a week ahead to freeze Mother said to me, "Now Ruth, we don't want to eat any 'old' potatoes."

At any rate, we would do as much as we could ahead so that all the time together would be as leisurely as possible and we could spend it just talking and sharing. However, a part of the special time together was the time spent in the kitchen finishing the cooking processes.

It seemed that most of the time "the home comers" would leave directly from work and drive straight through, which made their arrival well after bedtime. We saw lights turn the corner at Granny's and come down our little road. No, I don't expect that Mother slept a wink until her children were safe at home. No one wanted to go immediately to bed, so we would visit for a while and then go back for a brief rest before daylight again got us up. No one ever slept until 10:00 or probably even 8:00 a.m. and I do not have a sense that they even wanted to for the time at home was too precious.

I do remember some "catnaps" in the afternoon. In the early days, there was no couch and one never went back to bed unless ill, so naps were taken in a chair. Often the napper would straddle a straight chair and with crossed arms on the back for a pillow, would rest the head for a brief respite. Occasionally in later years, you might rest across the bed the short way. No one ever considered pulling back the spread and climbing under the covers or for the matter even putting the head on a pillow. How times have change! In the summer a pallet (old quilt) might be taken to the yard and we would stretch out to visit and of course catch a few winks.

When weather permitted, there were fields to be re-explored and especially Evah, but I expect everyone else too, wanted to walk back through the fields. There was always "border" at the edge where it was clear so we would walk there and admire the crops or the Queen Anne's lace or the goldenrod. There were also wild cherry trees to share their fruit in season and an apple tree or two for a treat. I also recall that some years Dad had a turnip patch back of the cornfield and he would pull a turnip, take out his pocket knife and peel it back for me leaving the tops as a handle. I shall never forget the sweetness of that juicy treat crisp from the icy weather.

Moods of the homecoming would vary with the season. As Thanksgiving is close at hand it is also close in mind. I was quite a grown girl before I knew that turkey was for Thanksgiving (maybe this was when the media or retailing decided). Even though we were told the Pilgrims had it and in school I made construction paper turkeys, we did not have turkey at Thanksgiving. The Pilgrims ate what was available to them and we ate what was available to us. Our Thanksgiving bird was chicken – a wonderful baked hen. Mother would have already chosen the hen and would kill and clean it the day before. Early on the day she would boil the hen in a large pot so that there would be broth for noodles and stuffing. When the chicken was tender it would be taken out of the pot and placed in the "bread pan" to be surrounded with the dressing and baked for 20-30 minutes just before mealtime. While it was boiling Mother would make the noodles and the dressing (stuffing).

There would, of course, be potatoes from the cellar, grown in our potato patch. I do not remember parsnips or turnips but this may be psychological. Desserts were always special perhaps persimmon pudding. Mother made her own mincemeat and it contained meat – probably hogs head and was absolutely delicious. I have tried several times to make mincemeat but it is never anything like Mother's. The pumpkin would have probably been grown in our cornfield and cooked by Mother. Persimmons we gathered from a tree which grew on the fence line between us and Granny and I believe there was also a tree on our property and we used whichever were at the right stage. Seems to me the Granny persimmons required a frost to be edible. Our recipe was the one Jan uses with the white cream sauce, a truly beautiful, bountiful meal of the harvest.

Christmas was much the same except more so and with lots of dessert changes. Mother did not make her famous prune cake until later, from a recipe Evah made first and brought home. Shortly after Thanksgiving we would have made a fruit cake to age for Christmas. As no spirits or fruit juice were used to moisten the cake, it was encased with pastry and then wrapped in a cloth for the aging process.

My favorite dessert without a doubt was suet pudding, a steamed mixture of batter, spices and raisins with chopped beef suet. Since we did not have modern steamers Mother always put the batter in a clean cloth, tied it at the top and submerged it into boiling water. The special thing that happened that doesn't happen in a steamer is that it formed an out layer like a thick skin which I thought was delicious. This was served hot, sliced and with a very thin, uncooked white sauce Mother called dip. This dip was made with rich, whole milk (not cream), sweetened with white sugar and flavored with lots of nutmeg. It was very simple and easy to make and a perfect sauce for her old fashioned suet pudding.

Mother made delicious fudge (especially peanut butter), taffy, cinnamon logs - nuggets of fondant rolled in cinnamon - and a wonderful divinity roll with peanut butter inside. That she could do all this without the benefit of electric beaters and heat controls on the stove seems quite remarkable to me. No candy thermometers either!! There were hard candies, including wonderful stick candy, thin shelled nuts such as pecans and English walnuts and oranges and tangerines. All of this was special at Christmas and generally not had at other times of the year as apples, hickory nuts and black walnuts were the available treats.

For the normal "homecomings" there were also special foods.....always a company meal and specialties geared to the tastes of those coming. Of course Nita and Floyd came often from Terre Haute for Sunday dinner (at noon) and because my first cooking attempts were in the dessert area I remember the stages we went through. Two of Floyd's favorite desserts were graham cracker pudding and angel food cake and Mother indulged him often with both. Then we went through a stage of chocolate mayonnaise cake which I learned to make, sometimes with fluffy icing, sometimes plain and Floyd would put this in a glass with milk poured over it!!!!!

Coming to table with family and/or friends gathered 'round was always a time for celebration and sharing and I always remember the meal shared following Mother's funeral as a time of comfort and therapy. There is truly communion in the breaking of bread together.

Section IV

CHILDREN'S ADULT LIFE CHAPTERS

Chapter 11

Leaving The Nest - Dale

None of the young Wolfes, children of Ora and Ann (except George Edward who as you may remember, died from scarlet fever at five years of age), left the nest before they graduated from high school.

A main focus of Mom and Dad and I think I could safely say, second to their being grounded in their Christian faith, was a good education for all of their children. That was ingrained deeply into our beings that it was not only important, it was expected of us. To re-enforce the importance of education, each child was promised (and received) a gold watch at graduation and our own personal Bible with our name engraved in gold on the cover.

Since Dale was the oldest, older by five years than Evah who was second in line due to the death of George Edward, Dale was the first to leave the nest. We were always a close-knit family and when he left for college in the fall following his graduation from high school it was a big event, viewed almost as a tragedy by his younger siblings. We knew it was a good thing for him, but that didn't seem as important to us at the time as his being gone.

Dale, by temperament, was a kind and thoughtful person, loved and looked up to by all of his brothers and sisters. By virtue of being the oldest, he sometime became a little bossy but that was usually when there was a fracas of some kind between the younger children or when they had done something he knew would not be approved by Mom and Dad.

Not only was Dale looked up to by his brothers and sisters, but by his younger cousins also. A cousin, Thelma Willis Norris, Uncle Cornie and Aunt Tilda's only daughter, told me a few years ago that when they were all growing up and younger than Dale (she was four years younger), if they had a problem or wanted to know if they should do something, they always said, "Let's ask Dale and he took us seriously, but he always said, I'll have to think about it". "Then",, she said "by the time he had thought about it, we probably had forgotten what it was we wanted or wanted to do."

Dale's absence at home was sorely felt by each younger child. I remember distinctly the first time he went off to college how we all cried. He came home for many weekends before that ritual ended when he left to go back.

In later years, after we were all married with growing children of our own, a family newsletter was started (more about that in a later chapter) and each of the seven siblings wrote a small article entitled "Leaving the Nest". Those notes, plus memories of the others now living, will be used to round out this chapter.

In his notes, Dale remembered working away from home at Grandpa Deckard's before he went to high school. He said it was standard procedure for him to stay overnight when he was working for Grandpa and that he earned enough money to buy a watch for $1.00. He also said Grandpa taught him to tell time by the sun by setting a stick straight up and you could tell what time it was by the length of its shadow. That was how they knew when it was time to come in from the fields for dinner (the noon meal).

The summer between Dale's junior and senior years in high school, he worked part of the summer for Lexie Robbins, a near-by prosperous farmer who needed some summer help. Dale's job included getting there early enough to curry and brush down the team of horses he would be working that day. Then he worked wherever Lexie needed him for the day.

Sometimes Dale would be cultivating corn which meant hitching his team of horses to the cultivator, a large piece of farm equipment with four small hoes on each side of a metal seat. With the cultivator eight long rows of corn could be hoed and weeded at the same time.

Then again, Dale might be harvesting hay, or when the wheat was ripe, he worked with the wheat-threshing crew. Hay was harvested, again with the team and a large mowing machine with a long cutting blade on each side of the metal seat and it is easy to see how much more hay could be cut in an hour than with the long handled, one-man scythe no matter how sharp the blade was. A large hay rake with several hay forks was used to pull the hay into wind-rows to dry for a few days in the hot sun before it was hauled to be stacked in the fields or put into the hay loft of the barn.

Threshing the wheat was more complicated and took more of a crew to get it completed in a day's time. The crew could be all hired workers or often it was mostly neighbors or relatives, or both, who gave a day's work for the return of a day's work.

These jobs, of course, were ready to be done during the hottest part of the summer and always in full sun. The work was hard and the days were long and the $0.75 a day Dale was paid for the regular work was upped to $1.00 a day during threshing time.

The Robbins' farm was on the way to Sullivan, near where State Road 54 intersected with US Highway 41. Dad drove Dale to work early every morning and picked him up at supper time every evening.

The summer following his graduation from high school, Dale worked at Princeton, Indiana, helping install a large gas pipeline for bringing gas into the city. Mom's brother, Uncle Floyd Deckard, held the job of Sullivan County Commissioner at that time and was able to get a job on the pipeline for his son, Winnie, who was about Dale's age, and for Dale.

This, again, was a job at hard manual labor. It included a lot of shoveling in a deep trench that had been dug a few feet below the freeze line of the ground with a trenching machine. He and Winnie shoveled out the loose dirt and prepared a fairly smooth and level base for the 12-inch gas pipe to be laid on. Since it was a seven-day-a-week job they didn't come home until the job was finished – about two or two and a half months.

The two cousins, Winnie and Dale, probably stayed with local people who opened their homes to out-of-town workers. That was a common practice in those days and it was a win-win situation. If someone had an extra bedroom, it meant some extra money for them as well as providing a reasonable rate for a sleeping room for workers. Most of the time the rate included the room, two men to a double bed, and board.

Dale didn't remember what his pay was on the pipeline but it was enough that it gave him the boost he needed to believe he could go to college at Purdue University, West Lafayette, Indiana. Always farm oriented, Dale had thought about college and wanted to go to Purdue and major in Agriculture. With that education a solid job as a County Agent was then a good possibility.

Before the first semester started, Dale went up to Purdue and landed two jobs. The first job he got was at the Grab and Run Restaurant where, after school hours, he washed pots and pans and sometimes waited on tables. The waiters' jobs usually went to the upper classmen, but when needed, Dale was available and willing. In fact he looked forward to waiting tables occasionally because that meant a little extra money in tips that was not available in the pots and pans department. The restaurant also was a place he could get his evening meal on school days.

For his room, Dale worked in the home of Dr. Carr, the chemistry professor in the Agriculture Department. His main jobs in the Carr's home were to take complete care of the lawn in the summer and to take care of the furnace in the winter. Most people today have no idea what taking care of a furnace entailed in those days. Unlike a gas-fired furnace, where its daily care means turning the thermostat up or down, a coal-fired furnace needed attention several times a day.

Coal had to be shoveled into the furnace during the day and the fire had to be "banked" at night which meant covering the existing fire with very fine coal or slack as it was called to smother the fire and with the draft closed it would smolder all night. Then every morning the coal had to be stirred up and when the crust was broken, the draft opened and the ashes were shaken down, it would burst into flames again. Soon, the house would be warm. Then, there were ashes, endless ashes, to be carried out daily.

Besides these two jobs at the Carr home, for his meals on the weekends, when the Carrs entertained, it was Dale's job to wash the dishes and pots and pans and to put the kitchen back in "ship-shape" condition. The Carrs were nice people and treated Dale with respect, as he did them, and it was a mutually satisfactory arrangement.

This arrangement for Dale at Purdue lasted for two years. For his third year, there just didn't seem to be enough financial resources for his tuition. However, sometime before this, the Macaulay family had moved to Flint, Michigan. We always wondered if this may have had some effect on Dale's desire to return to Purdue.

The Macaulays were our neighbors on the farm throughout our elementary and high school years and Dale and the older Macaulay daughter, Jeanette, had been dating for a while. Jeanette had a younger sister, Margaret, and three older brothers, Tom, Jim and Melvin. Since there weren't many work opportunities around the home area at that time, as the Macaulay boys graduated, they went to see if they could find jobs in Flint, Michigan, where work was thought to be plentiful because of the automobile factories. The Macaulay boys did find work in Flint and soon their whole family moved there.

Before the summer was over Tom Macaulay said he could get Dale a job at Graybar Electric Company where he worked. Word may have been sent from Tom by Jeanette in a letter to Dale, or since we did have an old fashioned box telephone that hung on the wall, that may have been important enough to warrant a phone call. It seemed to be a good opportunity for Dale so he went to Flint and was hired as a shipping clerk at Graybar. He bought room and board in the Macaulay home and started to work immediately. He worked as a shipping clerk at Graybar for eight and one-half years, then worked in Graybar's office for another year.

Bob has always said his "window to the world" was his and Max's visits to Flint to see Dale during Dale's earlier years at Graybar. One or two weeks in the city were a welcome change from the farm during summer vacation from school. Dale and Jeanette invited them to stay in their home and of course they were willing (even anxious) to do things around the house to show their appreciation.

Mrs. Macaulay (Jeanette's mother) was always mindful of them and tried to see that they had something to do when Dale and Jeanette were at work so they wouldn't become bored. Everything seemed so different and exciting that being bored was never a problem for these two young boys. Even electric lights were new and exciting for Max and Bob.

Dale always had a generous nature and during his years at Graybar, it was always a great celebration when he came home on vacation or even for just a weekend as he sometimes did. He often brought small gifts for everybody or gifts for the house which he knew would make life easier for all of us, but especially for Mom.

One of the most important gifts Dale brought home was an Aladdin lamp that made the brightest light we had ever seen. It was fueled by gasoline instead of kerosene. It had a mantle and a wick that had to be trimmed and cleaned every day. The mantle was made of a non-combustible substance that when placed over a flame, threw off a brilliant incandescent light. The lamp had a glass chimney similar to the chimneys on our kerosene lamps, but it was also fitted with a rather large shade that directed most of the light downward and certainly gave more light to study and work by than we had ever had.

I do remember that when we girls cleaned this chimney on the Aladdin lamp (that was always girl's work) we had to be very careful not to touch the mantle for it seemed very fragile. Gasoline, however, burned cleaner than kerosene and the chimney, sometimes, didn't need to be cleaned and polished every day.

Another gift Dale brought, especially for Mom and us girls, was a gasoline fueled iron. We were used to using flat-irons that were heated on the kitchen stove, picked up by the wooden handle and exchanged for a hot iron when the one we were using cooled down.

This new iron was a larger iron than we were used to. It had a gadget – I suppose it would be called a tank – that was fitted on the back of the iron. This made the iron very cumbersome. Although we didn't have to run back and forth to the kitchen, the temperature was hard to regulate and the little tank had to be refilled with gasoline every now and then. It really wasn't easy to use and sometimes we would just go back to the old flat-irons we were used to.

The REMC (Rural Electric Membership Corporation) had brought electricity into Greene and Sullivan counties and it was available now in rural neighborhoods. In about 1940-41, Dale provided all the electrical equipment from the meter ring to the in-house wire and fixtures to bring electricity to the Wolfe household.

Dad could always do almost anything and he knew the rudiments of wiring from his mining experience. So he was able to do all the wiring himself and installed flat ceiling fixtures in all the rooms except the living room. By that time, Max, Bob and Ruth were the only siblings living on the farm and what a blessing that was for them. Dad also ran electricity to the smokehouse and Mom was eventually able to get an electric washing machine. For several years she had used a washing machine with a gasoline motor.

In June of 1937 Dale and Jeanette were married and they bought a cute little house in Flint at 2010 Berkley Street. Dale, of course, was still at Graybar and Jeanette had been working as a bookkeeper in the office at A. Koegel Meat Packing Company for a number of years. With two salaries life was good. Dale and Jeanette were both careful with money and in that first year they not only bought a house, they bought an automobile too.

In Dale's "Wolfe Call" article he described the first car they bought. Dale wrote:

> *"The first car we purchased was a 1928 Chevrolet coupe with a rumble seat. The purchase price was $50.00. Jeanette's brother, Jim Macaulay, was selling used cars then, and this one had come through the dealership to the lot where he worked. It was well worth the $50.00 in 1937 and Jim was giving his commission back to any member of the family who bought their first car through him. So when*

we finished all the steps of making the sale and transferring the title Jim handed me back $8.00. Not bad!

This car was a gem for us. It was started with a hand crank. First we pulled out the choke then went around in the front and gave the crank a quarter hook a couple of times – three times if it was a cold morning. Then we went back and pushed the choke in half way and switched the key on. Then back to the crank to spin the motor with the crank and hope it started."

The always health conscious Dale had found a store in the downtown Flint area that impressed him and he had become a regular customer. It was a health food store and Dale was interested in every aspect of it. However, he thought it was very casually run because the owner, Frank Mythaler, was nearing retirement age and if he wanted to go fishing in the Upper Peninsula, it was not unusual to find the door locked and a sign in the front window that read, "Closed, Gone up North".

Frank's store not only had a health counter where vitamins and the like were sold, it also had a cafeteria and bakery where all bakery goods were made in the store with whole wheat flour and other whole grains, brown or raw sugar, real butter, etc. Mr. Mythaler had closed the cafeteria, probably because at his age it took more work than he wanted to put into it but the bakery was still operating.

Located in the front of the store was a Karmel Korn Shoppe. Mr. Mythaler had purchased a Karmel Korn franchise some years before his association with Dale and he not only sold delicious caramel corn which was made on site, he also made and sold some special candies.

Dale and Mr. Mythaler had long talks about the health food business. As Mr. Mythaler thought more about retirement, he thought more and more that Dale would be the best person he knew who was qualified to take over his store. He told Dale he wanted to sell it to someone he was sure would take care of it and be able to carry it on.

Finally, when he thought the time was right, Mr. Mythaler offered to sell his store to Dale. Dale had left Graybar about six months earlier and had started to work for Koegel's Meats selling cold cuts to grocery stores and had doubled his Graybar salary. Dale and Jeanette talked the offer over and the deal was struck. In a short time the name over the door was changed from Frank's Health Foods to Dale's Health Foods and Dale and Jeanette were in business.

Soon after they bought the store, Dale and Jeanette reopened the cafeteria. Dale's words:

"We opened the cafeteria and by golly, we were busy. It was a good thing we didn't know there was any other way to be!"

Of course, that meant hiring and training more employees; however, the other departments were pretty well staffed. But with a "built-in" professional bookkeeper (Jeanette) Dale didn't have to worry about the qualifications necessary for a bookkeeper nor about that end of the business. He could focus on changing the management style more to his liking. He hired and trained new people as well as training the older employees in every department to be clean, dependable and helpful to every customer that entered the store.

His emphasis however, as always was on the Health Food Department for more and more people were becoming aware of vitamins and healthy foods all the time. Because he had a long list of responsive customers, Dale's Health Food Store could attract the most famous speakers and lecturers of the day – among them, Paul Bragg, Walter Hodson, Gaylord Hauser, Betty Lee Morales, Adele Davis, etc. Dale and Jeannette became good friends with Betty Morales and her husband, John Grant, and visited some European spas with them.

A room upstairs at Dale's store was ample for the lectures he sponsored in the beginning but as time passed and more people heard about them and became interested in their health, the evening lectures were moved to a room in one of the downtown hotels.

Although Dale registered for the Selective Service Act for World War II, he was never drafted into service. For such a sensitive person, this bothered him quite a bit and Bob remembers Dale talking to him about it more than once. He kept wondering if he should enlist. Bob advised him to stay where he was. Dale was married but didn't have children yet. He was older, had a business and was more essential to the home front than young men just out of high school who were not settled down.

President Roosevelt had stated different times that the efforts of civilians at home to support the war through work and personal sacrifice was as critical to winning the war as the soldiers themselves. There were many ways civilians could help the war effort. The Civilian Air Patrol was formed to ensure that lights were either off or black curtains were drawn across the windows of homes, as well as businesses, at night. Early in the war, German U-boats were using the backlighting of coastal cities to destroy ships leaving their harbors.

Although it was the most necessary in coastal cities, blackouts were to be practiced in every city in the United States. One of the main purposes was to remind people there was a war on and to provide activities that would engage the civil spirit of millions of people not otherwise involved in the war effort.

Dale volunteered in the Civil Defense Patrol and patrolled his area every evening to ensure that all exterior lighting was extinguished or black curtains were drawn over the windows. If he could see light showing from any window, Dale tapped on the door and reminded the occupants that light was visible. People were very conscientious about this and Dale never encountered any resistance.

Various items, previously discarded, were saved after use for what is now called "recycling". Families were requested to save fat drippings from cooking for use in soap making. Neighborhood "scrap drives" collected scrap copper and brass for use in artillery. The milkweed was harvested by children to be used in life jackets.

The government sponsored eight War Bond drives that called on people to save now and redeem the bonds after the war when houses, cars and appliances would again be available. The War Bond campaign helped finance the war. Americans were challenged to put at least 10% of every paycheck into bonds. Compliance was high, with entire work places earning a "Minuteman" flag to fly over their plant if all workers belonged to" The Ten Percent Club".

In 1942 a rationing system was begun to assure that everyone would have the necessities, especially poor people and to prevent inflation. Tires were the first thing to be rationed because supplies of natural rubber were interrupted. Gasoline rationing followed and that was an even better way to allocate rubber.

To coordinate the worldwide supply of food to the Allies, especially to Britain, by 1943 ration coupons were issued to buy coffee, sugar, meat, cheese, butter, lard, margarine, canned goods, dried fruit, jam, gasoline, bicycles, fuel oil, clothing, silk and nylon stockings, shoes and many other items. To get a ration book, we had to appear before the ration board to register. Each person in the family got a book, including babies. Ration stamps were valid only for a set period to forestall hoarding.

After a few years, even though his business was growing, Dale realized there were still a lot of people who didn't know what "health foods" meant. He began to wonder if the name, "Dale's Health Foods" was presenting the image he wanted. He knew most people were interested in their own health and in eating healthy foods, so the name of the store was changed to "Dale's Foods For Health". That name still remains over the door.

With their business going strong, a nice house and car and money in the bank, it seemed everything was in place for Dale and Jeanette to start their family. They both loved children and had been trying for several years to get a family started but it just wasn't happening. They went to many doctors and clinics all over the country to whomever and wherever they thought or heard that they might get help but nothing happened. They read lots of fertility books and followed the instructions but nothing happened. They talked to the best known Health Food experts that were known at that time. Jeanette had a goiter and they had that removed - just in case. They both took "mountains" of vitamins to keep their bodies in good condition. For almost 11 years, nothing happened.

Then Dale and Jeanette's first child, Douglas Dale, appeared on the scene on February 14, 1948. I don't know what caused the change and to my knowledge no one else, not Dale and Jeanette nor their doctors knew. I would guess it to be a combination of things. But it happened. It was never talked about much in the family. We all knew of the struggle and we all hoped and prayed about it but those topics were not much talked about in those days. (What a difference a generation makes.) I do know this birth brought much joy to the whole family.

Both Dale and Jeanette wanted Jeanette to be at home and take care of the baby, but neither of them thought it was a good idea to hire a new bookkeeper for the business. Jeanette thought she could do her bookkeeping work at home if Dale could bring it home to her. So instead of Jeanette going into the office, her work came to her at home and that worked well. If she needed to, they could go into the office on Sunday afternoon, take the baby with them and she could catch up there.

In a few months Jeanette was pregnant again and Dale and Jeanette's second child, Sara Ann, was born on August 10, 1949. With two children just a year and a half apart, it was harder for Jeanette to get her bookkeeping done at home and she began to look around for a good, dependable, honest woman that she and Dale would be comfortable leaving their children with.

Before long, Jeanette was pregnant again and a second boy, Donald Alan, followed Sara Ann on July, 12, 1951. Dale and Jeanette's family was now complete but with three children, she knew she had to make some changes. She had found this nice Italian lady, Mary Bessolo, within her own age range that fit all the criteria so she hired her for one day a week.

It could not have worked out better. The children all grew to love Mary and she catered to their wishes. She came to the house every Thursday to take care of the children and Jeanette went into the store where she could close her office door and get her bookkeeping done without interference from the little people.

I asked Sara Ann recently what Mary did after the children were in school all day. She said, "Oh, anything Mom wanted her to but mostly she ironed. I can still remember Mom sprinkling and rolling the clothes every Wednesday night and packing them in a basket so they would be just damp enough for ironing the next day". (No wash and wear at that time). Sara also said, "I never remember Mary not being there on Thursdays. She was just always there. I was too small to remember when she came and she was still coming when I got married."

When I asked Doug about Mary he said, "When I think of the nicest women I have ever known in my whole life, I think of Mary Bessolo. She was just such a nice person. And boy could she ever iron. She was the best ironer I ever knew. And she made fantastic polenta which she served us for breakfast with milk and honey on it".

I also asked Doug about Dale and Jeanette's retirement. He answered, "Mom and Dad never really retired. They just came into the store less and less. As Don and I could handle more of the responsibility they didn't need to come in so much and finally they could spend two or three months each winter in Florida."

With Jeanette not there to oversee the purchasing and preparation of food for the cafeteria, it began to look like the cafeteria was not carrying its share of the load. It was decided to close the cafeteria. The Health Food Department was Dale's main focus anyhow and he was now able to expand that area.

As the children grew and started to school, both Dale and Jeanette began to wish he could be home for breakfast with the family. About this time the baker was also making some changes in her schedule and it seemed a pertinent time to close the bakery. What a wonderful change of pace for Dale not to have to be at the bakery every morning at 6:00 a.m. Even though he was pleased to have more time with his family, Dale had always enjoyed being the first person in the store every day where he mopped the floor himself and knew his customers would enter a clean store.

At this point the bakery and cafeteria equipment was sold, opening up more space to enlarge the Health Food area again which had always been the heart of the business. The Karmel Korn department was also enlarged. A specialty in that department was wonderful pecan pralines. Dale made the pralines right there in the back room, along with chocolate and vanilla fudges. At the end of the counter, he now put a large juicer and sold carrot and other vegetable juices by the glass, as ordered.

Sometimes, one of the unsettling aspects of owning a small building in the downtown business district is having to move to make room for larger businesses to expand. Because of a law called, Right of Eminent Domain, Dale had to relocate his business twice. The first move was to make room for a college campus and seven years later he had to move to make room for a downtown bank. Eminent Domain means the government has the power to take private property for public use. As the old saying goes, and I heard Dale say it too, "You can't fight City Hall." The city did, however, appraise Dale's building and paid him a fair price for it.

Dale and Jeanette enjoyed good health most of their lives. About 1982 or '83, Jeanette was diagnosed with congestive heart failure. She had some bouts with that and was in and out of the hospital a few times. She was not well enough to attend the 32nd annual Wolfe Family Reunion on Labor Day weekend of 1992. So her family took turns staying with her and her husband or one of her children was with her all during the reunion weekend. She passed away a few days later on September 13, 1992, about three weeks before her 79th birthday.

Just about a year after Jeanette's death, Dale had a heart attack. He was living alone in their lovely home on Court Street in Flint. It was a hot August late afternoon and Dale was cutting grass in his backyard when he felt pain in his chest. He went inside and laid down expecting it to get better. When it didn't get better, he called Doug who was nearby and Doug took him to the hospital immediately. Dale was in the hospital about a week but did not respond well to the treatment. He died on August 19, 1993, two months after his 82nd birthday.

This year of 1993, Dale and Jeanette's family was the chair-family for the reunion. Although we offered to cancel the reunion, Dale's family would have none of it. They had made their plans and they would carry them out. What a beautiful job they did! A stranger would not have known anything was amiss but the hearts of the whole Wolfe Family swelled with pride, sympathy and gratitude.

Chapter 12

Leaving The Nest - George Edward

Although he was born second to the oldest, George Edward was the first of Ora and Ann's children to leave the nest. Born in 1913, he died from Scarlet Fever in 1918 at five years of age.

Ora and Ann had three other small children when Scarlet Fever went through their neighborhood. Dale, the first born was seven years of age, Evah was two and James was still a nursing baby only a few months old. None of the four other children, Juanita, Max, Bob nor Ruth were born yet.

Dale and Evah both came down with Scarlet Fever along with George Edward, or "Brother" as we always called him. James, however, as a nursing baby was immune to the germs and escaped getting it.

Both Dale and Evah were so ill it was thought for a time they would not recover either.

Evah's fever ran so high during her illness that she lost all of her hair and although at two years of age she was walking she lost that ability too. She had to learn to walk again.

I'm sure Mom and Dad were overwhelmed, tired and weary but with two very sick children still to care for and a new baby, they hardly had time for grieving. Sick children need much tender, loving care and although James wasn't sick, a new baby is growing and constantly changing.

I never remember any of us calling George Edward by his given name. We all, Mom included, called him "Brother". Not "my brother" or "little brother", just Brother as if that were his name. "These flowers are for Brother's grave," "we need a marker for Brother's grave," etc.

Mom always believed Dr. Deputy brought the scarlet fever germs into our home. He had been called to our house because all three children had a cold. Mom noticed that he did not wash his hands before he left our house, so she thought it was very likely he had not washed his hands before he left the home of Silas Parks where he had attended their sick children. Mom later learned the Parks children had scarlet fever.

With a new baby coming every couple of years or so, a marker for Brother's grave was not as high on the priority list as food or clothing and Mom anguished for many years about not having a head stone for his little grave. It was not until the older children left to work away from home that a marker was put down. Dale, or possibly Dale and Evah, I'm not sure who, sent money home to purchase the stone and have it set. It is a small flat headstone with a glazed surface engraved with just his name, George Edward Wolfe, and the dates, 1913-1918.

George Edward was not usually mentioned when we were discussing the family. We always talked about our family of seven children. Dale was the only one with any memory of him whatsoever and his memory was very vague. I'm sure Mom never forgot him, but she never corrected us, either, when we spoke of "the seven". She was a very practical person and she just met us where we were and let it go at that.

Granny Brewer/Mosier, our nearest neighbor who was like a grandmother to all of us children, always spoke of how smart George Edward was. Her words were "He was just too smart for this world." I heard her say that many times.

Chapter 13

Leaving The Nest - Evah

Evah graduated from High School in 1934 and as the second oldest child due to the death of George Edward, she was third to leave the nest. Being the oldest child at home since Dale had gone off to college, she always seemed to feel some sense of responsibility to help out in any way she could, not only with her younger siblings but for keeping the house clean and in order. She learned how to clean, cook, make beds, iron and do general housework at an early age.

During her senior year in high school, Evah did a most selfless, unselfish thing that was very indicative of her priorities and the value she placed on material things. Union High School followed the pattern of all the high schools and a committee was elected from the class to choose a graduation class ring. Orders were taken from students who wanted class rings and could afford them and the rings were due to be delivered a short while before graduation. I believe now that senior rings are ordered during the junior year so they can be worn and enjoyed all during the senior year.

Not feeling that the family could afford it, Evah told Mom she didn't want a senior ring. Mom insisted that she order one and had saved enough money to pay for it. So Evah took the money and pretended to order the class ring. She did instead, take the money and order six dining room chairs from the Sears and Roebuck catalogue. Nothing more was said about the ring, but when the chairs were delivered to the house by the country mail carrier, Evah had to "fess up" and tell the truth about what she had done with the money for her class ring. Mom scolded her for it and I'm sure she felt really sorry that Evah would not have a class ring but Evah assured us all that she spent the money the way she really wanted to.

After graduation it was natural to spend the summer at home, but as fall neared Evah felt she should be doing something productive. Doris (Aunt Dulsee's daughter just across the field) had enrolled at Indiana State Teacher's College in Terre Haute and I'm sure that increased Evah's restlessness. There was an opening for a girl to work in the little store directly across the road from the high school and after checking, Dad found out that Evah could ride the school bus to work and back home again, so she got the job.

School hours were the only hours help was needed at the store, so it was a perfect set up. Mr. Lam, the seventy year old, white haired gentleman who owned the store was the father of Thelma Lam who had married our cousin, Winnie Deckard, Uncle Floyd's son. It was a pleasure to work for him but of course when school ended, the job ended. The only time Mr. Lam needed help was when there was an influx of students looking for snacks, gum, pencils, notebooks and possibly sandwiches at lunch time. She made $1.00 a day for the five days she worked each week.

Evah then got a job at a federally funded indoor recreation place in Dugger. This was a part of President Franklin D. Roosevelt's "New Deal" to get the country back on its feet after the Great Depression of 1929. She supervised a group of young kids and Bob remembers going to work with her occasionally where he played ping pong, caroms and other board games. This was always a special occasion for him to get to go into town and play games that were not available on the farm. This was always in a good atmosphere and well supervised. Evah's job was to get the games out and see that they were put away at the end of the day. There is no record of what she was paid but it was certainly minimal, possibly two or 3 dollars a week.

In the early summer of 1937 we got the news that Dale and Jeanette were planning a June wedding and they wanted Mom to come to Flint for the wedding. There was not even a thought that the whole family might go. Ruth was four years old at that time and Mom just couldn't see any way that she could be away for a number of days. So, after much discussion it was decided that Evah would go and represent the family at Dale's wedding.

Evah had never been farther away from home than Terre Haute and that, only a few times, but we took her to the depot in Sullivan and she boarded the train for Flint. The plan was that she would spend a week in the home of the Macaulay family since they were former neighbors at the farm, then come back home by train. Margaret, Jeanette's younger sister was near Evah's age, a couple of years younger, but Evah was thrilled at the idea of spending a week in the city.

Many people from our area had moved to Flint because there was much more opportunity there for young people than around Dugger or Sullivan. Evah met some high school friends there and one of the girls was going to apply for a job in the home of a family that lived several blocks out and off East Court Street. She told Evah she knew of another job in the same neighborhood and asked Evah to go with her. They rode a city bus out to the neighborhood and both girls were hired on the spot.

Evah worked in a lovely home and was quite amazed at the way city folks lived. Her description of the family and her job follows:

"I worked in the home of Harold and Naomi Peer who had two darling children, Jackie and Hal, who were pretty much my responsibility plus the general

housework. I did some cooking, but not a lot. Those were the days when the garbage man came to the back door, picked up your garbage can, carried it to his truck on the street, emptied it and carried it back behind the house. Also on Mondays the back door was always left open for Mr. Peer's shirts were picked up from the back entry way to be laundered. No need to worry, shirts were all that was ever taken."

Dale and Jeanette went to Oak Park Methodist Church and since Evah had Sundays off, she was able to attend church there with them. She took a bus to church then often went home with Dale and Jeanette and in the late afternoon or early evening - she would take a bus back to the Peer home.

At Oak Park, Evah met a girl she graduated from high school with, Margaret Haupt, and her sister, Faye who both worked at the Home Dairy in downtown Flint. Home Dairy was a big place with several departments. There was a lunch counter on the main floor, a dining room on the lower floor and a cafeteria upstairs.

A year or so after Evah went to Flint; there was an opening for a waitress at Home Dairy lunch counter. Evah applied for the job and was hired. Her main job was at the lunch counter but she also, when needed, worked in the dining room and cafeteria. One December when Dale and Jeanette were going home for Christmas, Evah asked her manager for time off to go home and he said she couldn't have the time off. After thinking it over, she figured another job would not be too hard to find, so she quit her job and went home for the holidays.

When she went back to Flint she went into the Home Dairy to see her friends and while she was sitting at the lunch counter her boss came by and said, "When are you coming back to work?" So she went into the back room, put on her apron and went back to work!

Working at Home Dairy was a job Evah liked. She always liked meeting the public and there was plenty of variety in a clean and pleasant atmosphere. She was working in the cafeteria one day when one of the Cafeteria's steady customers, Mr. Kramer, asked her as he came through the line, if she would like to come to work for him. Mr. Kramer was manager at Beecher, Peck and Lewis – a stationary store that carried office supplies and paper goods of various kinds.

That would mean working in an office all day and she wasn't at all sure she would like that, so she told him she would have to think about it. After thinking about it for a few days, she decided it would be nice to at least try it and see if she liked it. So she contacted Mr. Kramer and was hired as a file clerk. She also worked part time on the switchboard and this gave her experience in more than one field.

Evah's job at Beecher, Peck and Lewis had given her a lot of knowledge about the paper business and when she knew of an opening at R.P. Lewis for someone to work in the front office, it sounded more to her liking so she applied for the job – and was hired.

Actually, R.P. Lewis was a competitor of Beecher, Peck and Lewis, but they carried office furniture and Evah loved selling the furniture. However, when asked if she would take a job as a salesman, she said she would prefer to stay inside the store and sell over the counter. She was not confident that she could sell as well if her salary depended on commission. She chose to sell inside the store even though it may have meant a smaller salary.

After she had been at R.P. Lewis for a few years, maybe three or four, a friend in the office there secured a job at W.J. Phillips Insurance Agency. Before the date her friend was to start work at the insurance company, her husband was transferred to Detroit and of course, she had to move to Detroit with him. Since the insurance job was a small office with only one girl, Evah's friend felt very responsible and asked Evah if she would apply for the job. Evah applied for the job and soon started to work for Mr. W. J. Phillips at the insurance company.

The Phillips' had two sons, Bill and Jim who were both in the service when Evah started working for Mr. Phillips. The war ended and in early 1946 the boys came home and both went to work for their father.

In 1940 Bill had been working at A.C. Sparkplug in Flint where he took some math, drafting and blue print reading classes at General Motors Institute. He had registered for the draft in World War II as the president had required and in early 1941 it was beginning to look like the United States was going to become involved in the war.

Wondering what his options might be, Bill went down to the post office and talked to an army recruiting officer and learned that if he enlisted, he could choose what he wanted to do, but if he waited to be drafted the choice was no longer his, he would have to go where the army sent him. After talking it over with his parents, it was decided that, since it was obvious he would be called, enlistment might be the better option.

Bill signed up and became a member of the Army Air Corps on April 28, 1941 in Detroit. From there he was sent to Chanute Field at Champaign, Illinois where he was taught the army way to make a bed, store clothes in a foot locker, clean and unload the latrine, and other things. He had to wait some time for his uniform because there were not enough uniforms to go around, but he was issued underwear, socks, shirts, pants, fatigues, coveralls and last, but not least a toolbox with a set of airplane mechanic tools.

In school five days a week, Bill and his class studied electrical systems, hydraulic systems, engines and what makes an engine run. Bill's group was assigned a radial engine and the instructor said, "Now this engine has been put together beautifully by the previous class. Your job is to take it down, piece by piece, reassemble it piece by piece and hope that it runs when it's finished." The engine Bill worked on fired up the first time and ran like it was supposed to.

Bill was sent to Kessler Air Base, Biloxi, Mississippi on September 30, 1941, for a five month course on B-24 crew training. While he was there, the Japanese attacked Pearl Harbor on December 7, 1941 and war was declared the next day. After finishing the course, Bill was sent to Miami Beach, Florida on February 21, 1942. The army had taken over hotels there to be used for Officer Candidate School.

When Bill was discharged from the Air Force, he was anxious to get back to a normal life and went to work in his Dad's insurance agency. Evah was already working there. Bill needed a date for his sister Betty's wedding in 1946 and he invited Evah to be his date, but it was some time before they began dating seriously.

The story goes that in the meantime Mr. Phillips's wife, Ruth, who had met Evah several times and liked her, took Bill aside and had a conversation with him. Ruth said to her son, "That girl is a good one. You had better grab her before someone else does."

September 3, 1949, Bill and Evah were married at the Wolfe farm in Indiana and honeymooned in Michigan's Upper Peninsula. They went all the way to Copper Harbor and on the way home they stopped for an overnight at the Phillips' cottage on Chippewa Lake in Michigan. When they got back to the apartment at 1221 Mason Street where Evah was still living, they found a group of their friends there, decorating it with crepe paper for the return of the newlyweds. They quickly bought snacks and enjoyed their first evening together at home with friends.

By early 1950, Bill and Evah had found a spot they liked and were having a house built at 431 Warren Avenue, Flushing, Michigan, a small town on the outskirts of Flint. They were expecting their first baby in December. Evah quit her job in June to prepare for the move and the new baby and Gregory Holden Phillips made his appearance right on time on December 20, 1950.

Now, they were really anxious to move, but the new house wasn't finished until early March of 1951. I, (Juanita) left my two little girls, Susan, four years old and Janice, two and one-half, with my parents (Ora and Ann) and went to Flushing to help with the move and with the new baby boy.

The new subdivision had been cut through an apple orchard. It was a rainy, muddy spring and Evah felt far away from anyone or anything familiar. However, families were moving in as their houses were completed and two other couples moved in about the same week Bill and Evah moved. Everyone was anxious to neighbor and there was lots of borrowing of tools and helping each other in various ways.

Soon a card club was formed and Saturday evening parties were held in each other's homes. No one seemed to have a lot of extra money and this was a good way to get to know each other and to enjoy an inexpensive social life. New babies were being born to couples up and down the street and baby showers became common. Brian, baby boy number two, was born September 28, 1951.

Building across the street did not begin until about four years after Bill and Evah moved there and it seemed the mud was never ending. Mom told Evah how nice she though it would be to move into a house that no one else had ever lived in. There were times though that Evah thought it would have been nicer to move into an older home with a ready-made lawn, a garage already built and so many other things in place.

Eventually everyone had established lawns and the mud leveled off. The family across the street had three boys so Evah and Bill's boys never lacked playmates.

Stephen was born April 21, 1959 and the Phillips family was complete. Many of the original families on Warren Avenue lived in their homes for many years and the adults, as well as the children, are still friends.

After she was married, Evah never worked outside her home – at least not at a full time paying job. Her main focus was her family and she loved being at home when the children came from school. She was a faithful worker in the Parent Teacher Association at their schools and as a Room Mother she baked hundreds of cookies and cupcakes, and made herself available when needed.

Chippewa Lake and The Farm were probably the two places in the world Evah liked to go best. Bill was only nine years old when his parents, Jewett and Ruth Phillips, bought the cottage at Chippewa, Michigan, so from the time Evah and Bill were married, it was a favorite place to visit. When their children were small, Bill and Evah could spend their vacations there and Evah could go for a week to two at a time and stay with the children. After Mrs. Phillips was gone and the cottage became theirs, Evah could spend even more time there in the summer with their children.

The shallow water, with a sandy bottom around the edge of the lake where the cottages were, made a perfect place for children to play. You could wade way out before the water got deep and Bill made a large "float" to tie the boat to and for the kids to use. Some summers they were able to spend nearly all summer there.

The Farm was a favorite place to go on holidays as well as vacations. Mom and Dad were always there and loved having any of their children come home. Although even when they remodeled the house in 1960, they never put in a bathroom and everyone had to use the outdoor toilet – no one seemed to mind. We had all grown up using it and the in-laws all adapted.

Bill and Evah came home for Easter, Thanksgiving and Christmas until their children were of the age they needed to be home when Santa Claus came. Then they stayed home for Christmas, but The Farm remained a favorite place to go. One of Evah and Bill's sons told me recently, "Trips to the farm were the best. My brothers and I learned to hunt, fish, gig frogs and were free to explore the strip mining hills on our own. We all loved to go to The Farm, but Mom was the driving force that made it happen."

Evah filled her extra hours with various volunteer jobs in the community. Bill was a member of the Lions Club for many, many years and Evah, a member of the Lions Club Auxiliary, assisted with their paper drives and other projects.

As an Election Judge, Evah worked at the voting polls during many elections. She and Bill belonged and regularly attended the Flushing United Methodist Church and Evah worked in the Women's Organization there where she was a faithful worker at the rummage sales and other money making projects.

Philomathean Club was an "invitation only" club. Evah was invited to join the Club and she enjoyed working there, also.

Her love of children led Evah to become a storyteller. She took the training necessary to prepare for the Children's Story Hour at the local library. She would read and learn the story, then hold the book up and point out the pictures as she told the story to the children.

Evah was not sick when she passed away. In fact, she had had a great day. She was cleaning out her linen closet when Max called and wanted her to go shopping with him. She was the kind of person who would not say "no" to a brother who proposed a fun trip. No doubt they went to the Goody Barn and some of Max's favorite places and maybe hers too.

This was March and the Lenten Season. When Max and Evah got home, she prepared a casserole and she and Bill went to the Lenten dinner at church that evening. They came home and went to bed and Evah never woke up.

About 9 o'clock the next morning, Evah's daughter in law, Mary Jane, called to talk to her. When Bill went to tell her, he couldn't wake her up, so he called 911. She was taken to the hospital unconscious and passed away from a brain aneurism about 9 o'clock the evening of March 28, 2003. She was 86 years old.

The funeral for Evah was held at a funeral home in Flushing two days later and was attended by many friends and most of her extended family. Nieces and nephews came from as far away as Texas and New York. The ground at the cemetery in Chippewa was still frozen in late March, so her burial was postponed for about a month.

Evah was buried in the beautiful little cemetery by the United Methodist Church at Chippewa, Michigan, where the whole Phillips family has spent and enjoyed so much time and continues to do so, since 1927 when Bill's father, W. J. (Jewett) Phillips and his wife Ruth, bought the original cottage on Chippewa Lake.

Bill turned 98 this year in February, 2016. He was diagnosed with Parkinson's disease several years ago, so does not get around well anymore, however his mind is still active. He currently lives in an assisted living facility in Flushing where he is close to two of his sons, Greg and Stephen. His other son, Brian, lives in Kalamazoo, Michigan, some 130 miles away.

Evah's sudden death was a grave shock to all of her siblings. She had been healthy most of her life and I always thought she would live to be 100 years old. She was in good health the day before she went to the hospital for the last time, so it was a tremendous shock to all of her family.

After her funeral, Bob, who has a propensity to write poetry, wrote this "Ode to Evah Phillips" as he sat by the fireplace in his home that evening. It was read a month later at her burial.

I think it is one of the best poems Bob has written, in fact, I believe it rivals the poetry of the old masters. I liked it so well I read this poem over and over, until I, Juanita, who has a propensity to memorize poetry, memorized it.

I would like to preserve it here in this family history as a tribute, not only to my sister Evah, but to my brother, Bob, also.

ODE TO EVAH PHILLIPS 1916-2003

So many things taken for granted
As if they always will be.
And the days run past like a river
In its haste to get to the sea.

Then life can be changed in an instant,
When the phone brings a chill – like ice.
Perhaps that's the way the Lord wills it,
So each year is not robbed of its spice.

The spice of which I am speaking
Is the sister we all hold so dear.
She was woven so deep in our fabric
In ways that just now becomes clear.

As I sit by the fire here this evening,
And roll back the years in my mind,
I remember her gift to our family,
She was thoughtful and caring and kind.

As a kid brother, I'm sure that I irked her.
As kid brothers are prone to do.
Yet she always welcomed with a kindly smile
And shared much – when dollars were few.

I recall some past years in the thirties,
Some gifts and vacations in place.
The work, the effort and sacrifice,
Was done with a smile on her face.

With young families we spent time together,
"The Lake" or in places quite strange,
Isle Royale, Fontana, Deep Creek and the like,
But the love and respect did not change.

Her deep seated values, her strongly held faith
Her disdain for material things,
Was a shining example for all of us,
To relish whatever life brings.

We shared so much life together,
And all of it simple and fun,
Poems, the garden, health notes and more,
With her gone – it's like losing the sun.

A trait outstanding, I always recall
Her welcome was always so strong,
Her caring, her food, made sure that you knew
There was no time to come that was wrong.

To add to her welcome in similar ways
Were Bill and her family and all.
We sometimes worked hard, sometimes just had fun,
But as a group, we were having a ball!

The family reunion will not be the same,
Her cobblers, her smiles, her love pure,
Leaves a hole in the fabric of our gathered group,
That will never be filled – that is sure.

However, we know that to honor her life,
We must do what she wants us to do.
We must build on the bonds of the family tree,
And live by the faith that is true.

In spite of the loss that we feel in our heart,
We know there is heaven for her.

With family awaiting and loved ones galore,
Her coming will create a stir.

I have as a memory, some twigs I will keep,
Pussy willow and heather for me.
But each time I look at the vase on my desk,
It's a flood of those memories I see.

I hope that each one can gain solace from this,
She lived 86 years full and free.
If we use her example and follow the Lord,
We leave light – so that others may see.

A loving brother,
Bob Wolfe

Chapter 14 ═══════════════════════════════════

Leaving The Nest - James

The fourth sibling to leave the nest was James (Jim). He graduated from high school in the spring of 1936 with good grades and was presented with a gold watch and a Bible, as Dale and Evah had been. He had no special yen to go to college – none of his friends were going to college. The country was still in the throes of the Great Depression and, actually, college wasn't considered much of an option.

The summer following his graduation, Jim stayed at home helping Dad plant and tend the crops. Dale was already working and living in Michigan and Dad needed some help. However, in the fall Jim was restless and enrolled as a post graduate student at Union High. After one semester, he felt like he was wasting his time and he needed to do something more productive.

A tip from a friend led Jim to an interview with a German farmer in Freelandville, Indiana, a small town about 15 miles or so from the farm, as a general farm hand. He was hired by Mr. Volle and was to arrive early on Monday mornings and work until Friday evenings, with Saturdays and Sundays off.

Dad took Jim to work early each Monday morning and picked him up on Friday evenings. Hours were long and the work was hard but he was paid $1.50 per day, plus room and board. Most young farm hands were paid $1.00 to $1.25 per day with no room or board, so Jim felt like he was doing okay. Mr. Volle was a hard worker and from daylight to dark, he and Jim planted and tended the crops, planted trees, repaired farm equipment and kept everything running smoothly. Mrs. Volle was friendly and a good cook and Jim enjoyed the work and the family.

After the crops were laid by, Mr. Volle didn't need Jim's help anymore so Jim was free to start looking elsewhere for a job. One Saturday evening when Jim was in town (Sullivan) he ran into Jim (Jockey) Sevier, a friend from high school. Jockey had been told the automobile factories in Flint, Michigan were hiring and the two of them decided they would like to go up to Flint and get a job. Mom and Dad understood how Jim felt and made no strong objections.

On Monday morning, Jim and Jock Sevier started hitch-hiking to Flint and arrived on Wednesday. Dale and Jeanette were married by this time and Evah was in Flint also, so Jim felt like he had a good support group. Evah was living at Dale and Jeanette's and Jim stayed there until he got a job, then he and Evah got an apartment together.

Applications at the factories proved useless. Evah was still working at the Home Dairy and knew there was an opening there, so Jim applied for the job and was hired as a clerk for the candy and baked goods counter. His salary was about $10.00 a week and all the candy he wanted. But counter work was not Jim's "thing" and in a few weeks when he heard of an opening at Freeman Dairy, he put an application in there and was hired.

At Freeman Dairy, Jim worked with a six or seven man crew and made ice cream bars and popsicles. The company worked three shifts a day, six days a week, and paid $0.20 an hour. Ice cream bars and popsicles were pretty new at that time and Freeman produced 4,000 to 5,000 dozen bars per day. Although the work was more to Jim's liking, his pay was only $9.60 a week and his room rent was $3.00 weekly. He worked the 4:00 p.m. to midnight shift with a 15 minute break at 8:00 p.m. to get something to eat. This shift, however, afforded him time to look for something better.

Probably due to Jeanette's working for A. Koegel Meat Packing Company, after two weeks at Freeman, Jim was interviewed and hired at Koegel's where he helped make what he considered, as A. Koegel also did, the best sausage and cold cuts available anywhere. The starting wage at Koegels was $0.35 an hour and Jim stayed there for three and one half years. The work was hard but pleasant and with lots of hours and an occasional raise, Jim was happy there.

During his time at Koegel's, Jim bought two different used cars and late in 1940 he talked to Jim Macaulay (Jeanette's brother) at Summerfield Chevrolet about buying a new car. The only qualifying question was, "Do you make $120.00 a month?" Jim answered yes and bought a brand new Chevrolet Club Coupe with radio and heater for $965.00 using his used car as a down payment.

By mid-1940, the war in Europe was heating up and looking ominous. The peace-time US Army was small and the Selective Service and Training Act was introduced into Congress. Its purpose was "To provide for the common defense by increasing the personnel of the Armed Forces of the United States and provide for its training." On August 28, 1940, it passed in the Senate, 58 to 31. September 7, it passed in the House of Representatives, 263 to 149 – not a landslide but a fair margin. September 16, 1940, President Franklin D. Roosevelt signed into law that men between the ages of 21 and 35 must register for the draft.

This Selective Service Act was the first peace time conscription in the history of the United States. All American males between the age of 21 and 35 were required to register for the draft. The government selected men through a lottery system and according to provisions of the Act, a man drafted had to remain in the United States or its territories and service was limited to 12 months. Not more than 900,000 men were to be in training at any one time.

When the Japanese attacked Pearl Harbor, the attitude of the American people changed dramatically. Not only were men drafted but thousands of young men rushed to their draft boards and enlisted. A new Selective Service Act made men between 18 and 45 liable for military service and required all men between the ages of 18 and 65 to register. Limit of service was extended to six months after the war. From 1940 until 1947 – when the wartime Selective Service Act expired after extension by Congress – more than 10,000,000 men were inducted.

Jim was called in the first wave of draftees and started training in March of 1941. Francis Haupt, the youngest child of the Haupt family we all knew from high school, enlisted and hoped to stay near Jim, but Uncle Sam had other ideas.

In the May 1988 issue of the "Wolfe Call", our family newsletter, Jim wrote of his "stretch in the service" in such interesting detail, I am going to enter it here in his own words. No one could say it better.

Jim's story:

> "Life was great in Flint. Good job, family support group, a church family and I could go to Indiana to visit Mom and Dad every few months. However, earlier I had registered for "Selective Service" and could be called to serve a year in the branch of the Armed Services, but it would be some time before I would be called. Sure it would!!
>
> In early March I received my Greetings from Uncle Sam. So, I left Flint on March 11, 1941, along with 200 other draftees and traveled by train to Detroit. The next morning, in a cold empty warehouse we were asked to strip to the skin for physical exams. A loud speaker blared, "Wolfe, James L. report to station G". I am a prime, shivering candidate, 22 years old, 5 feet 11 inches, 160 pounds, single and warm to the touch of those cold hands. Welcome to the Army, Mr. Wolfe.
>
> We were sent to Camp Grant, at Rockford, Illinois, for clothing issue and formal inductions and I became NO. 36104883. I clearly remember green scrambled eggs for breakfast, but was assured "that is all there is available". Everyone looked at this with suspicion but that was the only color of eggs served. A few days later we were sent to Camp Livingston, Alexandria, Louisiana, and arrived at 11 p.m. as part of the very first draftees to arrive at a training camp anywhere in the United States. It was a wet cold place.
>
> The next several months are a story I am sure every ex-GI could write. We were paid $21.00 per month, less laundry charges of $3.00. Our equipment included 1903 Enfield WW I rifles, some of our jackets had high collars (WW I) fastened

on front with two metal hooks. Our pay increased to $30.00 per month after basic training. We didn't care for all the walking in the infantry, so Floyd Willis and I located the Motor Pool, transferred and were promoted to mechanics. I was now a specialist in the service: an "ordinary man a long way from home".

On December 7, 1941, Pearl Harbor was attacked by the Japanese and in a matter of days we were detached from the 32ⁿᵈ Infantry Division. We were all packed and loaded, lock, stock and trucks on a troop train. When war was declared, a prior Army decision to streamline infantry divisions was put into effect. Our 125ᵗʰ Regiment was one of the orphaned units sent to the west coast for guard and patrol duties. We were certainly available for any kind of duty. We went where we were asked to go, did all we were asked to do and we did it well.

After four or five days our troop train stopped at Pomona, California, where we were "housed" at the fairgrounds. We slept on cots in the livestock pens there and at Santa Anita Race Track nearby where we slept under the betting windows. The three battalions were organized as individual units with a Service Car Detachment of six or eight trucks with driver to furnish food and supplies and one mechanic responsible for the maintenance of the seventy or eighty vehicles involved.

I was attached to the Second Battalion, and within a few days our unit was sent to Barstow. Since it was the schools' Christmas break we were housed in the high school gymnasium. The high desert was snowy and cold and my work was done outdoors anywhere I could find shelter from the elements. We were to guard the railroad center there along with the top secret Air Force testing area of Murdoch Dry Lake near Mojave. This area is now known as Edward's Air Force Base, and famous as NASA's landirect area.

Before school reconvened we were ordered back to the Los Angeles area. My parent Service Company was housed at the National Guard Airport at Griffin Park. I went to North Hollywood with my battalion where our troops helped guard places such as Douglas Aircraft, Hughes Tool Plant, etc. I loved being on detached service. Although I was on 24 house call, I was on my own, responsible only for keeping the trucks running.

The general public was very hospitable and on our time off gave us rides anywhere we wanted to go and we enjoyed many free meals in homes around L.A. and Hollywood.

Arrangements were made for a training cadre to go to the Santa Barbara Polo Grounds to give basic Army training to 1600 recruits who were to be sent out later as replacements in units wherever they were needed.

The Captain in charge of transportation asked me to go along to take care of thirty trucks. I reported back to L.A. Service Co. (an 80 mile drive) each Saturday and returned on Sunday. All night driving on the coast was "blackout". Street lights in towns were very dim and transformers had been put on all civilian cars to dim lights, too. However, we did locate the little U.S.O. in Carpinteria – which was about three miles from the Polo Grounds. It had a ping pong table, juke box and dance floor and is now the local library. Pat was in one of the hostess groups and on Mother's Day, 1942, I was invited to dinner at her home, along with several other soldiers. That was our beginning.

After our troops were trained our regiment moved north to Gilroy and another group moved in to help protect the California coast line. When a convoy was on the road a mechanic followed and was responsible for getting all of them to their destination. On this five hour trip I had trouble with a couple of trucks and didn't arrive in Gilroy until the next day. In the next couple of years I became familiar with this since I was often assigned to follow trucks from a Quartermaster Unit out of San Francisco when they moved troops. In between times I made several trips to visit Pat in Carpinteria.

During the summer Dale, Jean (Jeanette-j.t.) and Evah drove to California on vacation – Pat always insisted the main reason they came that far (on gas rationing too) was to look her over and see if they approved. When they came to visit, our shop foreman (in Gilroy) put Dale's car on the lube rack to repair the muffler problem and then filled it with a free tank of Uncle Sam's gasoline. Dale was very uncomfortable the whole time the car was in there as he really did not want to visit a federal prison too.

In mid-1943 we were ordered to Fort Ord, California for overseas shipment. We packed our freight and put it on a train bound for Ft. Lewis, Washington and said our goodbyes. Next morning we boarded our train; it moved a few feet and stopped. After thirty minutes we were ordered off and trucked back to Gilroy. Pat and I had discussed marriage but decided to wait until the war was over, when I was ordered overseas. Now we could proceed with wedding plans and on October 23, 1943, we were married in Carpinteria Community Church. From then on I was permitted to live off the post and we found a nice little apartment in Gilroy.

Two months later we were transferred to Camp Maxey, Paris, Texas, and I traveled by train and Pat came a little later on a Greyhound bus. Our motor pool bordered a small orchard and wooded area and with snow on the ground I spotted rabbit tracks. So, I built two box traps and proceeded to reduce our food bill at our apartment in town. When I mentioned my good fortune about the meat to *our landlady, we were told "Whites did not eat rabbits. That was nigga' meat." However, with our allowance of $1.00 per day for food and the same for rent, this smoothed things out and we continued to enjoy our free meat.*

Pat shopped at the commissary with other Army wives where German POW's worked as box boys – carrying groceries out to cars etc. It was hot in Texas and at times we had to sprinkle the sheets with cool water before going to bed.

When we were in Gilroy the Army had started calling on our unit for overseas replacements and this was stepped up a notch here in Texas. Good mechanics and truck drivers were sent to front lines without combat training. In many cases we received word within days or weeks that friends had been killed in action. A request arrived for two Tech 4's (which is what I was at the time), and with only three of us left in the Company we were to flip coins. Lucky again, I had the odd coin and got to stay in the United States.

Next stop – but only a short one – was Camp Gruber, Oklahoma. We lived in the country and shared half of a large home with another couple. We had inside plumbing for the kitchen and bath only so it was "back to nature". I had taken my box traps with me but never was able to catch an "Okie" rabbit.

Before we had time to look around Muskogee and see what the town looked like we were transferred to Camp Rucker, at Ozark, Alabama. We lived in town in the Mayor's rentals which consisted of eight converted chicken houses about 6' x 12'. These were in a semi-circle behind the Mayor's home and inside was just enough room for a kitchen table, two chairs, apartment size stove and a bed. Outdoors in the center of the circle was a central bath and shower. All for $1.00 a day. At all our camps we had bus transportation to and from town at least every hour.

A major benefit of our service life was the special friendships we developed. I was drafted with Floyd Willis from Flint and he became one of the closest friends of my entire lifetime. He was best man at our wedding and we had applied for Warrant Officer's Examination together when we were still stationed in Gilroy. Because of a small tooth cavity I was denied the exam. He passed his and was assigned to the European Theatre from Camp Maxey, Texas. Our saddest day came several months later when we were in Alabama and received word that he had been ambushed behind the lines and killed just thirty days before the war in Europe ended.

Special friendships developed too with many of the married couples and some single men because of the special conditions under which we lived. Many of these friendships remain strong today even though one spouse is missing from some couples.

On a furlough from Alabama we went home to Indiana by train and while there we arranged to buy Floyd and Juanita's '36 Chevy. I overhauled it and we loaded it down with produce from the farm, canned goods from Mom's cellar and even some old curtains we could use in our Alabama chicken house. We felt on top of the world with wheels and all the goodies we had packed in as we went driving south to Alabama again.

While at Camp Rucker the war ended and we were sent to Camp Hood, Killeen, Texas, to await discharge from the Army. We found a room in Belton, Texas, with the local postmaster as we knew it would only be a short time before discharge papers would come through. And that date was November 18, 1945.

With our Chevy fully loaded we drove back to Indiana for a visit with Mom and Dad before we headed to Santa Ana, California, where a friend and I had agreed to open a garage. I did mechanical work in a Shell Service Station owned by Pat's cousin while we searched for a location. When it was clear that nothing was available, we moved to Carpinteria to the apartment in Mom and Dad Demaree's house (which we later bought) and settled in.

I had met the Chevy-Ford dealer in Carpinteria during our tour in California and had a standing offer to work for him, so when I showed up he put me to work. In 1946 we sold Fords and Chevrolets out of the same building. At the end of the year Mr. Humphrey was forced to make a decision and took the Ford sign down. Bob had stopped in to visit us on his way back to Indiana from the Pacific Theatre and life had become quite routine. However, a few months later on January 7, 1947, young Dennis arrived and our family was in progress."

Pat had never been out of California before she met and married Jim and Jim had never seen California until he was drafted into the Armed Forces. However, due to the time he spent in California during World War II, his experiences and the connections he made caused him to think it would be a good place to settle down.

That certainly was okay with Pat since most of her family lived in California and it was "home" to her.

Jim was discharged from the Army on November 18, 1945, and when he and Pat came to Indiana for a visit on their way back to California, Pat was so surprised to see the fall colors in the trees and landscape. She had never seen the seasons change as they do in the Midwest. She thought it was beautiful.

When Jim's plans to open an automobile service garage with his Army buddy didn't work out he decided to check back on the standing offer for work he had received from the Chevy-Ford dealer in Carpinteria. Pat's mother and dad, the Demarees, lived in Carpinteria and they had an apartment in their house that Pat and Jim moved into. Later, after Mr. Demaree passed away Pat and Jim bought the Demaree's house.

Jim worked as a Parts Department Manager all his working life, mostly for Chevrolet and General Motors (GM) dealers. In Carpinteria Mr. Humphrey sold both Chevrolets and Ford. A short time after Jim went there though, Mr. Humphrey had to make a choice and he chose to keep the Chevy dealership.

From Carpinteria, Jim went to Mel Smith Chevy in San Luis Obispo. From there he went to Fred Brieden Chevrolet in Paso Robles, then back to San Luis Obispo to Kimball Motors.

Jim's younger daughter, Becky, now a grandmother, told me, "In my brain, I thought my Daddy could fix any engine in the world. He knew all of the other GM Parts Department Managers in the southern part of California, so if he didn't have a specialty part for an older engine he would call around until he found it then have it shipped in by Greyhound bus."

Becky said, "He not only knew the department managers, he also knew all the salesmen who came through our area of central California and had genuine friendships with all of them."

"After Dad's death," Becky went on to say, "at the Celebration Service, there was a man who shared an experience from when he was in high school. He told us that Dad located a hard to find part for his late model Corvette somewhere in Los Angeles and had it sent by bus up to San Luis. Apparently the other dealerships had just shunned the young man because of his age and Dad took him seriously. He never forgot him for it either."

When Jim and Pat lived in Santa Margarita, they bought a house there with a big yard and lived there for a couple of years. They then found a place in a little berg named Garden Farms with some acreage and enough space for a big garden. It was close enough to Jim's work to be comfortable and they bought it.

Pat was never as comfortable with gardening though as Jim was. I remember her telling me how much trouble it was to clean, string and break the green beans Jim brought in from the garden. I laughed and we talked about it. She said, "Oh, but it's so much easier just to open a box of frozen ones." We all laughed and teased her about that, as we did about her being afraid to go to the outdoor toilet on the farm. She was always a bit of a city girl at heart.

The two bedroom house in Garden Farms became too small as Pat and Jim's family came along. Dennis, the first grandchild of Ora and Ann, was born January 7, 1947, and has lived in Camas Valley, Oregon, for many years. Cathy arrived September 28, 1950, and still lives in Atascadero, California. James, Jr., born March 31, 1952, also has been in Camas Valley for many years and Loren, April 8, 1956, has settled down in Camas Valley. Rebecca (Becky) born November 27, 1960, has spent most of her married life in Juneau, Alaska.

Undaunted by a house that was getting too small Jim set about making the house fit the family. He added more bedrooms, a big porch, more kitchen and dining area and extra space indoors to make room for the children and added more buildings outdoors to make room for the cows, horses, chickens, goats, cats and dogs. With five children and numerous animals she had not been used to, Pat learned to do many new jobs. She never worked outside the home, but along the way she started calling herself a Domestic Engineer.

Jim had a heart attack sometime around 1970 and shortly thereafter had open heart surgery when open heart surgery was a relatively new procedure. He retired about 1980 or so when all the children were out of the nest and on their own. After he retired, Jim and Pat sold their home in Garden Farms and moved into a mobile home in Atascadero to be near Cathy and her husband Jack. They also bought a small place in Desert Hot Springs and enjoyed the winters there.

After Jim's heart attack, he changed his diet to lower his cholesterol, apparently with some success. The prognosis for his lifetime at the time of his surgery was five to ten years. Although he had a few setbacks, Jim lived 26 more years. On Sunday, July 29, 2001, he got up, had breakfast and went out and watered his flowers and garden. He came back into the house and went to the bathroom, fell against the bathtub and passed away from a massive heart attack.

Pat stayed on in the mobile home for a couple of years. When her health began to fail, Dennis and Cathy looked for a good Assisted Living Facility for her. Dennis found one that was very suitable in Roseburg, Oregon, and they moved her there.

From her third floor window, Pat could look down on the Umpqua River where much of the Wolfe family fishes now and where two of Jim and Pat's grandsons, Richard and Scott, twin sons of Dennis, own a fishing guide business. They escort fisherman from all parts of the country to quality fishing areas. They fish mostly for salmon and steelhead but other seasonal fishes too - very successfully I might add. Many of Ora and Ann's third generation Wolfes have visited Oregon and enjoyed the services of their professional guide cousins.

Pat spent about two years in Oregon near Dennis, Jim Jr., Loren and her Oregon grandchildren and loved being near them. She had been diagnosed with congestive heart failure and her health continued to worsen some. She died in her sleep on November 25, 2005.

Jim and Pat had both requested to have their bodies cremated and their ashes scattered over the Umpqua River. Both of those wishes have now been granted.

Leaving The Nest - Juanita

By the time I (Juanita) was ready to leave the nest, the nest was nearly half empty.

I graduated from Union High School at Dugger the end of May, 1938, and received my gold watch and Bible from Mom and Dad, as my siblings before me had. I spent the summer at home trying to decide just what I would do after graduation. Dale, Evah and James were already working in Flint, but I had always wanted to go to business school and become a secretary.

When Evah was home that summer on vacation, we checked out Wabash Business College at Terre Haute for costs, classes, etc., and she was going to help out with financing for tuition and housing. We had thought I could get a room at the YWCA, maybe get a part-time job and we could make it work.

Evah's vacation ended and she went back to Michigan before the arrangements were all made and getting back and forth to Terre Haute to complete them was not easy. Before I could get the plans finalized, Elizabeth Wilson, a neighbor and church and school friend who was Evah's age, came home for a visit from her job in Terre Haute.

Elizabeth worked in the home of a business man and his family and she told me that a family who lived about six blocks from where she worked and was friends of her employer, needed a girl to work in their home. She said it was a doctor's home and would be a good place to work and she thought I would like it.

Now I was really in a dilemma! Should I continue with plans to go away to school when I could work in the same town and start immediately? Mom and I talked it over and we agreed that it was a good opportunity to have a job offered without even looking for one. So I told Elizabeth to tell Dr. and Mrs. William Baldridge I would take the job. Through Elizabeth, it was decided I would start on a Monday in early September.

Dad took me to a 6 a.m. bus at Sullivan and I rode to Terre Haute with much fear and trepidation, wondering if I had made the right decision. Since I had not talked with Mrs.

Baldridge personally, I was not sure just what to do when I arrived in Terre Haute, so I asked the bus driver to let me off at the corner where Elizabeth's older sister, Ellen, lived at 2424 South 7th Street. Ellen showed me where to catch the street car that went down her street, told me to take it uptown, ask for a transfer and take a city bus on to the stop on North 9th Street. I then walked about six blocks to the Baldridge home at 2510 North 8th Street.

Mrs. Baldridge was surprised to see me when I rang the doorbell for she had met the 6 a.m. bus at the station and thought I had either decided not to take the job or had missed the bus. She was planning to meet the 10:00 a.m. bus just in case. She was very nice, quickly put me at ease and this started a four year relationship that was mutually agreeable to all concerned.

Annabelle, a darling little blue eyed, blonde haired four year old daughter was at home when I arrived and at noon when school was out for lunch, I met Dolores, the brown eyed, blonde haired six year old daughter. Both little girls had long curls and from then on, one of my duties was to help the girls bathe, put them to bed each night, get them up in the morning, help them dress, brush those curls, fix their breakfast and get Dolores (and later Annabelle) off to school.

My other duties included going over the whole house every day, with deep cleaning every Friday and doing all the cooking, which at that point I had rarely, if ever, been on my own to do. I well remember the first time Mrs. Baldridge went off for a social afternoon, leaving me to cook dinner and bake a coconut cream pie for dessert. I got out the recipe book, looked up a recipe for pastry and proceeded from there. Everything was going fine until I looked into the oven to see how the pie crust was coming. To my surprise, and shock, I might add, I was baking a flat circle of dough. I had put the crust on the inside of the pan and crimped the edges, as I had seen Mom do many times, but my dough had slid down into the pan as it got hot. I thought, "Oh dear, what now?" I knew no pie would leave a gaping hole in the dinner menu, so I hid that crust in the trash, hurriedly got out the cookbook and started over again from scratch. Mrs. Baldridge never knew how I flubbed my first pie.

Most of the doctors and businessmen had Wednesday off. So every Wednesday afternoon was my day off and almost every doctor and businessman in town had a maid, so there were many young girls all over town with this afternoon off. It seemed most of us went to the post office at some point Wednesday afternoon to mail a letter home. Two of the girls I met at the post office, Ruth Trueblood from Carlisle, Indiana, and Hazel Arnett from Sullivan, Indiana became my lifelong friends.

My starting salary at Baldrige's was $5.00 a week and that was the norm. For the first month or two, I was permitted to go home every weekend. I took the bus home Saturday morning and Dad took me to the 6:00 a.m. bus on Monday. After that I could go home every other week, then as time went on, monthly. On the weekends I didn't go home, I had Sunday afternoon and evening off. After several months, my salary was raised to $6.00, then $7.00 and when I quit to get married, after almost four years, I was making $9.00 weekly.

Today that doesn't sound like much, but I really could buy quite a lot with it. My room and board were free, it cost $0.10 to go to a movie and the bus trip home was $0.60 cents, round trip. I remember some nice Sunday dresses, one in particular, a navy blue taffeta one with a rather large white collar, I bought for $1.98. So things were pretty much in perspective. I also remember a brown coat with a beautiful brown real mink collar that was square in the back, about eight inches long and came all the way down the front, to the waist. I don't remember what I paid for it, but I do remember that Dr. Baldrige's mother, Grand Mom Baldridge, the girls and I called her, got her nose a little out of joint when she saw it and the perky brown hat I bought to go with it. Her attitude was that if I could afford to buy a coat like that, her son was paying me too much money. She was a widow, lived alone in a big house and nothing ever seemed to be just right for her. I don't believe I ever saw her smile. Everyone just sort of took what she said "with a grain of salt".

After I had been working for the Baldridges for more than a year, I met Floyd Tryon in a small restaurant in downtown Terre Haute. Ruth, Hazel and I were having a bite to eat before we went home on a Wednesday evening, in this little restaurant that was a converted railroad passenger car, when Floyd and one of his friends came in. They sat down in a booth across the aisle from us and, of course, Floyd struck up a conversation. We had to leave before the buses stopped running, so they asked if they could drive us home.

The next afternoon Floyd called me on the telephone. I pretended I didn't know who he was and said, "Floyd who?" The conversation soon got friendly and before long, he took charge of my Wednesday and Sunday afternoons and evenings. Floyd's friend, Bob Price, and Hazel started dating and the boys had another friend Charles "Zip" Miller, for Ruth to date. The three couples did lots of fun things together. The Trianon Ballroom out on Wabash Avenue, Terre Haute's main street, had free Sunday night dances. None of us knew how to dance very well, but we had fun. We three girls had gone occasionally to a free dance on Wednesday evenings at the Arthur Murray Studio. There were no lessons but we always had fun.

Dating didn't cost a bunch of money in those days. There were several theaters here and there around town. Some were $0.10, some $0.15 and the best theater, right downtown with the latest movies, was $0.25 admission. Drugstores all had soda fountains where you could sit at the bar and watch the sodas, sundaes, fountain drinks, etc. made or at a booth. Sodas and sundaes were $0.15 each and you could get a sandwich or a large serving of tuna salad on a lettuce leaf with Ritz crackers, (this was my favorite), for $0.15. Several items on the menu were $0.10 and a fountain coke or drink or a cup of coffee was a nickel.

Dr. Baldridge always took the month of August off for vacation and it was spent at Lake Leelanau at Leland, Michigan. Friends of theirs owned a beautiful spot on the lake with two large cottages on the waterfront and a smaller cottage a few yards away, down the pretty lane lined with lilacs that ran from the highway back to the cottages.

The Pendergasts who owned all three cottages spent the summer there and other friends rented the other big cottage for two months. They each took maids with them so I always had someone to be with on my days off. On our Wednesday and Sunday afternoons, we usually walked up town and laid on the Lake Michigan beach and swam in Lake Michigan, walked back to the cottages, changed clothes and walked back uptown to the Bluebird Restaurant where we each could get a sandwich, talk with some of the local girls and dance if there were some local boys around.

In July 1941, Floyd and I became engaged and he wasn't very happy when I went off for a month's vacation. But I had no choice. If I wanted to keep my job, that was part of it. Tough job!! Floyd and I set our wedding date for March 28, 1942, and I continued to work until the week before the wedding. Floyd worked as a salesman for Union Laundry and Dry Cleaners, the one laundry in town. He had a special route that included part of downtown with restaurants and hotels and his job was to canvas the area, get new customers whenever he could and pick up laundry for anyone on his route who called in. Many people sent sheets, towels, etc., and sometimes dresses, underwear and the like. Men's white shirts were a big item.

Floyd's laundry route also included North Second Street which was known far and wide as Terre Haute's Red Light District. There were many houses of ill repute on both sides of the street and one hotel that catered to that kind of traffic. Day or night, if the red light in the window was on, they were open for business. Of course, that area provided many stories for Floyd to tell. One especially funny one he got a kick out of telling was about the gal who called for cleaning to be picked up. When he rang the bell, she opened the door. There on a chair beside the door were several items of clothing for him to take. As he picked them up, she said, "Oh, wait, I want to send this dress." peeled it off over her head and stood there naked as a jaybird. He grabbed the dresses and took off.

There was no air conditioning in those days and in summer the heat in the laundry was almost unbearable. The hot water in the huge washers and the large mangles threw off a tremendous amount of heat. One girl stood on each side of the heavy mangles, shook the sheets (and tablecloths) out, pulled the top of the sheet taught and fed it through the hot rollers, stretching and guiding it all the way through. Shirts and clothing were done on smaller mangles and sometimes special items had to be touched up or ironed by hand.

Floyd's mother, Edna, worked inside the laundry for many years. It was a hard job but steady, dependable work. She and Floyd's dad, Raymond, divorced when Floyd was eight years old and his sister, Virginia, was four. There was a day care center in Terre Haute where you could leave your children for $0.05 each a day and with that and the help of Grandma Nora Tryon, she was able to take care of the children. A few years later, she married Charles Goss, one of the truck drivers at the laundry.

Floyd and I were married in the evening after Floyd got off work, in the living room at The

Farm. I had rented two palms from a florist in Terre Haute and we had a few bouquets of cut flowers. Evah came home from Michigan to be maid of honor and she brought with her a large, three tiered wedding cake. The Haupt sisters, Faye, Margaret and Dottie (Dottie was my age but was working in Michigan), came with Evah. They were beautiful singers and presented the music for the service. After the reception, Floyd and I drove to Indianapolis, stayed overnight in a hotel and spent most of the day in Indy, but Floyd had to be back to work Monday morning.

We had bought our little house at 1309 North 6th Street a month before we were married for $2,580.00. The down payment was $75.00. Floyd's mother was in the process of getting a divorce from her second husband and as soon as the deal for the house closed, she and Virginia moved in. So when we got married we moved into our house that was already occupied by his mother and sister. The furniture all belonged to Floyd's mother except for a brand new gas kitchen range we had bought a year before for $69.95. That was not a big problem though. We expected to replace her furniture with ours as we could afford to buy it.

Floyd's salary at the laundry and dry cleaners was $16.50 a week, guaranteed, plus commission on all he picked up and delivered. With commission it was usually somewhere around $100.00 weekly and was adequate. The house payment was $28.00 a month, electricity of $2.50 a month and the gas bill was $1.50. We paid $3.00 per ton for coal for the furnace in the basement. I kept out $10.00 a week for food and there was enough left to buy a 1936 Chevrolet. We considered that a luxury since it was only five years old.

Life settled into a pretty easy routine. Life was good. Ruth and Zip and Hazel and Bob were married before we were and lived in Terre Haute. Floyd had friends from high school that became my friends too. We were always a little uneasy though about what was going to happen. War had been declared on December 8, 1941, the day after the Japanese attached Pearl Harbor and Floyd had been required to register for the draft.

In October 1942, Floyd received his "Greetings" from Uncle Sam telling him to report to Fort Benjamin Harrison near Indianapolis. Floyd's dad and stepmother, Mary, and I took him to the depot in Terre Haute on October 16th where he boarded the troop train and he was inducted into the Army October 17, 1942. We had no idea when we would see him again but because he had flat feet, he was held at the camp for six weeks waiting for special shoes to be made. During that time Floyd's Dad and Mary, drove me over twice to see him. Finally, his shoes arrived and he was shipped out to Fort Bliss at El Paso, Texas.

After Floyd left for camp I was so lonely. I started looking for a job. A friend who was manager of the Steak and Shake Restaurant downtown offered me a job as evening hostess and cashier and I jumped at the chance. Before Floyd left for camp we had taken our '36 Chevy down to the farm and he and Dad put it up on blocks to store it. I had no car to drive back and forth to work, so I found a small apartment about two blocks from the Steak and Shake. We never considered me keeping the car to use for I hoped to move wherever Floyd was stationed. When

I moved, Floyd's mother and sister moved into an apartment and I rented the house to Jim Graham, the manager at the Steak and Shake, for we had no idea how long Floyd would be gone.

In December, after Floyd was settled in at Fort Bliss, I bought a new red wool suit and a beige wraparound coat with a long, wide tie belt, packed up and spent three days and nights on a bus to Fort Bliss. Floyd had rented a room not too far by street car to camp and we spent our first Christmas together there. Gifts were not an option. We were so happy to be together that we wanted nothing more. We soon made friends with other Army couples.

One special couple, Charles and Iris Peers from Louisville, Kentucky, were in a rented room not far from ours. The boys could spend most of their days off the base as long as they returned each evening, so we had good times with Charles and Iris. Neither of us was allowed to cook in our rooms and we got mighty tired of plate lunches and Mexican food at the little restaurant near us. Charles and Iris had bought a hot plate and one day we were in their room heating some Campbell's soup for our lunch when there was a knock at the door. We hurriedly stashed the soup pot and hot plate under the bed and sat down. Charles opened the door and the landlady stepped in and said "Are you cooking in here?" Charles said, "Goodness, no." She couldn't see anything that looked like cooking, so she left. As soon as the coast was clear, we got the hot plate and soup out and enjoyed our lunch.

When Floyd was held in Indianapolis waiting for shoes, his Army pay was also held up. It was four months before his first check arrived and by that time we were so broke, the last week before he got paid we were short one dollar on our $6.00 a week rent. I had an old silver dollar Floyd had given me as a keepsake and we asked our landlady if she would hold it and let us buy it back when Floyd got paid. When we went to buy it back, she had it in her apron pocket. We figured because it was so tarnished and dirty looking she may have thought it was no good.

In El Paso, I found a job as a waitress at a lunch counter so we were able to rent a cute little apartment where we could cook and invite friends over. Shortly after I started as a waitress, I saw an ad for help at Western Union. I had just finished my training there when Floyd was shipped overseas with no warning at all. Western Union said no – I could not quit my job as they had put money into my training and if I left, I would have to pay them for my training. I wasn't about to stay in Texas alone, so I left El Paso anyhow. I visited the Baldridge's in California, where Dr. Baldridge was stationed, for two weeks, then took a bus to Flint.

When I arrived in Flint, bag and baggage, Evah was living with Dale and Jeanette in their little two bedroom home at 2010 Berkley Street. I moved in and shared Evah's bed until I found a job at one of the defense plants. The government had ordered all automobile factories to stop making automobiles and to change over to products for the war effort. I got a job at Buick Motors in the plant that made anti-aircraft shells. I stood at a drill press all day long and drilled the hole in the bottom of the shell casing. The casings came down an assembly line to me; I picked one up with my right hand, placed it over a jig, drilled the hole, removed it and set it back on the line with my left hand. This went on like clockwork eight hours every day – then the night shift came on. When the war ended the production of anti-aircraft shells stopped immediately and I, along with hundreds of other workers, was laid off.

I started looking for work again and was hired at Marvel Carburetor. The carburetor parts were made in other areas of the plant, and then sent to an assembly line of about eight or nine girls where the raw parts were assembled into the finished product. Each girl did one specific job – drill a small hole, put in a cotter key, attach something else, etc. and at the end of the line a completed carburetor was put into a box, then sent to the testing department. I was relief girl for the line and went up and down the line giving each girl a fifteen minute break in the morning and again in the afternoon. I had to learn to do each job properly, but it was not as monotonous as doing the same job all day long. I have no idea what the pay was for either job, but for the times it was good money.

With the allotment check Floyd sent me plus what I could save out of my pay, we were able to pay the house off and have enough for new furniture and to fix the house up when he came home.

When Floyd was shipped overseas so abruptly on March 12, 1942, from Fort Bliss in Texas we had been married about a year but had spent only about six months together. At that time we were told he would be gone for six months and would be home again. However, when six months were up, the time was extended for six more months and this was true for all enlisted men.

While they were aboard ship, heading overseas, the soldiers were not allowed to write letters and although he wrote every day when he could, his letters were censored and I rarely received one that didn't have several spaces cut out of it. They could not mention where they were nor say anything about what they were doing that had to do with the fighting. I am amazed today that we didn't talk more about where he was and about the fighting after he came home. He never wanted to talk about it and there were no children to ask questions so I learned very little about his time overseas. I believe it was very painful to remember and I never pressed him for information. I wanted to forget about it too.

Floyd's Separation Papers say he arrived in the Asiatic-Pacific Theater April 1, 1943. He received a ribbon with two bronze stars for his service there and a ribbon with one bronze star for the Philippine Liberation. He served as a cannoneer and a machine gunner before he was injured. Bronze stars were given for bravery under fire I believe.

When he had been in the Pacific for about a year, Floyd was badly burned with flaming gasoline. One of his buddy's poured gasoline from a five gallon can onto a smoldering fire, the can exploded and he threw the can. The can hit Floyd and flaming gas ran down his legs and he was engulfed in flames. They were in combat and there was no way to get him to a hospital immediately. In fact he was burned so badly, he was not expected to live, so he was laid in a trench. A guy from Marshall, Illinois, (a small town about 16 miles from Terre Haute) covered him with his raincoat to shield him from the rain. After three days and nights he was taken to a hospital where he remained for ten months.

Penicillin was a brand new drug at that time and Floyd was one of the first people to use it. He believed it saved his life. He had seventeen skin grafts on his legs, taken from the skin on his upper body. He said when his burns were healing, he could reach around his right leg, just above his knee with the finger and thumb of one hand and he joked and said he was so thin, if he drank tomato juice, he looked like a thermometer!

When he was ready to be released from the hospital, Floyd, as well as the rest of us, expected he would be sent home. Not true – the army had other ideas. They sent him back to duty, however not back into combat. He went to the Fiji Islands.

In the Fiji Islands, Floyd served as a radar operator. He operated a radar set scanner, scanning for enemy planes, enemy surface craft and for enemy gun positions in the hills. He and the radar crew also located friendly planes in distress and gave them directions to the airfield. Here they had to do their own maintenance and made minor adjustments on the sets. They also had to do their own cooking and he told how the natives came begging for food and how he bartered with them for a mattress for his bunk and other things they could use in their station.

When the Japanese surrendered on April 14, 1945, we expected Floyd to be sent back home soon. But again, that didn't happen. Of course there was no place to get any information about when they would return. So, we waited – and waited – and waited. Finally a telegram came and he was in the states on December 20, 1945. Now, we hoped for Christmas, but that didn't happen either. At least he could contact me by phone now so he kept me aware – as near as he could find out – what was happening.

People stateside were happy to welcome the troop's home and at Christmastime, they were especially benevolent. Movie stars and other people invited soldiers to their homes for Christmas dinner. Floyd was lucky enough, along with a number of other soldiers, to be invited to the home of Lucille Ball for Christmas dinner. They were wined and dined in festive fashion. It was not home – but it was far and away above army mess.

The days wore on, each day seeming like a week, and Floyd finally got his orders. He would come by troop train to Camp Atterbury at Indianapolis to be mustered out on January 3, 1946. We had planned that I would meet him there, so I took a bus to Indianapolis, arriving well before he was due to get out, rented a hotel room and waited. I was as nervous as a cat. Although I had slept with his 8 x 10 picture under my pillow every night since he had been gone, I wondered if I would recognize him – had he changed – would he still love me.

Finally there was a knock on the door and I jumped up and ran to answer it. The door opened, and he stepped in and it was as if he had never been gone. He had asked me to bring one of his suits, shirt and tie. Before we went out to dinner, he changed out of his Army uniform and that was the last day he ever wore it.

We went back to The Farm for a few days with Mom and Dad then on to Terre Haute to see Floyd's family. We had given notice to the people who had rented our house and while we waited for them to move out, we stayed with Floyd's Dad and Mary. Floyd went back to work at Union Laundry and within thirty days we were back in our own house. We just moved in the bare necessities and began to redo the whole house. We removed the wallpaper in every room, repapered and painted the woodwork and sanded all the floors except the kitchen. With our savings, we were able to buy new living room and kitchen furniture and some used furniture, dishes, etc. from one of Floyd's uncles and aunt who were moving to California.

By this time the family we wanted was on the way and our first beautiful little daughter, Susan, was born February 7, 1947, a little over a year after Floyd's discharge from the Army. I spent ten days in the hospital recuperating and learning how to nurse a newborn. I will be the first to admit those ten days in the hospital after any easy birth and a healthy baby, seem excessive but it was the norm. I didn't ask to stay ten days; the doctor just did not release me to go home earlier. Each morning the nurse brought a pan of water, soap and washcloth for me to clean up before breakfast was brought in. During the day my baby was carried to me every two hours to be nursed and each evening before bedtime, after the visitors had left the room and I was ready for bed, the nurse came in and rubbed my back with lotion and I slept through the night undisturbed.

The cost of my hospital room and all this care was $5.25 per day. Our hospitalization insurance payed $5.00 per day and we picked up the $0.25. My total doctor bill for all the prenatal care, the delivery and a six month checkup after the baby was born, totaled $50.00.

When I came home from the hospital, Mom came and stayed for a week to help me get settled in and when she left, reality began to set in! My days were consumed from early morning to night nursing the baby every two hours at first (then every three hours, then four as she got older), sterilizing bottles and making formula (recommended by the doctor in case nursing was not sufficient), housework and meals, washing and ironing and diapers, endless diapers to be washed every other day and hung on the clothesline to dry – outside in the summer or in the basement in the winter. No such thing as disposable diapers. All diapers were cloth and after use, were kept in a diaper pail filled with fresh water each day and a few drops of bleach. Dirty diapers were rinsed in the toilet bowl by hand and dropped into the diaper pail until they were rinsed again, by hand, and dropped into a tub of hot sudsy water.

By the time I could manage all these chores with ease, a second beautiful baby girl we named Janice Lee, was born on June 28, 1949. After a period of readjusting, to a new baby with a two and one-half year old running all over the house, life settled into a fairly easy routine. As the girls grew, ours was a neighborhood of young families and there was never a dull moment. There were 36 children on our block alone, counting both sides of the street.

Most of our friends had children around the ages of ours and that made for good times visiting or picnicking on the weekends at Deming Park.

When Floyd came home from the service, he joined the Masonic Lodge and became a Shriner, joined the local Elks Club and the Eagle and Moose Lodges. Most of our friends were Shriners or Elks and we spent many evenings square dancing during the week and going to dances on Saturday nights. We could get a babysitter for $0.25 an hour and there were no cover charges at either place so it was not an expensive evening. We also belonged to a Pinochle Club for several years, with three other couples that met once a month in our homes. That was a fun evening that was even less expensive.

When Janice and Susan were six and eight years old, Mike came along and completed our family. He was the joy of all of our lives. He was a happy and easy to care for baby. I expected the girls to be "crazy" about him, especially Janice who always said when she grew up she just wanted to be a mother and have twelve children. The big surprise I hadn't expected was how "crazy" Mike was about his sisters. From the time he was old enough, his eyes followed every move they made. Janice, little clown that she was, would stand in front of him and make funny faces and cavort around and he would go into a deep belly laugh that would cause us all to laugh.

When they were old enough, each of the three children went to Rea Elementary School just two blocks from our house. I was close enough to help with various things at school. I always thought when a teacher asked; "Whose Mother will serve as a room mother?" or "Whose Mother will bake cookies or cupcakes?" my children's hands went up. At some point during their school years, I served in every office in the Parent Teacher Association (PTA), but I didn't work outside our home as some mothers did and I always enjoyed doing it.

By the time the girls were in college and Mike was in Junior High where he didn't come home for lunch, I felt I had time on my hands so I should be doing something productive, but something I could do from home. I answered an ad in the newspaper for a Market Researcher. A woman from New York came down to Terre Haute to interview me.

She decided I was a good fit for the job and I was hired as a supervisor. I rounded up a crew of fifteen or sixteen women who wanted to work part time from home that I could call on as needed. Sometimes our surveys were by telephone and sometimes we went door to door. When we worked outside, I was instructed exactly which day to go, which streets to canvas, which houses to stop at and what questions to ask. Sometimes I needed ten or twelve women and sometimes only two or three. Although I worked the same jobs the other women did, I had other responsibilities. My job included calling the women together at my house, before the job started, to go over the survey in detail with them. Then after the surveys were completed I was to verify a certain number of each of the women's completed interview, to see if they were actually conducted in the manner they were supposed to be.

I enjoyed this work. I liked working with other women somewhat in my age group and I enjoyed the interaction of the respondents I interviewed. I determined from that experience, that as a whole, people are nice – that if they are approached in a kind and friendly manner, most of them will respond in like manner. I assured the occasional "grouch" it was perfectly alright, thanked him kindly for his time and went on to the next.

The occasional woman, who filled out the interviews herself and turned them in, was always found out, for I was religious about my verifications. After dealing with problems two or three times, I was careful to explain at our briefings that their interviews definitely would be verified, I seldom had further problems. The pay was not great but I thought it was fair. My part time work averaged about $50.00 a week which I considered money for extra clothing for the kids and things around the house that didn't fit into our budget.

After about two years doing market research, I was approached about a job on the Terre Haute Star newspaper. Frances Hughes, Society Editor on the Star, asked one of my friends, Betty Sheets, when she took some club news in for the society page, if she would be interested or if she knew someone who might be interested in working with her and eventually taking over her job. Betty told her she was not interested but she knew someone who could do the job if she was interested.

Betty told me about the conversation and said if I was interested I was to call Miss Hughes at work. I thought it over, gave Frances a call and made an appointment to talk to her. She explained to me that she was sixty one years old and wanted to retire at age sixty five. That she had worked on the paper as society editor for forty three years and wanted to do some regular news stories before she retired. She said upfront that she had no authority to hire anyone, but would like to have someone to recommend when she approached her boss, Lawrence Sawyer, about what she wanted to do. We talked and she asked me if I had had any journalism training. I told her I had had no formal training, but I always thought I could do anything I really wanted to. She liked my attitude and asked if she could set up an appointment for me with Mr. Sawyer.

The Terre Haute Star was the morning newspaper and all Star employees worked nights except the Society Editor. My appointment with Mr. Sawyer was at ten o'clock on a Wednesday evening and I stopped to see him on my way home from Pinochle Club. He asked me a few questions about writing, but mostly we just talked. I told him of my experience interviewing people and told him, as I had told Miss Hughes; I figured I could do anything I set my mind to. He said he would let me know.

Several weeks went by. Floyd kept asking me if I was going to take that job at the newspaper. I kept telling him it hadn't really been offered to me yet. Finally, on a Sunday afternoon, Mr. Sawyer called and asked if I was still interested in the job. I said I was as interested as I ever was, but I was not sure if I would like it or if they would like me. I asked if I could try it on a part time basis. He let me choose my hours and I worked four hours a day for three months, whatever hours Miss Hughes wanted me. At the end of the trial period, I liked the job. Both Frances and

Mr. Sawyer thought I was a good match and the job was mine. I then quit my market research job and worked eight to five at the newspaper.

I had only been working full time at the newspaper a week when Mrs. Hughes, Frances's mother, became very ill, was hospitalized and passed away. During the time Frances was away, I was completely in charge of the Society Page and was responsible for filling it each day with news of club meetings, weddings, dances and other society events in the city. Mr. Sawyer thought I did an exemplary job, complimented me and gave me a raise in pay, the first of several. But we were a union paper and the amount of a raise was stipulated in the contract.

After I had been at the paper a year or so, the Union Laundry closed and Floyd was out of work. After World War II ended and washing machines could be produced again, automatic washers and dryers replaced wringer washers and clothes lines and that was hard on the laundry business. Polyester and wash and wear clothing took the country by storm and that was hard on the dry cleaning business.

About this same time laundromats began to spring up all over the country. Some of the laundromats also had coin operated dry cleaning machines. Hotels and motels went to wash and wear sheets and pillow cases, large restaurants replaced their damask tablecloths and napkins with wash and wear and it became obvious the only alternative for Union Laundry was to close its doors.

Floyd had a Shrine buddy, George Doughty, who had opened a filter business in Terre Haute and the two of them, with another Shrine buddy, Bill Sheets, began to talk about opening another filter business. After doing some research, Evansville came up as the best place to start that type of business. So, George, Bill and Floyd began to talk about and plan for a filter business in Evansville. George already had a filter business in Terre Haute and Bill was manager of Seabury Tavern on South 7th Street in Terre Haute. Neither of the three had much money, but they each came up with $1,000.

The plan was to fashion the business after George's filter business, with a service department to wash metal filters picked up in restaurants and to replace dirty filters in commercial businesses with new ones and a sales department that stocked and sold all sorts of filters as well as other types of air cleaners.

As Floyd was the only one unemployed, it fell his lot to go down to Evansville, about 125 miles from Terre Haute, to get things started. George was busy in his business every day, but Bill worked mostly nights at the Seabury so he could go a couple or so days a week. Floyd was not on any kind of salary, so it was a good thing my job at the newspaper was secure for it was a constant drain on my salary. There was not much done in the way of bookkeeping and as you might know, $3,000 would not last long.

In the beginning, Floyd and Bill would drive down and back two or three days a week. They brought the dirty filters back to George's place in their cars, to be washed for a charge of so much per filter. Eventually they were able to buy a used Ford Econoline van and that was a big help. As time went on, they got the equipment to wash the dirty filters in Evansville. The sales department continued to grow enough to keep things going, but this went on for several years with no one realizing anything from it.

After being in business about five years Bill Sheets was killed in an accident. George, who was doing okay in his own business, was not interested in putting any work into the business and he and Floyd arranged for Floyd to buy the business.

Floyd found a larger place for the business and moved into it. He changed the name from Clean Air of Evansville to 3T Corporation, Clean Air Division. It still was hardly making its own way. I was still working at the Terre Haute Star, so I would leave Terre Haute on Friday evening after 5:00 p.m. and drive to Evansville. Floyd and I would go out to dinner, get up early on Saturday morning, put on the yellow rubber overalls and heavy rubber gloves that went up to the elbows and wash filters most of the day. We usually managed to go out some place nice for dinner Saturday evening. On Sunday, I would get the bookwork caught up and get up to leave Evansville about 5:00 a.m. Monday to be at work by 8:00 a.m. If someone asked me where I lived, I would say, "On the highway between Evansville and Terre Haute." That's what it felt like!

When I retired from the newspaper in 1980 at 60 years of age, I was able to move to Evansville. I had received a nice severance pay and started to work at Clean Air, as office manager. We took the severance pay and got the business on its feet, really, for the first time. I enjoyed the work there. When I first went, my desk was back to back with Floyd's, so we sat face to face. When someone asked me how we could get along working that close together, I would tell them, with a laugh, "I sleep with the boss, so I get special privileges!"

In the 1980s we hired a part time young woman that could work a couple of days a week and a full week now and then when I needed her. That worked well, especially since grandchildren were still coming and I needed time off for more grand-mothering.

Floyd finally made a small office for himself with a large window between it and the front office. We worked there until we were both 75 years old. Sometimes we were kidded about working so long. One of our customers laughed and said, "Aren't you two old people ever going to retire?" I answered, "Oh yes, if we ever get old enough – we're trying to get old enough to retire." In 1995, we both felt like it was time. Barbara had been with us for about 10 years and had been working full time for a few years, so we sold the business to Barbara and her husband, John, packed up our personal belongings and retired.

Floyd was only able to enjoy his retirement for a few years. He had a heart valve replacement in 1998 and passed away March 3, 1999, two weeks before his 78th birthday.

I, (Juanita) stayed on in Evansville for five more years, then when the ten room house with a big yard, lots of grass and mountains of leaves in the fall began to sound like a heavy load, I stayed in Indiana, but moved to Crown Point where I am less than ten minutes from our daughter, Janice and her husband, Jim Kosiba and maybe two hours from our son, Mike and his wife Cathy in Crystal Lake, Illinois. Our daughter, Susan McMurray, has lived in Dallas, Texas, for many years.

The 11 grandchildren I love so much, some now with families of their own, are scattered from the Midwest to California.

Chapter 16

Leaving The Nest - Max

Max's high school years were good! He wasn't a really serious student academically, but he loved sports and excelled at them. He played basketball, football and baseball, the only varsity sports that were offered at Union High School. He was tall, good-looking, well known and well liked - a "jock" - a BMOC (Big Man on Campus) in that crowd that always had lots of admirers.

As the center on the basketball team, Max played under the basket and made lots of goals. However, his percentage of shots made was not high because on rebounds he would try to tip the ball into the basket. Several tips would usually put it in, but each tip counted as a shot.

Football was probably Max's favorite sport. He was always a starting end and made his share of passes, receives and tackles. Dugger's football team, though, never did very well in any season, mostly because it was the smallest school, as well as the smallest team, on the circuit.

Sullivan High, the closest high school to Dugger, was an arch rival and could always beat us in football. Basketball, however, was a different story. Union High could usually outscore them, sometimes advancing to the finals or semi-finals.

As a tough farm boy, Max was willing to catch on the baseball team - not a coveted spot on a high school baseball team. This was not a spectator sport at Union High, but was played in the off season. Coach, Tom Leaman, used it mostly as a way to keep his team members busy and in shape for football and basketball.

The year 1941-1942, his senior year, was an especially good year for Max. His grades were good and he lettered in all the sports. The school letter is awarded for excellence and worn with honor by the sportsman. Black and gold were Union High's colors and the huge gold U, embroidered into a woven black background, looked very handsome on Max's gold sweater. Often, these sweaters are worn with much pride by the sportsman's high school sweetheart and this was the case with Max's sweater.

In his senior year, Max was dating Wanda Lee Jones. A pretty red-headed gal, she was the sister of John Paul Jones, Max's best friend. Wanda Lee and John Paul both lived with their grandmother, Aunt Kate Armstrong we called her, across the road from Park School. After Max wore his sweater for a short time, he let Wanda Lee wear it and it was never returned until many years later, after she had been married to someone else for a number of years.

Max was funny. He had an unusual way with words and usually had a little joke on the tip of his tongue or a little ditty he would sing. In the May 1988, "Wolfe Call" newsletter, he wrote about the jobs he had after he graduated from high school, before he was inducted into the Army in World II. It is "so Max" I think you will enjoy reading it just as he wrote it.

Max's Story: *"I'm supposed to let everyone know a little about my high school days, until my army days. So, please remember, my army days started much too quick for me. I sure wasn't ready for my army days!*

First off, I had had a pretty good time in high school playing basketball and football. In Dugger, we got out of school around the last of April. We had eight months of school and got off four. Sullivan had nine months of school and got off three. We were always quite happy about that. Just the breaks of the game, I guess. Or maybe we just didn't need that much schooling. Ha-ha. No comment.

Anyway, after I graduated I wanted a little of that stuff you call money, but it wasn't all that easy. There weren't that many jobs around. In the meantime, Camp Atterbury was being built for the Army, not too far from home, close to Columbus, Indiana. I'm sure Dick and Ruth and family know just where it is – Rick has probably hunted around that locale.

A fellow who lived in Jericho, Soldier Collins, and his son Billie were working at Camp Atterbury at the time. So John Paul Jones, a friend of mine from school, and I went back with Soldier and his son on a Monday morning to get us a job. They seemed to be making quite a large amount of money per week and we thought we should cash in on some of the loot. The thing we didn't know was how hard they had to work to get it. They didn't want you to sit down or stop at any time.

We went to work later that Monday morning picking up wood from around the building. There must have been six or seven of us. Later that morning, we all sat down in the shade of one of the buildings for a little rest and when the foreman came by, we were all fired on the spot.

But in those days you were sort of frozen on the job. So, they gave us another job that same day - pushing a wheelbarrow in the motor pool. Well, I guess you know John Paul and I couldn't see that we had gained a great deal by that. So that afternoon, we just quit. This all happened in one day. I guess we didn't want a job as bad as we thought.

That evening around 8:00 p.m., we started thumbing for Toledo, Ohio, where John Paul's mother, dad and sister happened to be living at the time. We got on the other side of Indianapolis about 9:30 and then our luck changed for the better. A fellow in a big new car going to New York picked us up and gave us a ride to Toledo. We had stopped on the way and he had gotten us something to eat.

I can remember getting in to Toledo. We sure thought we were in the land of plenty. But that's just when the hard part started, taking care of myself. Mother and Dad weren't around to put any grub on the table.

Jobs were quite easy to come by, so it wasn't very long until I had a job working in the shipyards building ships and living downtown in Toledo at the Melrose Hotel. I guess at that time, I thought that was pretty hot stuff. I know I sure felt better about myself and the rest of the world and was having a fine time. Then winter came and it sure was cold in the shipyards. We were on Lake Erie and the wind was sure coming off that big lake. But I guess that was life in the big city.

I remember coming home that Christmas and I had gifts for all who were at home and Mother thought I was doing okay in my old age. I also remember telling Mother I was still a country boy. I have sure never been sorry for having been raised on The Farm. I don't want to take anything away from the city boys, it's just that I like a little more room to breathe.

That winter was just about all I wanted of that, so I quit the shipyards and the boss and I went around again about being frozen on the job. When I didn't show up any more I'm sure he got the message. I went to work in the Overland Factory building Jeeps. It was only a matter of weeks 'til my old, dear Uncle Sam called and I went. I might add, with great reluctance. I suppose back in those days I was just plain hard to please. I had no problem keeping my army job. Just couldn't find any way to get out.

When the war was over, I understood what Dad meant when he used to say, "I wouldn't take a million dollars for my experience and I wouldn't give a nickel to do it again."

I wish there were more known about Max's Army life, but many of the men who served overseas on the frontlines never talked about it after they came home. Max was like that, as was my husband, Floyd. I always thought it was too painful to remember and they just chose to avoid it. I'm sure they never forgot it.

Max's birthday was April 23, so he was barely 18 when he graduated from high school in the spring of 1943. At age 18, he had to register for the draft then waited for his call. The Japanese had attacked Pearl Harbor on December 7, 1941, and the United States declared war on Japan the next day. The War in Germany had heated up and Hitler jumped in and declared war on the United States on December 9, 1941. Now there were two fronts and troops had to be sent, not only into the Pacific Theater but also into Europe.

As Max said, he spent the winter after his graduation working in the shipyards at Toledo. Just weeks after he quit the shipyards and started working in an automobile factory in Toledo, he was called up.

The protocol for all draftees was a rigid classification system to insure that each individual was directed to the specific job he was fitted for and that he was fit physically and mentally to fulfill that duty. The first screening was at the Selective Service Board. Men essential to industry were deferred, so as not to cause disruption of the vital economic effort.

The draftees were then sent to an Induction Center and there the physically fit were separated from those with physical or mental problems who failed to meet the minimum standards for military service. Men were usually processed through the Induction Center in 24 hours or less. They were then inducted into the Armed Forces.

Next stop was the Reception Center where each inductee received his first classification to determine his civilian skills and aptitudes. This was determined through a series of trade tests - clerical, mechanical, etc. This could take as long as two weeks. Some were inducted into the military service from the Reception Center and used on staff. The enlisted men were sent to the Replacement Center and settled in for twelve or thirteen weeks of Basic Training.

During this basic military training they were converted from civilians to soldiers. Upon completion of these training courses, they were ready for assignment to a particular unit.

The inductees were trained not only in their crafts, but in the life of a soldier. When they left for replacement in a tactile unit, they knew how to shoot straight, to march like a soldier, pitch a tent, make a bed, defend against chemical warfare and use a bayonet. They knew about interior guard duty, first aid, military sanitation and map reading, among a host of other things.

Physical requirements for selectees required them to be at least five feet tall, weigh at least 105 pounds, be firmly muscled, vigorous and healthy. Their hearing needed to be only 10/20 in one ear and 20/20 in the other. They had to read 20/100 in one eye and 20/40 in the other. In 1941, the time limit of service was extended from six months to eighteen months. Enlisted men's pay of $21.00 monthly was raised $10.00 after one year. In 1942, limitation of the number of soldiers that could be in the service at any one time was removed completely.

After Max received his Greetings from Uncle Sam (the form letter to all draftees began with one word - GREETINGS - in big, bold, black letters) and passed through the Induction Center where he became a soldier in the Armed Forces, he was sent to Battle Creek, Michigan, for his Basic Training. After thirteen weeks there, he was assigned to the 44th Infantry Division at Fort Lewis, Washington. The 44th Infantry Division was under the command of General William Dean.

During the weeks of intensive training at Ft. Lewis, Max and his fellow inductees were taught not only how to function in the Army, but how to function in combat. They were reminded they had taken an oath "To defend my nation and the people I love". It was impressed on them that every man's life depended on how well his buddy had learned his job. They were told their main job was "To hit the enemy and hit him again". His purpose was to "move forward, always forward". They knew they were in for the duration.

There at Fort Lewis, Max and the other soldiers learned about and were issued many of the implements of war. They were told that "any weapon is only as good as the man behind it". Part of each man's issue was a 45 pistol, 30 caliber carbine (a rifle with a short barrel), and a 50 caliber carbine that he would learn was his best friend day in and day out. They were issued incendiary grenades, fragmentation grenades that made smoke screens, Molotov Cocktails, 105 Howitzers and bazookas. The bazookas could stop a tank all by itself and the 105 Howitzer was light and easy to handle and had a range of three miles.

Bob read a letter Max wrote to Jim while he was at Ft. Lewis and Jim was on active duty in California. Max was complaining bitterly that the 44th was famous for overtraining. One of his big gripes was that their grains - oats, cornmeal, cereal, etc., had worms in it, but was cooked and served anyway. Of course there were other typical G. I. Joe gripes, but Max assured Jim he did not tell Mom any of this. He just wrote positive things to her.

Max and the 44th Infantry Division, with General Dean in command, went by troop ship to Europe. They landed in German Occupied France via Omaha Beach on September 15, 1944, and trained for a month before entering combat on October 18, when they relieved the 79th Division in the vicinity of Luneville. It went on to secure several passes in the Vosges Mountains. The 44th was hit by a heavy counter attack by forces of Nazi Germany on October 25th and 26th. The attack was repulsed and the 44th remained in the area for several weeks.

On November 13, 1944, the 44th Division attacked northeast, advancing through the mountains capturing and liberating cities along the Marginot Line. On December 19th the 44th was forced to retreat to defensive positions but on December 23rd and 24th, it threw back three attempts by the Germans to cross the Blies River. An aggressive defense of the area was continued by the 44th through January, February and most of March.

In Jim's letter from Max, Bob remembers that Max told of that terrible winter in 1944 (it was known to be the worst on record at that time). Max told of 21 consecutive days on the front line without any relief or a hot meal. At that time, that was thought to be the longest any division had been on the frontlines with no relief. Max also described night patrols into German lines and nights when they could hear Germans talking, just inches from their foxholes. They would stay deathly quiet and hope no German would stumble into their foxhole.

During those cold and nasty months, nightly fire fights were a regular occurrence for the division. Max told of one especially grueling night when he was the only man in his platoon of eight men to answer roll call the next morning.

When Max was first attached to the 44th Infantry Division, he disliked General Dean immensely, but as time went on, especially during combat, Max gained much respect and admiration for him. General Dean was on the front line with his men more than most commanders. It was said he didn't believe the front lines were for enlisted men only and his actions proved that to be true. He issued aluminum cyanide capsules to his men so they could carry them in their mouths and bite down on them if they were captured. General Dean was thought to carry them himself.

For his service that terrible winter in France, Max was awarded two bronze stars for "unusual bravery under fire".

After a short period of occupation, the 44th Division returned to the United States in July, 1945 and began training for deployment to the Pacific Theater. It was intended that General Dean would lead his division during the planned invasion of Honshu, Japan but the war ended before that took place.

General Dean was well known for his encouragement, loyal devotion to his men and his complete disregard for his personal safety. For his dedicated service in France, General Dean was awarded The Distinguished Service Cross and a Medal of Honor, among other awards.

When the war in Europe ended on VE Day, August 14, 1945, Max was discharged shortly thereafter and went home to The Farm for some much needed rest. I don't believe he ever talked to Mom and Dad about his service in German occupied France. He was anxious to get back into a normal life again and after spending some time at home, he went to Flint where Evah and Dale were living to look for work there.

Post war Flint, however, was not the same as it had been before the war. Work had been plentiful then with all the automobile factories going full steam ahead. And during the war, with most of the able bodied men in the service, there was work for anyone who wanted to work, male or female.

Automobiles were the biggest industry in the city and the production of automobiles was banned from 1941 to 1946. All automobile factories had been retooled to make military vehicles and other products for the war effort. Now that the war was over, they had to be retooled again to get back into civilian automobile production.

Not only automobile production, but the production of most other durable goods such as kitchen appliances, vacuum cleaners, new housing, to name a few, was banned. Many items such a meat, sugar, clothing, shoes, tires and gasoline were tightly rationed.

Tires were the first item to be rationed in 1942 because supplies of natural rubber were interrupted. Gasoline rationing also proved to be a good way to allocate scarce rubber. In June

1942, the combined Food Board was set up to coordinate the world-wide supply of food to the Allies. Special flows were set up from the United States and Canada to Great Britain.

By 1943, the government issued ration coupons to purchase coffee, sugar, meat, cheese, butter, lard, margarine, canned goods, dried fruits, jam, gasoline, bicycles, fuel oil, clothing, silk or nylon stockings, shoes and many other items. The rationing system did not apply to used goods like clothes or cars, but they became more expensive since these items were not subject to price controls.

To get a classification and a book of ration stamps, civilians had to appear before a rationing board. Each person in a household received a ration book, including babies and children. To buy gasoline, the driver had to present a gas card along with a ration book and cash. The ration stamps were only good for a set period of time to keep people from hoarding. Most families were only allowed three gallons of gas a week.

All forms of automobile racing were banned, including the Indianapolis 500 which was canceled from 1942 to 1945, when the war ended. All sightseeing driving was banned, too.

In industrial areas, housing was in short supply, so many families doubled up and lived in cramped quarter. Prices and wages were controlled, therefore, Americans were able to save a large portion of their incomes. In turn, this led to renewed growth after the war.

When Max went to Flint after the war, the economy was in somewhat of a state of limbo. The automobile factories were not back into full production yet. When production resumed, the 1947 models were the first ones off the production lines.

Max worked some in Dale's Health Food Store, then he saw an ad in the newspaper by Steelco Corporation asking for salesmen to sell their waterless, stainless steel cookware. One of Steelco's requirements for salesmen was to be able to cook and serve an actual meal to prospective customers and their guests. Max had served as an Army cook during part of his Basic Training, so he felt confident this was a job he could handle.

As Max went door to door, he carried part of the set of cookware with him, showed it to the lady of the house and set up appointments to prepare meals. This of course, could be done during the daytime, but most of the meals were set for the evening dinner hour.

Steelco was among the first makers of waterless cookware. Their pots and pans were designed so that the lids would seal tightly to the pans when the food was started on high with a very small amount of water, then the heat was adjusted to very low temperature and the food cooked in steam as opposed to boiling water. This, according to Steelco, kept more vitamins, minerals and other nutrients in the food and was not poured off with the water.

Steelco's cookware was beautiful, made of several plies of stainless steel and the food that came out of it was delicious, but it was expensive. Max enjoyed the cooking and the interaction with the prospective customers and their guests, but anyone who has spent much time in the kitchen knows that cooking a special meal for six or eight people is not child's play. Since the bottom line is usually the cost, the cookware was not easy to sell and Max was not making the money he had hoped to. I feel sure he was happy when the automobile factories reopened and began hiring again.

Max applied and was hired in at General Motors at Chevrolet Manufacturing and worked there until he retired. He worked in Skilled Trades as a building repairman. His job included several duties, some of which were operating a backhoe, replacing wood floor blocks, pouring concrete foundations for machinery and repairing concrete inside and outside of all the buildings. There were approximately 10 plants at Chevrolet Manufacturing.

After Max's retirement, there were many changes in the automobile industry. Chevrolet Manufacturing no longer stands on Chevrolet Avenue in Flint. All but two of the production plants were closed in the late 1990s and early 2000s. One of the remaining buildings was donated to Kettering Institute - originally General Motors Institute.

While working at Chevrolet, Max met Marie Reno, a long- time employee of Chevrolet. Marie worked in and managed the main dining room and often worked in the executive dining room. They were married July 29, 1967. When they married, Marie had seven children from a previous marriage. However, all the children were grown and had homes of their own at that time, except the two youngest, Darlene and Danny. They lived with Max and Marie. Marie's five other children lived in the Flint area and Max enjoyed a good relationship with all of them.

Max and Marie's children, all born to Marie in a previous marriage, are: Richard (Dick) Reno, born July 12, 1938; Dennis Reno, born December 20, 1940; David Reno, December 2, 1942; Denver Reno, 1944; Diane Reno Weston, September 9, 1946; Darlene Reno Fall, September 8, 1948 and Daniel (Danny) Reno, April 8, 1952.

Max was always active, even after his retirement, with a variety of things, outside as well as inside, his home. He particularly enjoyed fishing, golfing and small game hunting. He built a small cabin on a plot of ground he bought in Sears, Michigan, less than two hours from his home in Flint. He had enough ground there to put in a nice garden and enjoyed working the soil for several years. He soon found, however, that since he could only be there a few days a month that the deer and other wild animals rendered it less than profitable.

Honeybees were a passion of Max's. He raised them in his backyard in Flint and at the cabin up north. He loved donning his beekeeper's hat and working among his bees. The hat was a large brimmed straw hat with a fine mesh veil all around the brim with a drawstring at the neck. With a long sleeved shirt, gloves and long pants tied with a string at the ankles, he could open the hives and take out the honey without getting stung by the bees. Max liked to think that occasionally he could gather the honey without all the paraphernalia. Sometimes, he could, but on occasion, a bee would make its mark.

Bill and Evah had a large garden spot at their one and one-half acres in Flushing and they assigned a nice plot of it to Max after his retirement so he could have a garden closer to home without the troublesome deer. Max was always on hand in the spring to carry the large, heavy buckets of sap from Bill and Evah's maple trees to Bill's maple syrup shed and to help boil it down into maple syrup. This was always a good time for Max, as well as for any of the rest of the siblings who could get there to help with it.

Max loved to collect and he collected a large variety of old things. Old mowers were a specialty of his and he would fix them up and sell them. The Goody Barn in the Flint area was a favorite haunt of Max's. It was a big warehouse-like building and it was stuffed with almost anything you could think of - all used items, I believe. There were piles of used lumber, old windows taken out of buildings, furniture, buckets, tools - you name it. Almost any time you visited in Flint, at some point, Max would say, "Come on let's take a run out to the Goody Barn". He loved to roam through the aisles. Sometimes he bought something, sometimes he didn't. He loved to browse and it was always fun.

With such a good natured, funny personality, Max was well liked by everyone. He was always a favorite with all his nieces and nephews. He didn't get married until he was 44 years old and when his nieces and nephews were growing up, he lived alone in an apartment in Flint. He loved children and always paid a lot of attention to them and of course they all loved that. His funny little jokes and ditties kept them laughing.

One of Max's quirky little songs that my daughters, Susan and Janice - both grandmothers now - still remember is, "Had a little collie pup. Dug a hole and covered him up. Now I sit here by the hour, waiting for my collie flower." Most of his other nieces and nephews probably remember this too. They also still remember, talk and laugh with affection about "the purple bathtub and pink telephone Uncle Max had in his apartment". Max's youngest step-daughter, Darlene, reminded me recently of one of his funny sayings. It goes like this, "If your feet smell and your nose runs, you're built upside down".

For several years after their retirement, Max and Marie lived on in their pretty little house on Winona Street in Flint. Marie had had congestive heart failure for some years and passed away in the hospital on January 13, 2004.

Max had some trouble with his eyes a short while before Marie's death but cataract surgery made that much better and he thought they were alright. However, shortly after Marie's death, more trouble with his eyes erupted.

Danny took Max to the eye doctor but it was some time before the problem was diagnosed. During this time Max's eyesight was so bad he went to live with Danny and his wife Stephanie. His sight continued to worsen and he was finally diagnosed with some sort of auto-immune disease that settled in his eyes. It was thought if the diagnosis could have been made earlier some medication might have helped however by this time it was too late!

Max then spent several weeks in a nursing home and his siblings went to see him as often as they could. Danny and Stephanie finally took him back to their home where he had a heart attack and passed away on October 4, 2004.

Arrangements were made for Max's funeral by Danny who had researched his World War II records and displayed his awards at his funeral at a funeral home in Flint. Max had requested to be buried in the Hickory Cemetery where his parents were laid to rest, and his family honored that wish.

Following the funeral, Max's body was driven to Sullivan, Indiana and his siblings who had attended his funeral and several nieces and nephews as well as grand nieces and nephews drove to Sullivan and spent the night in a motel there. We all attended the 10:00 a.m. burial ceremony led by Denny at the Hickory Cemetery.

Danny also had made arrangements for the interment at the cemetery near The Farm and Denny, Max's second oldest stepson, presented a brief, meaningful and heartfelt meditation and prayer. Max was laid to rest in the Wolfe Cemetery Plot at Hickory Cemetery with his brother George Edward and his Mother and Father.

After the burial, we then met for a lovely luncheon at Stoll's Restaurant in Linton hosted by Dick and Ruth Johnson. Then, we all drove out to The Farm for a last look around before leaving for our respective homes.

Chapter 17

Leaving The Nest - Bob

Bob was always a good student in school and high school was no different. In 1942 – '43 as he started his senior year in high school, he realized it was anticlimactic - a period of increasing anticipation and excitement. As the only "country boy" in a group of five of the most competitive students in his class, he realized he was doing well but was not outstanding.

Not much thought had been given to his future, for the Japanese had attacked Pearl Harbor on December 7, 1941, war had been declared by President Franklin D. Roosevelt and World War II was in full swing. Everything seemed to be concentrated on the war effort. With two brothers and one brother-in-law serving in the Army, Bob felt his future for the next few years was certain. He liked the country, so he could stay around The Farm and work in some phase of farming or go to Flint, Michigan and find work as Dale, Evah and James had done before him.

Bob's senior year was progressing well. He was liked by his teachers because he was a serious student and caused little trouble. He was liked by other serious students and was ignored by the "jocks" - and that was okay with him.

About the middle of his senior year, something happened that changed Bob's life in a positive and permanent way. The Sullivan Daily Times newspaper published a list of names of the seniors who were awarded county scholarships in the State of Indiana and he was named the Sullivan County winner. Bob had not even known of the scholarship, had not applied for it - but here it was. It seemed to him a bomb had dropped out of the sky.

The scholarship amounted to paid tuition - $30.00 per semester, $60.00 per year - to one of the four state colleges in Indiana, but it offered hope. The choices were Purdue University at West Lafayette, Indiana State College at Terre Haute, Indiana University at Bloomington or Ball State at Muncie.

It was some years later when Bob finally figured out how the scholarship came about. When he was in seventh grade at Park School, the elementary school where all his siblings had gone, the seventh and eighth grades were transferred and transported by bus to the Junior High School on the Union High School property at Dugger. Harold McCammon was the teacher at Park elementary and stayed there with grades one through six.

Mr. McCammon had total responsibility, not only to teach the classes but to take care of the building as well. That was not unusual but was the pattern in those days. Mr. McCammon lived in Dugger, so he hired Bob to do his janitor work. That meant Bob had to get up early, have breakfast at home, walk the three-fourth mile to the school, open the school, stir up the fire in winter and get it going good and be sure that the coal bucket was full of coal. When he was finished, he took the bus to school.

On the daily return trip, Bob got off the bus at the school, banked the fire, tidied up the room a bit and walked the three-fourth mile back home. In real cold weather, on the weekends he needed to go back up to the school house once or twice each day to check the fire and keep it active all weekend. For two years, Bob faithfully performed these duties, all for $0.75 a week and received many accolades from Mr. McCammon for a job well done.

By the time Bob finished junior high, Mr. McCammon had been transferred to the high school where he was Bob's math teacher. This is when Bob became certain that Mr. McCammon had made application for the scholarship for him. Much to his chagrin, Bob never mentioned it to Mr. McCammon or thanked him for it, but it has served often as a reminder of how important it is to do the most insignificant job to the best of one's ability. We never know who is watching and how it may influence our lives. An avid reader, Bob read every book or magazine he could get his hands on, as well as the weekly Grit Newspaper and had sometimes dreamed of going to college. His reading a book published by Farm Journal entitled, "How To Do Things" and reading an ad in the Grit Newspaper by International Correspondence School describing how to get a diploma in Mechanical Engineering and Drafting, had fired his dream.

Now that full tuition could be paid through the scholarship to Purdue University, the school of Bob's dreams, a college education seemed within reach. His direction was set. If all he had to do was take care of his room, board and books, he felt that would be easy - a "piece of cake".

The Sullivan Daily Times was the area newspaper read by most people in the community and at church the following Sunday, Aunt Dulsee and Aunt Tilda came to Bob to congratulate him and said "Oh Bob, we are so proud of you for winning that scholarship. What a shame you won't be able to use it." Their assumption was that college was out of the question for financial reasons, an opinion shared by most of our family and friends.

That assumption added fuel to the fire and steel to Bob's will and he was determined to make it happen. In family discussions, Mom wanted him to go but thought it would be very difficult. All his siblings were on his side, if he could pull it off. Dad thought it was a waste of time and reminded Bob that he owed him a corn crop "planted and laid by". Dad had bought an old used tractor from Dale Creager, an old friend, and thought great things could be accomplished with it. Bob wanted to discharge his obligation and since he would not be draft age of 18 until the end of December, he still had time.

The school year ended, graduation was over and Bob and Dad rushed into the corn crop. Bob said, "The old tractor with steel tires was barely better than the team of horses. When it didn't get bogged down in wet clay, it plowed more ground. We got a little extra corn planted and used the team, Maude and Tom, to cultivate it. The corn crop was laid by in mid-July, which gave Bob a month to earn money.

Purdue's first semester in 1943 began August 28 and Dale, having been a student there previously, advised Bob to go up to Purdue a week early, find a room, get a job and register before the campus rush began. That became Bob's number one goal.

When the corn crop was laid by, a cousin, Benton Deckard and Bob got an opportunity to join two neighbors, Bill Pirtle and Johnny Boone, cutting mine props. The coal company owned several acres of second growth timber and needed the props cut five feet, five and one-half feet and six feet long and at least three inches in diameter on the small end. They were to be cut and stacked in piles along the road that ran through the woods. Second growth timber is the saplings that grow up a few years after quality trees have been cut. The heat in that kind of woods in July and August in Indiana is terrific and the boys' bib overalls were soaking wet within the first hour and remained that way the rest of the day. At night, they were hung outside on the porch to shield them from rain and dew and were never quite dry by morning but they were worn anyhow. Clean ones were a delight on Sunday and Monday mornings.

At seven cents a prop, money didn't add up very fast. It took fourteen or fifteen props cut to make a dollar. However, in about four weeks Bob had earned about $45.00 to $50.00. This seemed to him to be an adequate amount for an optimistic farm boy to enter college with.

Bob's first trip to Purdue and the following years have been described by him and the following words are his own:

> "Acting on Dale's advice, I went to Purdue a week or so early, promising Mom and Dad and Ruth I would return before the semester started. Mom, as usual, trusted my judgment. Dad thought I would spend all my money and come back broke.
>
> Dad drove me to Sullivan and I took a bus to West Lafayette. Finding a bus to West Lafayette and Purdue took much questioning. I sat by the bus driver and I'm sure I added humor to his day by asking if a couple of large church buildings were Purdue University. When he dumped me off at the correct corner, I started walking up the curved sidewalk in front of Purdue Hall. Meeting a guy a little older than I, I asked him to direct me to Purdue University. By his smile, I knew I had

asked a dumb question but I didn't realize just how dumb. He rightly assumed I wanted the Administration Building.

With battered suitcase in hand, letter of Scholarship in pocket, I went into the Registrar's, Dr. Pebbles, office. He was an old hand at this, called me Mr. Wolfe and welcomed me as a student. He asked if he could help, so I quickly told him I needed a job as I was working my way through college. Dale's advice was so good, because all these offices were empty and I had no competition.

Walking down Grant Street, suitcase in hand, I came to 525, a house with a "Room For Rent" sign in the window. A knock brought the lady of the house and when I said I wanted to rent a room for a week (I didn't want a long term arrangement without more info) she tried to shoo me away. However, when she found I was to be a student in a week, she warmed considerably.

She took me upstairs to a bedroom with an upper-class roommate. He was away for the semester break. The room included a double-decker bed, a closet for my roommate and a cardboard "closet" about 4 feet long for me. Two small tables with the universal florescent desk lamp completed the accessories - all a new student could hope for! Cost, $11.00/month.

Now my quest to be sure I had the cheapest room (should have been best buy). I started walking the street knocking on doors with Room for Rent signs. That would take a day or two. I ate at the restaurant in the Student Union which meant I could see a few students, which I carefully observed.

Finally, four or five blocks farther away from campus was a room for $10.00 a month. Surprising, even to me now, that $1.00 difference loomed large. The landlady assured me I would like my roommate. The room was much as the other except for one double bed we would share. As we talked while I was leaving, she shared that the roommate was Turkish, smoked big ropey cigars in bed and had burned lots of holes in the bed clothes. I thanked her and left. Believe it or not, I still considered saving the $1.00 but couldn't quite bring myself to do it.

I now believe that was the best $1.00 I ever spent, for my roommate, Bob Bundy, a farm boy from Clifton, Indiana, was a great influence on me. He, an upper classman, practiced "the seat of the pants to the seat of the chair". I learned to do likewise.

The second day of my visit was the date of my job appointment. With no alarm clock, I was concerned about my 6:00 a.m. appointment. I put my watch around the bedpost of my upper bunk and watched it thru the night. As you might suspect, I overslept and rushed to the kitchen of North West Cary Hall about 7:00 a.m. I apologized profusely and was assured all was OK. The manager was busy in the middle of serving the Navy V-12 members who Purdue was training as Engineering Officers to serve in the Pacific Theater, WW II. I had a delicious breakfast - eggs et al and was soon interviewed for the job. They needed help and a strong eager farm boy fit in.

Most wanted an easy job of serving but I preferred to be a bus boy, running back and forth bringing full trays to the serving line and cleaning up. That also required more hours. We were paid by the hour and charged a stipend for each meal. I could net $5.00 or $6.00 per week and that was fine.

I started to work immediately and since all my immediate problems were solved, I worked several hours the next few days. I returned to the farm on schedule with $11.00 more than I left with. Dad had no comment.

After a few days at home, I packed Dale's old brown suitcase, took his laundry case and agreed to meet Uncle Cornie at the Park School corner for a ride to Sullivan to catch the Greyhound bus. Dad had chores, walked to work and needed to be there before 7:00 a.m. We quickly said early goodbyes.

Later, Mom walked with me to the hollow in the lane. She said, "Bob, you are leaving home for good. I want you to be a good boy". I said, "Oh Mom, I'll be back". She said, "Yes, but it will be as a visitor". I said, "No, Mom, it will be the same". By then, we were both teary eyed. As usual, she was far more perceptive than I, for at 17, I was "out of the nest".

August 28, 1943, was a real eye opener. Math and Science studies at Union High School were woefully inadequate. I had taken all I could, but had to take a non-credit math class that I should have had in high school and I had had Physics, no Chemistry.

Chem 101 came to dominate my life. Dr. Martin taught the lecture course with about 450 in a huge lecture hall. Seated by last names, I was way up and far away from his demonstrations. He opened by asking us to look right and left and said that after one year only one of us would be there.

I barely knew what a molecule was, knew nothing of electrons and neutrons and had never heard of Valence. By mid-term, I knew I was floundering. I took hat in hand, made an appointment and went in to see the renowned Professor. I told him my story, said I knew I was not doing well and asked if there were other things I could do to be sure of passing. (I felt I was carrying the family honor.) He said, "Let me check your record," studied it and then said, "Mr. Wolfe, Purdue does not use my course to teach chemistry, but to weed out those who will not make successful engineers. I think you will make it." Huge sigh of relief - but I *still worked hard. However, my friend from Brooklyn Polytech High School, Jack Gardner, knew more chemistry at the beginning of the course than I, at the finish.*

One other important event. In high school all boys were invited to take the test for Officer's Candidate School. I did, passed and had checked Army. I guess this was natural for a farm boy from the Midwest who had never seen an ocean and had two brothers in the Army. However, here at Purdue, watching real live trainees of both Army and Navy, it was apparent the Navy was to be preferred.

The Navy trainees wore civilian clothes and went to civilian classes just as civilian students did. We had Naval History and Naval Tactics in place of civilian optional classes, did regular morning calisthenics with Navy leaders, practiced marching, inspections, etc., on Saturday mornings, but by and large had much freedom and the college instructors treated us like civilians. The Army trainees were marched to class and had separate classes, although I understood they did get college credits for their studies.

Since I was only 17 (until the end of December), I re-took the test and chose Navy. Before the semester ended, I volunteered and was enlisted in the Navy V-12 program. After I became a Navy student (March 1944), a transfer to Illinois Institute of Technology (IIT) took me away from the school of my dreams to Chicago. There the "education" of a country boy continued - in many respects.

I, who thought all blacks (Negros in those days) lived in the deep south and picked cotton, arrived in the heart of Chicago's colored district - where the school was located. That was home while I finished a Mechanical Engineering (M. E.) degree going straight through summers and all, with only school vacation at the end of semesters as leave. It was the best possible opportunity for me to finish school while Max, Floyd and millions of others were doing front line duty to protect my rights and country. I will always be grateful!

During this time, President F. D. Roosevelt passed away and Harry Truman took office. V-E Day (Victory in Europe - May 8, 1945) came and the streets were awash with people all night shouting and celebrating. Then just as graduation and commissioning was approaching came V-J Day (Victory in Japan - August 14, 1945). We had expected to be required to storm the home island of Japan. That was expected to require all hands - new recruits, new officers and the full force of those released from the European front.

This was so much better duty than the Army units had been so accurately described by Stephen Ambrose in his book, "Citizen Soldier". He did thorough research for the book and explained the need for soldiers during the Battle of the

Bulge when Hitler made his last ditch stand in the Belgium Forest in the horrible winter (coldest winter on record) of 1944/'45. Ambrose describes this very vividly.

Ambrose thought it was a serious mistake to take raw recruits to the front lines without more careful integration. The strategists expected the experienced soldier to help recruits understand the "ways of the front-line soldier". Actually, the college boys, used to studying and discussing life wanted to stay in small groups. Experienced soldiers knew that was the way to get killed. To stay alive, they, and sometimes a buddy, stayed separate from the group in their foxholes. That is why many of our finest young men were killed during their first month in Germany.

The Lord surely had his hand on me here and looking back, it seems at so many other times. Max and many others were suffering on the Western Front in Europe and Floyd was in the Pacific Theater.

So 1945 rolled along. We could see that we who were scheduled to graduate in '46 would likely be headed for the Pacific Theater. Some of the Navy V-12 men were in from the fleet and maintained contact with friends familiar with island fighting. Not something to look forward to.

I joined Pi Kappa Phi Fraternity late in my IIT career, largely because I was friends with Wally Briesh, Jim Woodling, Cal Zhender and Don Helbling. This allowed me a little social life with friends. Wally had a girlfriend with a good friend from high school, so he and I double dated in my senior year. Both were great gals and we had a great time. Both were Catholic which didn't bother Wally, who later married La Verne for a long and happy marriage. At that time a Catholic gal was not an option for me so I never really had serious thoughts.

I regret to say that because of a failure in calculus I did not graduate on time. I took a correspondence course from the University of Wisconsin when I returned home and graduated late.

When the Germans finally capitulated, we were given a day off with no curfew. Everyone celebrated in downtown Chicago. Only foot traffic in the Loop, wall to wall people with confetti from high buildings. Much drunkenness and much activity with abandon as the pent up concerns were turned loose. Most of us were happy to limp back to quarters about 2 a.m. and turn in.

This of course increased our concern about the Pacific war for it looked as if the United States would need "all hands" to invade and capture the home islands of Japan. We really didn't know until later just how bad it would be. We later learned that Iwo Jima was the Japanese experiment on how to defend an island. This from "Flags of Our Fathers" by James Bradley, son of John (Doc) Bradley, one of the flag raisers and survivors of Iwo Jima, from United States perspective. "So

Bad to Fall in Battle," by Tadamechi Kuribayashi, the Japanese General of Iwo where every Japanese "sold" his life as dearly as possible.

All 22,000 Japanese died on the island and the United States lost 6,000 plus in six days. Since he, General Kuribayashi, (and none) of the Japanese survived, this book is a compilation of letters he sent to his wife while preparing the island for resistance for it was known that this island airport was crucial to the success of the battle for the Japanese home island.

It had been the pattern of Japanese soldiers who believed death in battle gave them automatic entrance to a glorious afterlife and being captured was a disgrace. Therefore, if they felt a battle was lost, those who remained just stormed the enemy, killing a few but becoming easy targets themselves.

General Kuribayashi was given the task of changing tactics to learn how to defend an island to the maximum. Iwo was the learning experience. He took the job knowing it was a suicide mission. Here, each Japanese was taught to "sell" his life as dearly as possible. He taught them, "So sad to fall in battle". Hence the island was full of concrete bunkers that resisted aircraft bombs and the Navy's 16-inch guns. Every enemy soldier would pop out, shoot and retreat. None left the island alive and I believe we lost upwards of 5,000 men.

One oft repeated story emphasing the value of the airstrip: While the Americans had just gotten control of the airstrip and the front was approximately 100 yards away, an American bomber was heard coming in, engines sputtering and fuselage shot up. The pilot landed and the crew got out and kissed the ground. Their only other choice was the ocean. The infantryman who was questioning the value of this battle got a new perspective.

While this was not known to the general public until these books were printed after the war, it tends to verify the estimates of the human casualty cost, both United States and enemy, to storm the home islands. While there are revisionists, of all kinds, who drum up reasons why the Japanese were weak, ready to give up, etc. there was no indication of that in their repeated refusals to surrender.

Make no mistake! Everyone I knew in uniform was delighted when the two atom bombs ended the war. V-J Day was even a bigger celebration for us than V-E Day. From a personal viewpoint both Max and I were scheduled for that action.

My class graduated in May, 1946 and shipped out into the Pacific Theater to relieve those who had earned early release. Everyone I knew was glad to do it.

In June of 1946, I traveled as a newly minted Naval Officer, Ensign, by train to San Francisco, enjoyed the beautiful cattle country along the North Platte River in Nebraska and on into Wyoming. Here the train ran along the river and the flat river bottoms, with many stacks of hay that foretold the cattle moving down from the mountains - a few already on site. Later that evening, I enjoyed dinner and a beautiful sunset across Salt Lake in Utah.

After a few days in San Francisco, I was assigned to the Mars, (a plane for carrying troops), the last amphibian plane in the Navy, then a C-54 (a troop transport plane) to Guam out of Hickum Field in Hawaii. A little drama gave me a personal understanding of the value of some of the small, seemingly useless islands.

We had just passed the point of no return (closer to Guam than to Hawaii) when one of our two engines failed and we started losing altitude. The flight crew scurried around, gathered all of our luggage and announced that the pilot was heading for Johnston Island and if we continued to lose altitude all luggage would be cast off. Essentially, everything I owned at the time was in a duffle bag and a Valpak (canvas suitcase) piled against the plane door. The pilot stabilized the plane with one engine and we had a three-day stay at Johnston Island. The island looked like concrete from the air but was a corral atoll with only two Quonset Huts and a runway of corral, one and one-half miles long, approximately. Under one of the huts was an excavated living quarters for kitchen, dining and sleeping. With plenty of time, I walked every inch of the island and the only living plant I saw was one castor bean (mole bean) in the shade of a Quonset Hut. Then I went on to Guam for my assigned ship, a Patrol Craft Escort PCE 897.

Little to do but I needed more fresh food than Navy mess provided. So with our jeep and a fire axe, I went into the jungle and got coconuts, bananas and breadfruit. I knew about coconuts, kept a stalk of bananas hanging in my state room but could never bring myself to taste the breadfruit. I knew my tropical fruits from "Mutiny on the Bounty" and other Nordolf and Hall stories. Everyone told me I would get attacked by a tarantula or one of the Japanese still living in the jungle, but I didn't.

This PCE897 was moored "Port side to Dock Peter" and was not moved during my watch. Later that year with the Navy winding down, I was no longer needed. Thousands of us returned on the Oglethorpe, a refrigerator ship converted to a troop carrier to bring servicemen home. As officers in transit, we lived four to a stateroom. I took my turn on watch in the lower decks, where the enlisted men were on hammocks five deep and narrow aisles. I was very thankful. We towed a barge to Kuaduleen for reasons not obvious, which made for slow going.

Even as very young adults, our family always tried to visit every family member possible. As an officer, I could choose where I mustered out, so I chose

Mare Island, a Navy base in Valero, California, close to Jim and Pat in Santa Barbara. I took a plane to Paso Robles, California, (nearest airport) and was met by Jim and spent ten days or so with Jim and Pat living with Mrs. Demaree (Pat's mother) in Santa Barbara.

I knew I would get home to The Farm during hunting season. I wanted a gun of my own but because of the war no new shotguns were available. Jim found a slightly used Winchester, Model 12, for $75.00 and I was delighted. That was my gun throughout my hunting life. It suited me perfectly. I gave that to Ken when we moved from our Ellington, Connecticut, home to Covenant Village in Cromwell, Connecticut.

I flew from Paso Robles to Flint, Michigan, to visit Dale and Jeanette and Evah. I spent some days there to renew bonds, then flew to Terre Haute and took a bus to Sullivan. Dad met me for this trip to The Farm. Nita and Floyd were in Terre Haute and Ruth in Indianapolis - close enough to visit.

I stayed on the farm like a Royal Guest until after Christmas. My mornings were spent studying the correspondence course I needed to finish my degree. Each morning Mom would bring me a popper of popcorn while I studied. When finished, I would mail the completed lesson and then would help in the kitchen or on The Farm outside.

This was one of the highlight periods of my life."

When Bob was mustered out of the Navy, the war had already ended in 1945 and the boys (men) who had served in the military - at home and abroad - were already back home and settled in. Since his tour of duty didn't begin until after the war was over, by the time he got home in 1947, life in the peace-time world was pretty much back to normal.

Bob particularly enjoyed the freedom of not having a job or any special duties while he worked on the correspondence course he needed to complete his engineering degree. Now he would be graduated properly and have a Mechanical Engineering diploma in his hands. However, he felt very much at loose ends, even restless, after all the lessons were completed and mailed.

Juanita and Floyd were back in their little home on North 6th Street in Terre Haute and offered him a place to stay while he looked for a job. Bob's first job offer came from Winslow Scales Company and although he knew this was not his desired field, it would provide experience as well as some ready cash. So he compromised and took the job, feeling certain something better would come along.

The job at Winslow was designing scales for trucks, but was not the engineering job Bob was looking for. He had put an application in at Visking Corporation and in about six weeks or so he got a call from them. That was a real engineering job and Bob accepted it. The job paid $55.00 a week to start and that was a good starting salary for the times.

Bob had been going with Juanita (me) to Fourth Avenue Methodist Church just around the corner from the Tryon home and he had taken much notice of a beautiful young woman named Virginia (Ginnie) Whitesell who led the choir there. With Bob's new job, everything seemed to be falling into place and he felt confident enough to ask her out. Ginnie lived with her parents in the 1400 block of North 4th Street, just a couple of blocks from our home on North 6th Street.

When Bob and Ginnie began dating, they found they had much in common. They were both devout Christians, both were hard workers, both loved children and music and liked the same sort of entertainment. Ginnie had just graduated a couple of years earlier from Indiana State College as a music major and was teaching at a small school in Newman, Illinois. The one-room building housed grades one through twelve and Ginnie taught music to the elementary students and chorus and band to the high schoolers. There was no middle school at that time.

Bob and Ginnie dated for several months and then decided to make their relationship permanent. They were married in a beautiful ceremony on July 17, 1949, at Fourth Avenue Methodist Church. A lovely reception in the church's downstairs Fellowship Room followed the ceremony. The ceremony and reception were attended by all of Bob's siblings and their families, except Jim and Pat who lived in California, by Mom and Dad, Mr. and Mrs. Whitesell, several relatives and many friends of the couple. Aunt Dulsee and Doris were the only members of the extended Wolfe/Deckard family to attend.

When the newlyweds returned from a honeymoon at Grand Lake, Michigan, Bob and Ginnie moved into an apartment on North 9th Street in Terre Haute. But by the following spring they had found a place more to their liking in North Terre Haute. Since it was an upstairs apartment, they had no grass to cut and the large garden spot behind the house was assigned to them since the couple who lived downstairs didn't want it. That was all Bob needed to keep him busy and happy. He enjoyed being able to till the soil again.

During the first year of their marriage, Ginnie continued to teach, but moved to a small school in Fontanet, Indiana, a small town about eight miles from their home. Again, the small school housed grades one through twelve and again, Ginnie taught music to the elementary students and chorus and band to the students in the high school grades. She soon quit teaching and kept busy canning vegetables from Bob's big garden, sewing, cleaning and becoming a good homemaker.

Although she was the only child in her family, Ginnie adapted to life in the big, boisterous Wolfe family like a duck to water. She learned her way around her kitchen in record time and became an excellent cook. She sewed curtains for the apartment, weeded in their garden and enjoyed canning and storing the extra produce. She carried her own weight in all aspects of life when they visited The Farm and I am sure that wasn't always easy. Being raised in the city, I doubt that she ever became comfortable with the outdoor toilet, although she never complained about it. She seemed to love all of us as much as we all loved her.

Bob's job at Visking continued to be exciting and challenging for him. His technical assignments gradually shifted to management and supervision. The plastic film industry was in its infancy then and Bob was at the forefront and a major influence in its fast growth. He developed and got patents on many innovative pieces of equipment he designed that furthered the growth of the industry. He was the recipient of many promotions over the years. More often than not, a promotion was accompanied by a move to a different part of the country,

Starting his career at Visking Corporation (later to become Union Carbide Corporation) in Terre Haute in 1947, Bob stayed there for seven years. His first move was in 1954 to Ringoes, New Jersey, where he was in complete charge of building a new plastics plant from the ground up at Flemington, New Jersey. This was the day when one man was sent to supervise all aspects of the building from the mechanical and electrical contractors to the foundations that were being dug in a wheat field when Bob and his wife, Ginnie, arrived in New Jersey. Seven months later, the building was complete and Bob had ten polyethylene plastic film machines up and running.

Here in Ringoes, Bob and Ginnie bought their first house, started their family, established themselves in a Baptist Church of their own choosing, and became fully functioning members of a community apart from family and friends. Their first daughter Linda Kay, was born February 20, 1955, and Karen Jean followed on December 28, 1957. Bob and Ginnie had thought of their home in New Jersey as a permanent location, but Union Carbide had other ideas. In 1960 they found themselves back in Terre Haute where their last child, a boy they named Kenneth Dale, was born July 15, 1961.

Union Carbide still had lots of moves in store for Bob. Most of the moves were to build new plants or to work out problems of various kinds in existing plants. From Terre Haute, Bob was sent to Cartersville, Georgia, 1961 - 1964. Then, to Ottawa, Illinois, 1964 – 1970; Downers Grove, Illinois, with the office of Visking Division of Union Carbide in Chicago, Illinois, 1970 – 1971; Bay Village, Ohio, with office in Rocky River, Ohio, 1971 – 1974; Mountain Lakes, New Jersey, office in Wayne, New Jersey, 1974 – 1981; Ellington, Connecticut, office in East Hartford, Connecticut, 1981 – 1986.

Bob retired from Union Carbide in 1986. He and Ginnie stayed on at the home they bought when they moved to Ellington. They had enough acreage for Bob's large garden, some berry vines and fruit trees and Ginnie "decorated" their large yard with "oceans" of perennial flowers and fresh annuals every summer. They are close to both Linda and Ken and their four grandchildren, two for each child. Karen has since married, lives in Hawaii and has brought them two "ready-made" grandchildren.

When asked about his retirement, Bob said:

"*Early retirement at 62 was generated by the sale of our Division resulting from a disastrous accident at Union Carbide in Bhopal, India.*

I enjoyed many friends in the plastic industry but was not ready for fishing full time.

I started a consulting business which soon morphed into a sales agency for plastic recycling machinery. Soon Ken and his wife, Barb, were added to the business and we sold throughout the United States and Canada with a network of agents. Our major principal went bankrupt in the slump following the bombing in New York on September 11, 2001. We closed shortly after that.

I found working with Ken and a small compatible group, in our own business was a high point in an interesting and exciting career.

In September 2013 we sold the house and garden we had grown to love but found difficult to care for. We moved to Covenant Village of Cromwell in Cromwell, Connecticut, and we made the best decision possible for this time in our lives. It allows us to continue enjoying each other, our family and has the freedom and services we both enjoy."

They are still a short drive (about forty minutes) from both Linda and Del and Ken and Barbara. Karen is still in Hawaii.

Chapter 18

Leaving The Nest - Ruth

My story will be one written by my sister and brother, as it was written by the two of them, Bob and Nita, as a gift for my 80th birthday. What a fun gift it was too.

Juanita called and interviewed me, not saying the real reason she was asking all those questions. And, of course, I the "innocent baby sister" didn't have a clue as to what was actually happening. I think, in truth, I must have been just delighted to talk about myself!! Then she talked to Bob also and together they compiled the narrative. *(Nita's Note: I must jump in right here and say - it was Bob's idea entirely. I am never the idea person but the moment he mentioned it I knew it would please Ruth more than any piece of jewelry or "girl thing" I could have thought of.)*

It was so much fun to read it all put into one story and immediately, I could see how the entire family story could be a compelling read. I hope you who are our descendants find it to be interesting, more for the historical value of "the way things were" and the values espoused that we all have held so dear, than for the personal happenings although that is an immense part of it.

When it was time for me to "leave the nest" the pattern had been pretty well established as all the others had gone before and I had been there for most of them. The first one I remember vividly was when Jim left. I vividly remember Mother and me walking down the little road from our farm home toward the corner. Jim must have been catching a ride with someone into town. I do remember that we thought he would be going away "just for a year" as that is what he had been told as he was part of the first draft in World War II. I remembered Mother's tears as we hugged him and kissed goodbye. It was the same for all of us, as I remember it. She did the same thing several years later when I left for Terre Haute.

I was leaving to go to Indiana State Teachers College and would be living with Juanita and Floyd but Mother, as some of you will remember, always seemed to have a real true sense of what the situation really was. She knew this was a break, a separation point of no return. My memory says that this was what was expected as I had heard many times that "no house was meant for two families" and I understood that when I finished my education, it was expected that I would find a job and become a productive adult. No other option seemed appropriate.

I had been given a state scholarship for one year at Indiana State, which covered tuition only, so I would be living "free" with my sister and enough money would be available for text books and trips back to the farm. There was never extra money but I had all I really needed and I didn't think about working for extra. I was not as dedicated to education as to finding meaningful employment and at that time it was not imperative to have a college degree for work.

The fact that it was not considered necessary to have a degree to get a good job was probably one of the reasons it was easy for me not to return the next year. I had a pretty good job which I loved, when it was time to return to school the next fall. I had a secure job and was living in my own apartment in a large city. What an exciting life for a farm girl. Mother had given us the courage of "her" convictions that we could do "anything" we put our minds to. What a blessed gift for a parent to give a child – confidence! I believe we all felt that we could learn any job that any other person could learn and we were all willing to work hard and apply much effort to succeed.

I have also been very grateful to several of my teachers throughout my school years for the confidence they showed me in my ability to do what was expected of me. Do not hesitate to pass that on to any young person who crosses your path when they show ability and desire to succeed. It is a priceless gift and costs no dollars. Be a person who encourages others. There are folks… adults included…who often just need a bit of encouragement from another human being. We all have the opportunity to give this gift to others…probably every day. I am thankful to many of you, older and younger, who have given me that gift.

This is a bit about my leaving the nest but Nita and Bob's story which follows takes us all the way back to my beginning:

> *"In the winter of 1932-1933, an event of great importance happened in the Ora and Ann Wolfe family. This event brought exquisite joy to the two young girls, namely, Evah, 16 years of age and Juanita, 12, as well as to the four boys, Dale – 21; James – 14; Max – 9 and Robert who had just turned 7 on December 30, 1932.*
>
> *On January 23, 1933, the birth of a new baby girl into this family of six rowdy children, all approximately two to two and one half years apart in age, seemed remarkable. In those days, the word pregnant was rarely spoken in mixed company, and never to children. Pregnancy was usually referred to discreetly as "being in the family way". Mothers- to- be were very modest and unassuming but babies were held in high esteem and treated as precious commodities.*
>
> *I don't remember Mom being "in the family way" ever being talked about in our home or with aunts or cousins. I can imagine though that Evah and Doris*

might have discussed it some for I expect it might have been talked about at Aunt Dulsee's because Doris and Freda were both older. I do remember once when we came home from church and Mom was changing her clothes that I thought her stomach looked big when she raised her arms over her head to take her dress off.

Then on Christmas Eve, before Ruth was born in January, I woke up in the night and realized Evah was not in bed with me. As I lay there wondering about that, I heard quiet voices and got up and peeked into the living room, and there were Mom and Evah whispering and putting gifts under the Christmas tree. I am almost embarrassed to say that at twelve years old this was the first time I was ever really SURE who Santa Claus was. Evah, at 16, would have realized some facts about expecting a new baby and was probably delighted to be able to help Mom in this way.

The girls, who were old enough to be called on to help in various ways, looked on this as a special gift – much like a new baby doll – but far better because it lived and breathed, cried occasionally and demanded much attention both day and night. However, in the absence of a baby bed, this little one slept in the bed with Mom and Dad and help from the girls was never needed during the night time hours.

All three young boys who were still at home seemed to be as delighted as the girls were and Dale who was away at Purdue University in West Lafayette, Indiana, was anxious to come home to see this new arrival. It was plain to see, she was definitely the "apple" of everyone's eyes.

When it came to naming this remarkable baby, I distinctly remember Granny Brewer-Mosier, a near neighbor who lived in the house at the corner where the lane leading to the house met the county road, announcing to Miss Ann – as she ALWAYS respectfully called our mother – that she had the perfect name for our precious baby girl – Bonetta Aretta.

Personally, I thought I had the perfect name for this wonder child. At the time she was born, I was reading the book "The Five Little Peppers and How They Grew". The youngest girl in the Pepper family was called Phronsie, short for Serfronia, and I wanted my little sister to be exactly like her.

Although none of us seriously considered Granny's name suggestion, I was passionate about Phronsie. Mom never discouraged me but she had ideas of her own. In 1933, Franklin D. Roosevelt was president of our country and Mom had a high regard for his wife, Eleanor, whom we had heard speak on the radio and read about in the newspapers. I suspect the name Ruth came from the Bible and Mom added Eleanor to that and we all liked and accepted Ruth Eleanor as a suitable name for this special baby.

When Ruthie began to talk, we would ask her what her name was and her answer would be Fifi Annanor. We all loved to hear her say that, so we would ask her often. I still sometimes call her Fifi in jest.

If Mom and Dad were anything but happy by this turn of events, they never showed it by word or deed. In retrospect, however, knowing what I know today, I wouldn't be surprised if they were quite stressed out when the news became apparent. At 42 years of age Mom was nearly past the child bearing stage and due to the financial crash of 1929, times were hard. But as true and faithful parents, they carried on, and led by them, we all knew that one more member in the family would never be a burden.

Dad had worked for many years at Shirley Hill Mine, just across Uncle George and Aunt Dulsee's field to the north. With the faltering, failing economy, Dad was laid off at the mine and with nothing but what the farm could produce as sustenance, all hands were pressed into service. The girls, with the baby in tow, worked in the garden and house with Mom, cleaning, cooking and canning. The boys trapped rabbits, hunted and fished and worked in the fields with Dad.

The summer Ruth was three or four years old, Mom and Dad decided to have a family portrait taken by a professional photographer in Dugger. I can't recall the date the picture was taken but I do remember the weather was really hot. I believe it was toward the end of summer. We surely had an appointment for I remember the pressure of getting everyone ready on time. Because I liked to fix Ruth's hair, I had washed it and waved it with a comb.

With all the hubbub Ruthie didn't have time for her nap and fell asleep in the car on the way to Dugger. When we reached the photographer's studio and Ruth had to be awakened, she was hot and sweaty and her new dress was scratchy. She had such a sweet little face and I remember Mom and the photographer trying to get her to smile. But she would have none of it. Hence, she was captured for posterity with a small frown on her forehead and a slight pout on her lips. (Still, cute as a button!)

I remember distinctly the clothes worn on this day, for this auspicious occasion, by the women folk. Mom wore a pretty, pink seersucker with scallops down the front. Evah's lovely dress was of navy voile with white polka dots, wide, white organdy collar and very large short balloon sleeves of white organdy with navy trim. Being of organdy, the sleeves held their shape beautifully and we all thought they were very special. My turquoise dotted Swiss had little capped sleeves and my *memory tells me it cost $2.98. Ruthie's scratchy little dress was white organdy with a wide collar and navy trim on the collar and above the hemline. If I remember correctly it cost $0.98.*

The two older boys, Dale and James, wore their three piece suits with vests that buttoned down the front, white shirts and long ties held down by the vests but pulled forward between the knot and the vest to give a puffed look. The tying of the ties and getting that puff just right were tasks to be reckoned with. The young boys, Max and Robert, and Dad all were just in shirt sleeves, white shirts of course, since no other color was considered a dress shirt in those days. I suspect the boys' ties and possibly Dads were the ready-tied ties with a little hook to keep them in place or an elastic band under the collar.

During Ruth's very young years, when she was about three years old, a stray tom cat came to the farm and naturally, she immediately fell in love with this small soft furry animal. Mom had a particular dislike of cats for when she was a young mother with two children, her mother (our Grandmother Deckard) died from blood poisoning caused by a cat scratch. However, she finally relented and said Ruthie could keep this cat as a pet. She promptly named him Tom Berry.

As there were no small children in the neighborhood, Tom Berry soon became a member of the family and permitted Ruth to treat him as such. He was a sweet, mild mannered cat and Ruth would dress him in her doll's clothes, rock him to sleep and put him to bed and he never so much as fussed at her. He was her constant companion and she enjoyed him as a playmate for several years. They were fast friends as long as Tom Berry lived.

Bob's note: Many years later, when Tom Berry developed mange we could not cure, Mom asked me to dispose of him, country style. With gun and shovel he was interred in the field west of the house. (For Ruth, he just "didn't come home".)

Speaking of Tom Berry's and Ruth's firm, loving relationship, Ruthie had a soft spot for all animals. When she was about four years old, Dad, who was a big tease, was playing with a new puppy on the dining room floor. He would put his foot on the pup's ear and make him cry and then release. Ruth, who was watching this from the next room, promptly ran into the kitchen, got the broom, stomped back into the dining room and hit Dad over the head with the broom. She has told me how shocked and scared she was after she did it. She thought she would surely be spanked or reprimanded in some way. Dad, however, seemed to be as shocked and surprised as Ruth was by this reflex action. The teasing stopped and no punishment was forthcoming.

In the fall of 1938, after I had graduated from high school that spring, I started to work in Terre Haute in the home of a doctor and his wife who had two small girls about Ruth's age. Of course I told them many stories of my little sister and they wanted to meet her. Arrangements were made in the summer of 1940 when Ruth was seven years old. I brought her – by bus – back to Terre Haute with me to spend the week and took her home again by bus the following weekend. Dad ferried us back and forth to the bus station in Sullivan as he did me on my frequent trips home.

Even at seven, Ruth enjoyed some of the comforts of this large city home that we did not have on the farm. Warm running water in a large built in porcelain bathtub replaced the round No 3 wash tub that had to be brought into the house and filled by carrying warm water from the kitchen stove reservoir in a bucket. The indoor toilet in the bathroom that flushed everything down the drain was a far cry from the old wooden outhouse in the chicken lot at the farm. Still, I am sure Ruth was happy to get back to her familiar surroundings and to Mom and Dad on the farm. As Dorothy says in the Wizard of Oz, "there's no place like home, there's no place like home, there's no place like home". I know that feeling. I felt it many times over the years when I worked away from home.

In 1939 I had begun to date Floyd Tryon, a native of Terre Haute, and he would often drive me down home when I had a weekend off. He and Ruth became the best of friends and he, as well as her brothers and sisters, thought she deserved special treatment. Ruth had a "sweet tooth" and used to stash little bags of candy in a special hiding place. So for her ninth birthday, Floyd bought her a full box of 24 candy bars. She was ecstatic. Who at that age could even IMAGINE owning a whole box of candy bars all for yourself!!

Ruth started to school in the fall of 1939 at Park Elementary School, the neighborhood school, where the formal education of all her siblings had begun. Most of the older children spent grades one through eight at this same school. Although we all walked the three quarters of a mile every day, rain or shine, sleet or snow, Ruth was bussed to school daily. She didn't even have to walk to the corner. The bus came down the road, passed by our house and went on down the road to turn around in Johnnie and Ellen Boone's barn lot. At this time the Sanderson family lived in the house on the hill at the end of the road where previously Charlie Boone and Bill Pirtle had lived. The Sanderson twins walked down and boarded the school bus. Therefore, Ruth had time to get her coat and hat, books, etc. before it returned and picked her up in front of the house.

As the years wore on, the school grew older and somewhat in disrepair and the population of the neighborhood had declined. There was much talk of closing the school and after her fourth grade the school was disbanded. Ruth was then bussed to Central School in Dugger and spent the next four years there preparing to enter Union High School, the school she and each of her siblings graduated from.

Ruth remembers her fourth grade teacher, Mr. Whitlock, a sweet, kind older gentlemen, suggesting to Mom that since Ruth liked to sing and was musically inclined, piano lessons would be a good activity for her. After much discussion concerning the strength of the floor in the living room, Dad was able to find a used upright piano and Ruth started taking piano lessons from Dorothy Dugger, the high school music teacher. Although none of the rest of the Wolfe children played a musical instrument in school, Jim later taught himself to play guitar on a $2.00 guitar mail ordered from Sears Roebuck. Most of the siblings did participate in Glee Club and other classes taught by Miss Dugger at Union High.

During high school, Ruth was a good student and participated in several extracurricular activities. She learned to play the trombone and played and marched in the high school band. She had some trombone lessons but for the most part, practiced at home and taught herself. Since she had learned to read music while taking piano lessons at an earlier age that proved to be helpful during her years in the band.

Getting back and forth to band practice or play practice or other nighttime activities at school was not always easy since parents in those days didn't serve as a taxi service. Many times Ruth would have to stay overnight with a friend when there were evening activities.

Evah always made every effort to come to The Farm, from Flint, at any break. In the summer of 1944 she was home and talked Mom and Dad into allowing Ruth to go home to Michigan with her, on the train, for a week. That meant the C&EI Railway from Sullivan to Dearborn Station in Chicago, a layover, then on to Michigan.

As always, family met when at all possible. During layover, Evah and Ruth decided to take a bus, straight up Michigan Avenue to visit Bob in Navy training at Illinois Institute of Technology. He was living in Navy Quarters No. 2 on 33rd Street. This area was solid black long before much effort was made for Civil Rights.

A policeman noticed the two of them alone, stopped them and told them that this was not a suitable area for them to be walking in. They had dismounted the bus at 32nd Street so they only had one block to walk which was mostly populated by Navy trainees so he allowed them to continue. They enjoyed a brief visit, then took the bus back down Michigan Avenue to the station for the Grand Trunk Western to Flint.

One week later Ruth made the return trip, alone, but wisely did not visit Bob. Evah charged the Conductor with the responsibility of helping Ruth change trains at Dearborn Station. She arrived on schedule in Sullivan much to her relief and that of Dad and Mom no doubt. Wonder why she likes to travel???

Ruth graduated from high school in 1950 and spent that summer at home with Mom and Dad. She wanted to go to college and Indiana State Teachers College in Terre Haute seemed to be a good option. Since she had won a partial state scholarship, it was decided that she would attend Indiana State and live with us, Floyd and Nita. That worked well since the bus route was only a block from our house and almost a straight shot to the college downtown. We were happy to have her in our home but I expect the presence of two small girls somewhere around the ages of two and four were quite a distraction when it came to study time. The girls loved Aunt Ruthie and wanted to be with her whenever she was with us.

When the college year ended, Ruth went home to The Farm for the summer. While she was looking for a summer job, she ran into two of her friends from high school who worked for Dun and Bradstreet in Indianapolis. They were home for the weekend and in the course of the conversation they wanted to know what she was doing. Ruth said, "Well, I'm looking for a job right now". They said if she would come back with them they could get her a job where they worked.

So Ruth packed up her clothes and went back to Indy with her friends. Of course, she had no other place to stay so they said she could stay with them. She went into Dun and Bradstreet with them on Monday morning, was hired and put to work immediately. Pretty gutsy for a young girl of 19 whom was practically straight off the farm. Ruth had no idea at the time that this summer job would be the end of her college career. But she liked the work at Dun and Bradstreet, it was steady work, the pay was good so she just stayed there.

After living two weeks with these girls, Ruth knew she didn't like their lifestyle. She had been paid a week's salary so she struck out to look for a place of her own. She found a small one-room efficiency apartment in a home which had been divided into four living spaces and rented it. Her one room had a couch that she made into a bed at night, a hot plate, a small refrigerator and a table and two chairs. It wasn't fancy but she could afford it.

At least she was alone and could live her own lifestyle without interference. Many may think it remarkable that a young girl would recognize that living with a different lifestyle would influence who she was. It would have been so easy and less expensive to live with two roommates. However, her values had been established during her years on The Farm by being reared by a Godly mother and by regular attendance at the little one room Hickory Methodist Church in the neighborhood. These values were very important to Ruth and this determination has stayed with her for life.

Naturally, for Ruth it wasn't hard to make friends in this apartment house where two other women lived. One of the women was married but her husband was in service. She and Ruth became good friends and she was Ruth's matron of honor when she married. The other tenant was Vi Bruner and she and Ruth became lifelong friends. Vi was a forty five year old and became a substitute "mother" to Ruth when one was needed.

After Ruth had been at Dun and Bradstreet about a year, Vi, who worked in the office of Shell Oil Company, told Ruth there was an opening in the office and urged her to apply for it because it paid more money than Ruth was making and had more opportunity for advancement.

She was hired and worked for Shell Oil for several years. Here she gained wide experience. One of her jobs was to edit the company newsletter titled "The Hoosier Colonel" – so named because it covered Shell personnel of Indiana and Kentucky. Her main job was performing secretarial duties for two of the managers at Shell. In this job she often was relied upon to write personal letters such as "thank yous" to those who planned parties for them and know what to say even though she was not a participant in the event. A "bit of a challenge", she said.

Ruth had been at Shell Oil for some time when one of the men she worked with called her and said he had a nice young man he wanted her to meet. He told Ruth this young man was a jobber for Shell Oil and had a Thunderbird. She told me she thought – Yeah, a guy with a business of his own and a Thunderbird – probably some old guy with a bald head wanting to make an impression with his Thunderbird! She said she was getting ready to go to a sorority convention and she told him she didn't have much time but would meet them at the Sheffield Inn for a drink.

This young man with the business of his own and a (used) Thunderbird turned out to be Dick Johnson and the rest is history. In six months they were married.

Before Ruth and Dick were married, they came to Terre Haute for dinner and a visit with us during the summer of 1958. Susan, 11, and Janice, 9, immediately fell in love with the Thunderbird and wanted to go for a ride. I remember Dick and Floyd lifting the one piece top off the car and laying it on the grass in the front yard. Dick took the girls for a spin and they were thrilled. In fact, Janice was so *impressed she embarrassed us all by asking Dick if he was going to marry Aunt Ruthie. Floyd and Dick lifted the top back on the body of the Thunderbird, fastened it down and Ruth and Dick were soon on their way.*

January 18, 1959, Ruth and Dick were married at Robert's Park United Methodist Church in Indianapolis with Mom and Dad and all siblings and their families in attendance. The one exception was Jim, who lived in California. It was a beautiful wedding followed by a reception in Fellowship Hall at the church. Our family all stayed in the same hotel in Indianapolis and true to form everyone enjoyed this special occasion. Aunt Dulsee (Mom's sister) and Doris (Aunt Dulsee's daughter who was Evah's age) also attended the wedding and the reception. They stayed overnight at the home of Harold Deckard, (Uncle Lon's son and a cousin of Ruth and her siblings as well as of Doris) who lived in Indianapolis.

Nieces and nephews of Ruth, ranging in age from nearly two to twelve, took advantage of the situation and the long, sleek floor in the reception hall and had to be corralled and corrected a few times. Dale and Jeanette's three, Doug, Sara and Donnie; Evah and Bill's Greg and Brian; Bob and Ginnie's, Linda (Karen was not yet two) and our Susan, Janice and Mike all loved to be together as much as the adults did.

After I had helped Susan, Janice and Mike get dressed for the wedding, I finished dressing myself and then I missed Mike. I started looking for him and found him in the hotel lobby sitting in one of the lounge chairs with his legs crossed and a cigarette butt from one of the ash trays between his fingers. He was three and one half years old and was mimicking Grandpa Wolfe! During the ceremony he embarrassed us by picking up the hearing aid from the back of the pew in front of us and speaking into it – "ten-four" he said – an expression from a television show with actor Broderick Crawford as the police chief."

Back to Ruth: Our wedding was a bit exciting for both Dick and me, as Dick had fallen asleep at the wheel and had an accident the night before the wedding. Fortunately, he was not badly injured – just a big cut on his chin – so the wedding went off much as planned except for a large bandage on Dick's chin. The honeymoon to Florida did not occur as planned and the night following the wedding we went to the Johnson family home in Fort Wayne as Dick's father left for Chicago following the wedding where he was due for a meeting on Monday.

After a couple of days, we went home to Columbus to the small apartment we had made ready to begin our life together. I don't suppose either of us realized that this was much the same pattern we would follow for many years to come. We made plans and needed to change them for "business reasons". When you are a business owner and responsible for it, your plans are often pushed into the background for events that occur or the plans of other people. The owners do not begin to reap the benefits of all the hard work and sacrifice until the business is well established. I was ready to pitch in and do whatever needed done alongside Dick and enjoyed that our entire life and I hope he did too. It is nice to be able to trust the other person you are counting on and I never forgot who was in charge in the office.

As the marriage progressed and Rick and Jenny came along, I had plenty to manage at home. Rick was born on October 26, 1959, and Jenny came along just 19 months later on July 14, 1961. There was plenty to do at home, so I was fortunate to be able to stay home with our children for many years. I did help with any office needs when I could and always typed all the contracts and major projects when needed.

As the children became old enough, they even helped by stuffing statements into envelopes, affixing stamps and getting the bills ready to mail. When Daddy had to go door to door to collect bills, we rode along and waited in the car. Sometimes we even got to have an ice cream cone on the way home. A treat to assure that we knew it wasn't all work but a little fun too. Dick continued that procedure even as the children were older. If we needed to go on a trip that was not "for fun", such as a family funeral or event that children might hate doing, he would plan a little side trip if only for a couple of hours to do something fun along the way. I enjoyed it too, and I'm sure he did as well.

We did all sorts of things to keep the family close as the children went away to college and established their own homes. Both Dick and I were very close to our families and wanted to keep the extended family close too. I remember when we established the Wolfe Family Reunion that Dick asked me if this was what we would be doing on Labor Day weekend for the rest of our lives. And, of course, it has been so for the past 50 years. I was equally ready to visit his relatives in Tennessee each summer and we did that as well, especially when his father retired there.

For our own children and grandchildren, we have continued a family Sunday dinner policy for all these years and as I have grown older it has been such a source of comfort and support. I especially felt the joy of the close family when Dick was diagnosed with cancer in 2008.

I suppose that should not have been a shock, as his mother, father and only brother had already succumbed to the disease, but somehow we want to ignore those things until we MUST face them. At least, with all of us working together we were able to grant Dick's wish to stay at home and give him the best quality of life that was possible until his death on July 30, 2009. We did have outside help who came to the house to assist but it was family that made it bearable for me.

We lived in three homes during our married life. From our three room apartment where we began marriage, we moved into a National Home on Lucas Way in Columbus, where both children were born. When Jenny was not yet one year old, we moved to a small house on Harrison Lake. A few years later we were able to move to a home also on Harrison Lake that was a bit larger and better constructed and although we have done many remodels to it, I am happy to say I still live in it today (at 83 years old).

How blessed I am to have both children living nearby and my grandchildren Annie, a junior at Indiana University and Ricky, a junior at Columbus East High School near as well. God has been very good to me and I am filled with gratitude. I decided that facing each day with an "attitude of gratitude" would be my New Year's resolution for 2016.

Section V

THE MATURE YEARS

Chapter 19

Remodeling The Farm Home

I am looking at the Mature Years as the years after World War II when the boys were all home from their "stretch in the service" and we were all getting on with our adult lives. Some of these years are after Mom and Dad (Ora and Ann) are gone and our children (at least some of them) were born and growing up.

Our children nor their lives are the focus of this section but there were several events and activities that took place that I feel are worthy to be mentioned and written about before I close the book.

Although our family has never been close in proximity we have held close family ties and bonds always and visited and gotten together every chance we could get. Even with just one other family – or as many as could get together – but the best of all times were when we could get together at The Farm. It was not because The Farm was a lovely home with neatly maintained grounds, cool in the summer and warm in the winter. It was none of those things. It was an old run down house with cast off furniture, that some family member had taken there because it was no longer useful to them and we needed beds, tables, chairs and the bare necessities in furnishings there.

To me, it was the most peaceful, quiet place in the whole world and it was "home" to all of us. I feel like I can truthfully say my siblings all felt as I did about The Farm. I'm sure it wasn't all those things to the in-laws but they all adjusted to it when necessary and I never heard any one of them complain. I really believe my husband, Floyd, loved it as much as I did.

We were a family that had grown up going to family reunions. As long as I can remember from elementary through my high school years, and even after I was married, we went every summer to a Deckard and a Robertson (both sides of Mom's family) family reunion. The Deckard reunion was always held at the city park in Linton, a little town about ten miles east of The Farm and the Robertson reunion was always at the Sullivan City Park at Sullivan, a small town about ten miles west of The Farm. They were always on the same Sunday every year, one on the second and one on the third Sunday, so you planned from one year to the next. Many of the people, probably most of them, we only saw at the reunions, but they were cousins, first, second or maybe even third cousins but Mom and Dad went, so, since we were close enough, we felt it was important for us to go.

The first major get together at The Farm of our immediate family after we were all married, except for Ruth and Max, was in 1954. It centered on a visit from James and Pat on the week of July 4th. Neither Max nor Ruth were married yet and each of the other siblings except Bob and Ginnie had small children. Ruth was married in 1959 and Max held onto his bachelorhood until 1967 when he married Marie Reno who had six children from a previous marriage. Marie's children were all grown and away from home except the two youngest ones, Darlene and Danny, when she and Max married.

By 1954, Evah and I were beginning to think about Mom and Dad's 50th Wedding Anniversary which was coming up in 1960 and to talk about plans for a 50th Anniversary Celebration. Mom also was looking forward to the celebration and she had started a savings "kitty" for a remodeling job she had had in mind for some time. About 1959 she called a construction company in Sullivan and they sent a man out to give an estimate. She made plans with him and settled on a price. When she knew she had enough money to complete the project, she called and got the job started so it would be finished well before September of 1960.

Extensive remodeling took several weeks before the redecorating began. The old front porch on the north side of the living room was torn off and the door that led out to it was removed and sealed up. The door between the living room and the girls' bedroom, which was one of the three original large rooms was closed and sealed up too.

The major construction in the living room included tearing out the south wall and adding eight feet of floor and walls to the south. A new concrete walk out to the driveway and a concrete step were poured to enhance the new south door and entryway. A decorative canopy over the front door and step added an attractive appearance to the entry.

The old chimneys were torn out of the living room and the old kitchen which was now the dining room. These were the other two large original rooms and about a five foot opening was left between them as a doorway. The wall between the rooms had a large window, open to both rooms, where Mom put a long, narrow gold planter with live green philodendron which she kept trimmed to her liking. It flourished beautifully in the light from the newly installed large picture window that replaced the window in the east wall of the living room. Live greenery hung down on both sides of the open window.

The contractor removed the door in the boy's bedroom and sealed the wall making more useable room there and installed an oil fired furnace in the east end of the closet that had been built between the two small bedrooms when the three small rooms were built in 1932, just before

Ruth was born. Dad built a large closet from the east end of the south wall all the way to the door in the girl's bedroom with a linen closet in the west end of it. He put shelves above the hanging space, enclosed them and built two large sliding doors of pressed wood. The construction crew finished their work by covering the exterior of the house with a mottled green salt siding.

When the construction work was completed, Mom and I were ready to begin the redecorating. Mike was not in kindergarten yet, so I was free all week long until Susan and Janice got home from school in the afternoon. I belonged to a women's evening bowling league and I asked my team to get a replacement for me so I wouldn't be constricted to having to be home early even one day a week.

So as many days a week as I could, Mike and I started out as soon as the girls went off to school in the mornings and drove the one hour to The Farm, worked the day with Mom and Dad, then drove back home to be there by the time they got home from school or shortly thereafter. They were about 11 and 13 years of age and could be trusted for a short time in our neighborhood of friends if Mike and I were a little late. Every day, Mom handed me a $1.00 bill and that paid for my gas. At $0.20 cents a gallon, five gallon got me home and back again.

As I look back, I see this as one of the best times of my life. I was not quite 40 years old, I had a wonderful family, husband and three children, we were all well and happy and there was no place I would rather be than on The Farm with Mom and Dad. It was always a pleasure to be there with them. I always felt I was the luckiest of all my siblings to be only 25 miles from home and I was blessed to be able to help them when I could.

Mom and I began shopping for wallpaper, paint, curtains and carpet for the enlarged living room. We repapered and painted (or varnished) the woodwork in every room in the house. Ruth came home from Columbus and helped with that as often as she could. Mom and I chose pale green wallpaper with a small white design in it for the living room and a matching paper for the dining room. The ceiling in the living room had been lowered during the construction and Floyd went down home in the evenings and on weekends and helped Dad lower the ceiling in the dining room to match the living room.

We found beautiful pink wallpaper for the girl's bedroom that had small flowers that looked like apple blossoms that Mom and I both liked and there was the prettiest pink paint called Cotton Candy to go with it. We both knew that Dad thought all new wood, woodwork, doors or whatever should be varnished. We talked it over and Mom thought if I wanted the pink paint, I should have the pink paint. She said we just wouldn't say anything to Dad about it and maybe he wouldn't notice it. Fat chance!

When Dad came into the bedroom and saw what I was doing he exclaimed in a loud voice, "Lord, God, you're not covering that new wood with paint!" I said, "But Dad, this is so pretty!" He shook his head, put a wry smile on his face, walked out of the room and never mentioned it again. We let him finish the two big rolling doors on the closet with varnish. (I would have liked pink paint on them too).

Dad had brought running water into the kitchen a few years before this. He piped the water from the well by the front door around the south end of the house to the back stoop where he built a little pump house for the electric pump that moved the water. He built modern kitchen cabinets all along the south wall of the kitchen and filled in the north wall from the stove to the west window with a nice cabinet. Ruth and I papered the kitchen with pretty ivy wallpaper we all liked.

The small kitchen had a back door to the west and the front door to the east that went out to the screened porch where Mom used to sit and do her letter writing in the early, cool summer mornings.

The two little bedrooms were so small wallpaper remnants were enough to cover them. When the painting and papering was all finished, Floyd rented a floor sander in Terre Haute and we took it down home and he and Dad sanded the floor in the girl's bedroom and the floor around the carpet in the dining room. Floyd and Dad finished them with some good floor varnish. All that was ever used in the girl's bedroom were some new throw rugs.

By the time these were done wall-to-wall salt and pepper (black and white) carpet had been laid in the living room. A new living room suite, new tables and lamps were purchased for the living room. Mom kept the big floor-style record player that stood against the wall in the living room which the grandchildren loved. They still remember the big 78 records that Grandma let them play.

A new Duncan Phyfe drop leaf table in the dining room opened to seat twelve people and when the leaves were down, it was flanked by two new easy chairs, one for Mom and one for Dad to watch their new television they had placed across the room on the south wall of the dining room.

Mom had foresight enough to see that these jobs were all completed in time to make preparations for the 50th Wedding Anniversary Celebration. Mom took good care of everything and it was lovely as long as Mom and Dad lived there. After Mom died and Dad moved to Michigan, none of us ever wanted to change it, so it always seemed like home.

There was absolutely nothing I liked to do better than go down home and open The Farm in the late spring and clean that old house and get it ready for family members and guests in the summer. We usually had someone there for Memorial Day weekend and I always had the house ready by then. I loved to wash and wax the wood floor in the girl's bedroom and the linoleum floors in the two little bedrooms and the kitchen. I always thought about Mom and wondered how many times she had done that before me.

From the time Mike and Cathy were married, through their years with young children, they liked to come to The Farm on Memorial weekend. One year, Cathy's Mom and Dad, John and Elsie Batjes, drove their big RV down and spent the weekend with us. A few times, Cathy's brother, John and his wife, Kathy, spent Memorial weekend there with us. Cathy's sister Pat and her husband Larry also came to visit once.

Of course, the most special times were when any of the siblings came. I always knew it was not just another old house to them, it was special to them as it was to me. I believe every year, some of them came. I believe a few times, all the siblings made it, but not all at the same time. I believe, well......actually, I know......there was no place on earth more special to me and I believe my siblings felt the same.

We did have trouble with people breaking into the garage from time to time. There were mostly just things of sentimental value there that I was saving to see if the kids wanted them. I had a fair sized collection of Avon perfume bottles of 20 or so and LaVerna Fisher had given Mike a collection of their son's horses I thought he might want some day, but someone, I will never know who, took them all.

The house finally was broken into too. We could see a large boot print where someone has stood on the front step and with a heavy boot or shoe, had kicked the door about where the door handle was and the door just gave way. They had stolen Mom's Duncan Fyfe table and her buffet full of dishes and locked the house back up.

When I went down the next time and saw the damage and what had been stolen, I sat down and cried, then it seemed as if I could hear Mom say to me, "My goodness, Nita, those are just things. They can all be replaced." Of course my Mom's things couldn't be replaced, but I got her message. I dried my tears and have been forever thankful for being able to have The Farm and use it as long as we did.

Chapter 20

50Th Wedding Anniversary Celebration

Mom and Dad's 50th Wedding Anniversary had been talked about and some tentative plans made for a couple of years. By the time the remodeling was complete it was time to get down to business and start some real planning.

Everyone had a part in the planning with Evah and Juanita (me) as the main planners. Of course a 50th anniversary celebration follows very much the same plan as a wedding reception so we had our work cut out for us.

Since the whole family planned to attend and stay on the farm for the whole week, the planning included much more than the day of the celebration. The house certainly was not large enough for 30 people to eat or to sleep comfortably and so plans were made for extra eating and sleeping arrangements.

Floyd belonged to Zorah Shrine and was a member for many years of its Drum and Bugle Corps. He always had plenty of friends who enjoyed getting together and helping each other. When he decided to build a "cook shack" so we could have a place large enough for everyone to eat together, he had no trouble getting enough friends together to get the job done.

So Floyd and a few of his Shrine buddies built a 16 foot by 20 foot cook shack that would hold enough chairs and tables for everyone to sit comfortably for meals. They put a screen door on each side of the shack and had room enough in one end for some hot plates and work tables and Floyd had an outdoor grill he had made from one half of a barrel that would hold plenty of chicken, hot dogs or hamburgers for the group.

Dad had started early in the spring cutting the grass and trimming around the trees in the little sassafras grove and old calf lot so it would be ready to use. Floyd and I had checked in Terre Haute and found a trailer rental place that would rent us five small one room trailers that would each be sleeping quarters for one family and Max and Ruth, Dick and baby Ricky would sleep in the house with Mom and Dad. The little house trailers would be delivered and set up by the time we needed them.

The cook shack was located about 50 feet due west of the house in the center of the calf lot. Floyd had found enough used 2x4's for the framing, Masonite siding half way up, a Visqueen plastic roof and mosquito netting would be used to close up all the holes and keep the flies and bugs out but that would be put on later. Floyd and Danny Griffith, a Shrine buddy, with the help of Dad and Uncle Bob Robertson, who was about 90 years old at the time, worked several evenings, sometimes as late as midnight, to get the shack completed in plenty of time.

I was surprised and pleased to find 20 or more small notebook pages in Ginnie's handwriting among Bob's saved material describing the celebration. When she gave up her daily scribing at the farm, it was finished in the car on the way home with Bob talking and Ginnie writing. Much of that will be used here. While these preparations were going on at The Farm, there were many other points of activity going on from New Jersey to California preparing for this same event.

In Atascadero, California, the six and one half Wolfes (Pat was pregnant with Becky) were busily scurrying around selling calves, installing a new septic tank, completely emptying the kitchen for remolding and doing a thousand and one other jobs to prepare a one and one-half acre garden farm for a two week vacation and a house for a remodeling job which would have a new kitchen largely finished when they returned. Jim was busy getting the parts department at the Ford/Chevrolet dealership ready to leave for his longest vacation in the last few years, as well as working at home on emergency trips to put out fires in a burning creek, etc. Pat was kept busy sorting clothes and limiting the quantity that each member of the family would be allocated on the plane. Someone even took time to ship a crate of oranges and lemons from California to sunny southern Indiana and to have a 20 pound turkey smoked and prepared for its first and last flight to our rendezvous.

In Flint, Michigan, the five Dale Wolfe's were busy getting the health food store ready to leave, studying plans for their proposed remodeling job with the architect, loading up papaya juice, baking cookies, fudge cakes, preparing lasagna, the border collie and Hammy the hamster, so they could join us on our family outing. On a previous trip Dale and Jeanette had brought down a lovely circulating juice cooler which contributed a lot to the pleasure of the children and adults throughout the week. Cold papaya juice, cider, Kool Aid, tea and other drinks were always circulating and available.

Max was busy putting Bill's boat carriers on his car top, loading Bill's canoe, buying games like the pitch and catch that he provided and storing away overflow of food and luggage from both Dale and Bill's cars. He even brought an overflow child, Greg, who wouldn't fit into the Phillips' car.

In Flushing, Michigan, the Phillips family was busy preparing to have red raspberries picked, making blueberry spice, cherry, strawberry and rhubarb jam for breakfast for 30 hungry mouths. Evah also baked banana nut cake, cookies, organized the menu, approved the duty roster, generally did all the correspondence in tying the group together, scheduling activities, etc. They were up until the wee small hours of the morning loading down the carrier with fishing tackle, camp stools, air mattresses, sleeping bags plus a thousand and one articles required for two year old Stephen. Bill and Bob agreed that it was a shame that a man had to take so much lip to get packing done for a trip. As usual the Phillips' came completely equipped and everyone knew that if any additional towels, sheets, rope, tools, flashlights or miscellaneous items were needed, Bill and Evah could produce them.

In Columbus, Indiana, the Dick Johnson's were taking care of house guests for a week, preparing for Bob and Ginnie to stop by enroute, baking cookies for the mob, helping in the preparation by mail and taking care of their only son, nine month old, Ricky. Pressure from Dick's business kept him from spending the entire time with the group.

On the east coast the Bob Wolfe's were kept busy preparing and waterproofing a tent, a last minute phone order to Detroit Michigan for a Miller car top carrier, building a plain wood box and having a canvas cover made for a car top carrier in addition to last minute operation in putting their one and one-fourth acre garden farm in wraps for two weeks, including spreading 50 bales of mulch in the garden, pruning and tying the raspberries, adding woodchip mulch to the fruit trees and last minute spraying and propping up the peach trees, heavily laden with fruit. Ginnie was busy several evenings sewing for the girls and packing the suitcases. Bob spent those last evenings organizing his job in hopes that Visking engineering group would function well in his absence. Bob had also assisted some in the general preparation by proposing a duty roster for the group, suggesting camp style menus based on the just closed Boy Scout Jamboree in Colorado Springs. Interestingly enough scouting celebrated its 50th year in America at the same time Ora and Ann Wolfe celebrated their 50th Wedding Anniversary. Although a 10:00 p.m. deadline had been set for loading, it was way past midnight when the tent and tent poles, air mattresses, sleeping bags, fishing bag, luggage and toys were safely packed for an early morning start.

In Terre Haute the Tryon's had done numerous things previously mentioned in reference to setting up the tent sites. In addition, it was Nita's lot to do most of the purchasing of the food. (No small task for 30 people.) She whipped up 90 cupcakes at the last minute and arranged for the anniversary cake after the Sullivan Bakery had cancelled with only a week to spare and purchased nuts, mints and flowers. She also tied bows on bells to be used as favors for 300 expected guests at the anniversary celebration. Floyd had nearly a full time job getting tables, chairs, table service from the Shrine, pots and pans from Frank's Restaurant and anything else needed from his friends in Terre Haute.

Mom and Dad were busy with final cleaning, and caring for a large garden (including beets, onion, beans, cucumbers, tomatoes, and cabbage). They helped as much as possible with all preparations but were kept busy at least half the time by avoiding the crush created by the converging multitude.

ARRIVAL:

The first from out of state to arrive at the farmstead were from the east, Bob and Ginnie with Linda, five and one-half years and Karen two and one-half. They left New Jersey early Saturday morning, arrived at Dick and Ruth's for Sunday dinner, visited for a few hours and had their Sunday evening meal with Mom and Dad on The Farm.

Monday evening Floyd and Bob took a load of chairs, tables, and utensils down to the farm. They worked late installing the Masonite wainscot on the cook shack. Bob and Nita went down Wednesday and spent the day. Nita did curtains, cleaned, etc., and Bob sawed down the kefir pear tree and helped Dad and Brad Ellis haul trash away, burning brush, mowing weeds and the last bit of outdoor clean up.

The next group to arrive was the Phillips' and Max. Bill and Evah, Greg, ten years old, Brian, eight and Stephen, one and one-half. They came down in convoy from Flint, leaving early Wednesday morning and arrived at Floyd and Nita's about 2:00 p.m. Since only Janice and Susan were there, they called down home and they found only Nita and Mom were there. Max left immediately after the phone call while Bill and Evah paused only long enough to raid the ice box. They arrived at 3:30 and 4:00 p.m. respectively. Max was immediately drafted into service using axe, lawn mower and scythe. Floyd arrived later in the evening with the stoves, mosquito netting, etc. Three trailers arrived at 7:00 p.m. and went into place along the sassafras fence row for Dale, Evah, and Jim. After leaving a long list for new arrivals to complete the following day, those from Terre Haute returned there.

Early on Thursday morning while Max was cranking the tractor over the protests of Dad, the crank back fired causing a hair line fracture in Max's right wrist. Dr. Joe Dukes put it in a cast. Although it dampened all our enthusiasm a little, it did not curtail Max's activity very much. He swam, pitched quoits, played badminton and did more work with only his left hand than most of us did with two hands. This was the first and only bone break on the farm while our family lived there. On Thursday Bill and Max, the lefties, cleaned up the grill, put up the mosquito netting and got everything ship shape.

Next to arrive were the Dale Wolfe's leaving Flint, Michigan, on Thursday with Dale and Jean were Doug, twelve years, Sara, eleven and Donnie, nine, along with Lassie the Border collie, and Hammy the hamster. They arrived Friday night and set up camp as soon as possible.

The group from Columbus, Indiana, Dick and Ruth with Ricky, nine months, arrived on Friday afternoon and were permitted to stay with Mom and Max in the house. There they lived with beds, chairs, and floors like royalty.

Coming from Atascadero, California, were the western Wolfes, Jim and Pat, Denny, thirteen,

Cathy, ten, Jimmy, eight, and Loren, four, plus Smokey the 20 pound turkey with the one way ticket. They drove to San Francisco, boarded the flight, and arrived in St. Louis the afternoon of July 15th. They had a car waiting for them and stayed at the motel overnight. The following day they drove to Hoosier Land. They arrived at Terre Haute approximately at 11:00 a.m. and arrived on the farm about 12:30 p.m.

Early Saturday afternoon the Terre Haute group, Floyd and Nita with Susan, thirteen, Janice, eleven, and Mike, five, arrived with food, refrigeration and the final requirements for a wonderful week.

Bob and Ginnie then came in from Ginnie's parents' home in Terre Haute for permanent residence with the gypsy band.

By cooperative effort, under Evah's direction, a delicious meal was served to the group consisting of Koegal's ring bologna, cold cuts and cookies. The last two trailers arrived about 8:00 p.m. and were lined up with the others at the south end of the row. This made five in line, all alike, assigned to the siblings according to ages except for Ruth and Max who stayed in the "big house". Amongst much talking and excitement, beds were made, children put to bed and the adults gathered in the cook shack for the first official "cracker barrel" session. A schedule was worked out and duties were assigned for the Golden Wedding Anniversary Celebration the following day.

Sunday morning, July 17, 1960, dawned bright and clear with much activity in the assembled group. A quick breakfast was eaten with everyone dolled up in their best finery. Everywhere you could see ladies combing children's hair, men getting dressed and children walking around stiff as if they might break. Promptly at 9:20 a.m., cars were loaded for the procession to Hickory Church. Those from the "big house" led off in Dick's car with others following with the California group bringing up the rear in Max's car.

We arrived a few minutes late and waited outside in formation while prayer was finished. We then marched in 31 strong taking the places that had been reserved for us. The entire service revolved around the Golden Wedding Anniversary and the need for Christian guidance in family relationships. The minister called Mom and Dad to the platform and commended them on their 50 years together and the group that had gotten together in their home. The youth choir stood and sang a song and Leona Willis played "I Love You Truly" and "Let Me Call You Sweetheart" on the piano. Aunt Dulsee then presented the celebrating couple with flowers and a bouquet from Hickory Church and from the Women's Society of Christian Service (WSCS). Other flowers were at the church and in their home. Mother introduced the family groups and children almost forgetting Max in the excitement.

Immediately after the church service, the Wolfe Family rushed back to The Farm where the photographer, Mr. Booth, was waiting. Several poses were taken of the entire family group. Bob then suggested that we find the picture taken of the family July 3, 1936, and duplicate it as nearly as possible. The contrast was startling. Someone suggested the in-laws pose in their respective places.

Lunch again was a well-planned affair, taking as little time as possible and final arrangements were made for guests, tables arranged with cakes, punch, nuts and napkins. The first couple arrived between 1:00 and 1:30 p.m.

By 12:45 p.m. all hands took their assignments as follows: Mom and Dad at the door greeting guests with Ruth pinning on favors; Evah and Nita manning the inside of the house, greeting guests; Susan was in charge of the guest register; Jeanette unwrapped and recorded gifts; Pat was assigned to the punch bowl; Ginnie did the honors on the cake; the sons and sons-in-law kept busy assisting the parking, greeting guests and generally assisting as needed. Many commented on the lovely weather and the smooth cooperation of the affair. What a nice celebration it was.

Most of the guests had heard of our arrangements for the following week so most of them took the liberty to wander out to the cook shack and the trailer area to take a look.

Many lovely gifts were received by Ann and Ora and they derived much pleasure from seeing friends and family who hadn't gotten together for many years. The last guest left about 6:00 p.m.

An evening meal had previously been prepared by group effort with Evah's direction consisting of a whole ham prepared by Evah, baked beans prepared by Ruth, and cookies and cake by Jeanette. After supper the children were tucked away. Ginnie helped Ruth clean up the debris from the celebration, washed cups, etc., while the other ladies cleaned up the cook shack.

On Monday morning cooks and kids were up at 6:00 a.m. The kids were anxious to get started on activities, fishing, playing in the stripper hills, running through the corn fields and playing together. The cooks, Pat, Jim, Bob, Ginnie, and Max, were anxious to get underway to have all meals on schedule. For breakfast there were oranges and pancakes with link sausages presided over by Jim and Max. Bob assisted with sorghum syrup and assorted jellies with the ladies helping where needed. Once the serving was completed, the cooks were free to eat. Evah and Bill were responsible for clean up along with assistance from Susan and Dennis.

Shortly after breakfast on Monday with the activities underway, Ginnie gave up trying to capture all of the events with pencil and paper. Menus had been prepared by Nita and a duty roster for cooking and cleanup for the week included all family members above ten years of age. It was felt the work parties would allow time for visiting and also for getting the younger generation involved by giving them a real and significant job as was true with all who grew up on The Farm.

Bob managed the beef stew with carrots and potatoes, a cabbage salad (slaw) with full support of the rest of the assigned team. Dick and Floyd presided over the grill for one meal of barbecued chicken and baked potatoes and each person - young or older - took his/her assigned places as they came up on the roster. Nothing could have worked smoother. If there was a complaint, even by a teenager or near teenager, it was kept under wraps. Working seemed to be as much fun as playing for young and old alike.

The exact menus for the remainder of the week are not available but it is known that all menus were hardy, country food and in generous quantity, satisfying all. Of course, the 20 pound smoked turkey from California was relished by all. Ample produce from The Farm garden fit in well and rounded out every meal.

At the end of the day the adults met in the cook shack for a time of winding down with a simple snack called "cracker barrel time".

Older cousins slept in tents pitched on the outer edges of the site to relieve people density in the trailers.

Adults were happy just to talk, work together, share life and review old times. Mom and Dad came and went as they pleased with no responsibility. Mom loved to be close just to see the family together while Dad enjoyed driving his homemade tractor back to a good fishing strip pit.

The kids enjoyed their activities, often with a loosely supervised couple of adults while roaming. The only very strict supervision was in one small deep clean stripper pit which Max had named "The Texas Bathtub".

One specific activity worthy of mention was a skit put on for entertainment for parents and grandparents by the third generation members. This was organized and led by Susan and was enjoyed by all.

These are memories that are permanently etched in the minds of all who participated. As we have reviewed this, all have been astounded at the work each one did so willingly to honor our parents and grandparents and create a memorable time together.

Ora's 80Th Birthday Celebration
Ora And Ann's Final Days

It had been more than five years since the family had all been together for the 50th Wedding Anniversary Celebration of Mom and Dad and most of the family was getting anxious for another get together.

Being only 25 miles away from The Farm, I didn't miss Mom and Dad like the other family members did, but I did miss my siblings.

Bob was not the farthest away from home, but due to the nature of his job in the fast growing plastics industry, he moved around a lot and I think that may have given him a feeling of being unsettled and he missed the stability we all felt growing up in one place and the closeness of a large family. We all missed that.

Being a great planner, which Bob had to be to fulfill the requirements of a plant manager for Visking Corporation and traveling the country to build new plastic plants, it came natural for him to plan family get togethers.

With Dad's 80th birthday coming up on September 18th, Labor Day weekend seemed like a perfect opportunity for another get together. So Bob talked to his siblings who were all in agreement, wrote Dad a letter and another celebration was under way. Bob did most of the planning for this himself, but there were always plenty of willing hands in this group when anybody needed help.

Bob chose Pokagon State Park in northern Indiana for the celebration. Pokagon seemed like a good, centrally located place and was agreeable to everyone. Mom and Dad came to Terre Haute and spent Friday night with us so we could get an early start on Saturday morning. We had never been to Pokagon but knew it was north, near Fort Wayne. A friend of Floyd's said – oh yes, he knew exactly where it was and gave us his directions. By the time we discovered we were going north but definitely not heading toward Pokagon, we knew we would miss the picnic lunch with the group. We weren't too worried about food however for we had a full picnic lunch with us and the party wasn't until evening.

All the family was able to attend Dad's 80th Birthday weekend except James and Pat and their family in California. It was a beautiful fall weekend and it was thoroughly enjoyed by all those attending.

Bob and Ginnie made a booklet of the weekend complete with the story and pictures of the celebration and gave each of us a copy for our 1967 Christmas gift.

No one expected this to be our last family get together with Mom and Dad both. Mom had had problems with her heart for a few years and had been to see Dr. Betty Dukes, wife of Joe Dukes who went all through high school and graduated with Evah. Joe was now the resident doctor in Dugger, following in the footsteps of his father, Fred Dukes, who had been our family doctor for many years.

Mom, however, seemed to prefer the treatment of Dr. Ramsey a chiropractor with her office in Sullivan. She went regularly for treatments for her heart by Dr. Ramsey and thought they helped her more than Dr. Betty, wife of Dr. Joe and a medical doctor did.

Floyd and I had been to the Shrine Temple the night Dad called and said he was taking Mom to the hospital. I had been shopping that day and Floyd had stopped at the Shrine on his way home from work and ran into Bert and Mary Ellen Wimmer, some friends from Rockville, Indiana. He called me and asked me to come down to the Shrine and we would have dinner with them. I did and we sat after dinner and talked with them and other friends that were there.

When we got ready to leave the Shrine, Floyd asked Bert and Mary Ellen to go home with us for bacon and eggs which wasn't unusual, he often did that. We were sitting there finishing our food when the phone rang. It was Dad telling us he had just called an ambulance to take Mom to the hospital, because she was having chest pains. I just said, "Okay Dad we will meet you there." We hurriedly said goodbye to our guests, got our coats on and left for the Mary Sherman Hospital at Sullivan.

It was close to an hour's drive for us and we got to the hospital just as they had put Mom on the gurney and were wheeling her into the hospital. So we went in with them and helped check her in.

It was March and the ground was just thawing out good and the ambulance had gotten stuck in the driveway at home and Dad had had to call someone to help them get it out. It was past midnight by this time and Mom was pretty uncomfortable all the while. After she was settled in, I stayed in the room with her and Floyd and Dad went down to the hospital lobby.

I had bought a new red knit dress on sale for $5.00 when I was shopping that afternoon and had worn it down to the Shrine for dinner that evening. Mom told me how pretty it looked, then as we talked she said, "Now Nita I don't want you to worry, if it is my time to go I am ready." I said, "Oh Mom, we're not going to talk about that. You'll be okay."

I have thought of that conversation a million times and wished I had talked with her about it. I don't worry though, because I know she was ready. She was only 78 years old and I hoped she had more years to be with us. I just didn't want to accept the fact that she might be going to die so soon.

Sometime during the early morning hours, when the doctor came in, they moved Mom to a different room and hooked her up to a bunch of wires and did a lot of tests. When I asked the nurses how she was doing they told me she was not responding like they had hoped she would.

Floyd and Dad called all of the kids, at least one of Mom's sisters, probably Aunt Dulsee, and about eight o'clock the next morning Aunt Tilda, Aunt Dulsee and Aunt Ina all came to the hospital together. They came up to her room and Mom was pleased to see them. She said, "Someone get a chair for Ina, she can't stand on her feet very long." They stayed in the room awhile then went back down to the lobby. I have thought so many times, how like Mom to be putting others first, right up to the very end. Just before noon as I stood beside her bed, wetting her lips with a water-soaked small pink sponge, she took a last long breath and passed away.

Floyd had taken Dad to a nearby motel so he could get some much needed sleep and rest. Bob and Ruth got there sometime in the late morning, but none of the Michigan group made it before nightfall. During the night we had the last snowfall of the season and the Michigan children and their families drove in heavy snowfall the night of March 23rd. They drove in tandem so they could help each other see the way.

Mom's body was held in state at Newkirk's Funeral Home in Dugger for visitation and the funeral was held at Hickory Church on Tuesday, March 26, 1968. She was carried across the road and laid to rest beside her five year old son, George Edward.

A lovely luncheon was carried in at The Farm by the Hickory Women's Society of Christian Service (WSCS) for Ora and his children, grandchildren and friends of the family following the funeral.

Ora decided to stay on at The Farm but it was far lonelier than he expected it would be. There were no close neighbors anymore. Aunt Dulsee was the closest and she was about a quarter of a mile west and another quarter mile north. He knew that the people all around the area knew he had sold his property to Peabody Coal Company for strip mining and he once told me he sometimes wondered if strangers might think a lone old man had his money tucked under his mattress and would try to rob him. He kept his shotgun standing behind his bedroom door.

Dad had loved to roam over the stripper hills among the pits. When he found a pretty rock, an Indian arrow head or something special, he would put it in his pocket and take it home to Mom and tell her about where he had found it. He said, "When I see something nice,

I immediately think – oh, I must go tell Mom about this. Then I remember she is not there anymore and that takes all the fun out of it." That always made him sad, as well as lonely.

On Memorial Day of that year, 1968, most of the siblings and their families went to Bob and Ginnie's in Ottawa, Illinois, for the weekend. Floyd and I went down and picked up Dad and took him with us to Bob and Ginnie's.

When we came back the evening of Memorial Day it was getting dark when we got back to The Farm with Dad. We had to work the next day, so we just pulled into the driveway, up near the kitchen door, said our goodbyes and let Dad out of the car. We backed out of the driveway and turned around to wave goodbye as we always did when Mom was there and Dad had stepped back into the house, closed the door and through the glass I could see him locking it. It made me feel sad.

The next day I called Evah and told her about it. I asked her if she thought we should talk to Dad to see if he wanted to move and she thought we should. Dad said he thought it might be a good idea. We talked to the other kids about it, so we all began to look around. I found a little three room house a few blocks from our home in Terre Haute that I thought would suit Dad and the Michigan kids found a small apartment in Flushing, a long walk from Evah and Bill's house.

Dad made the choice. He thought it made more sense to move to Michigan and be nearer three of his children and I had to agree with him. So we made plans for a move. About the middle of August everyone that could, went to The Farm to help with the move.

Everybody agreed it was time for Dad to move but no one liked the idea of giving up The Farm. When Peabody Coal bought The Farm, they had given Mom and Dad rights to live there as long as they wanted to. Floyd and I were the only ones close enough to take care of the place so Dad and I talked about it and Dad suggested he and I go over to Peabody's office, which was close to Aunt Dulsee's house, and talk to them.

So, with no thought about it ahead of time or without even talking to Floyd about it, Dad and I went and talked to Peabody. Dad did the talking, some phone calls were made, I wrote a check for $50.00 and The Farm was the Wolfe family's to use for as long as we wanted it. Floyd was as delighted as all of the siblings were. He loved that old place too.

Dad moved in August 1968 to his apartment in Flushing shortly before his 81st birthday and lived in Flushing the rest of his life. There was never any reason for any of us to regret Dad's decision or to think Flushing was not the best choice for him during the last 12 years that he lived.

His first apartment was a few blocks from town, but he could walk downtown to shop or to a small restaurant if he wanted to eat out. He could walk down to the Flint River if he wanted to fish for an hour or two. There was a field in back of his apartment house where in season he could smell the new mown hay. It seemed a good fit for Dad and he liked it.

However, when it became too long a walk downtown for him, he found an apartment in the Flushing downtown district. He did have to walk a flight of stairs every time he went out or came home, but his legs seemed to handle that pretty well. It was, however, too far to walk to Evah and Bill's house anymore so they picked him up in the car when he went to visit them.

Dad had given his car up before he moved away from The Farm. We never knew what, if anything, happened to cause him to make that decision, but we were visiting him one Sunday when I had fixed dinner for all of us and taken it down to have dinner with him, when out of a clear blue sky he said, "I've decided it's time for me to quit driving and I want Janice to have my car." I said, "But Dad, you need your car, don't you?" He answered, "Nope, it's time for me to give it up and I want Janice to have it."

Since we were looking for a used car for Janice, both of our problems were solved. So Jan's first car was her Grandpa's old 1957 Chevrolet Bellaire and she was happy with it. We always suspected that something had happened, a near accident, or something that made Dad so sure it was time for him to give up his car. For the short time he had left on The Farm, he rode to church and to town with Aunt Dulsee and Doris.

There was a Senior Citizens Center in downtown Flushing but Dad didn't seem to want much to do with it until someone suggested he set up a card table near the front window where he could make fishing flies and teach anyone that wanted to learn how to do his craft. He was well into his 80's when he decided to give others who might be interested the benefit of his years of fishing. By this time his fingers were pretty stiff and he couldn't tie the small knots anymore or wrap the threads as tightly as he could in his younger years, but he still enjoyed doing it.

A reporter from the little Flushing Observer newspaper came into the Senior Citizens Center one day to interview Dad and talk to him about his years of fishing, tying flies and making other fishing lures. He took a picture of him and ran it on the front page of his newspaper with a short story about Dad. This of course added to Dad's enjoyment of the Senior Center.

Dad seemed to get along well in Michigan and liked being close to his family. Bill was an avid fisherman and had several good places to fish. He understood Dad's love of fishing and was good about taking him to Chippewa Lake or to some of his fishing spots.

On Saturday May 10, 1980, Bill took Dad on a little fishing jaunt and they had a good time. However, when Dad got out of bed on Sunday morning, his stomach was giving him some trouble and he called Dale. He felt like he should go into the hospital and Dale took him into the hospital in Flint.

Since it happened to be Mother's Day, Dale and Jeanette and Bill and Evah all changed their plans and stayed with Dad at the hospital. Dad seemed to be getting along okay and on Thursday of that week, Bill and Evah went to Brian and Sue's house to celebrate Mother's Day, then on to Chippewa Lake. They came back to Flint on Sunday morning, May 18th and went to the hospital to see how Dad was doing.

Evah could see Dad was not doing well and she asked Bill to call Greg and have him call

Dale and Jeanette, who were at Sara's house for their Mother's Day celebration and to call the rest of the family to let them know Dad seemed to have taken a turn for the worse. Dad asked Evah not to leave him alone in the hospital, so someone stayed with him all the time from then on. Dad didn't seem to understand that the people in the hospital were there to help him, he wanted to go home.

The doctors had discovered a bleeding in Dad's stomach which they thought could be ulcers and wanted to operate on him. Even they weren't sure that procedure would help him and vacillated back and forth – yes, then no, then yes. The next Thursday they did perform surgery on Dad, but by that time his body was too weak to recover.

Dad passed away on Friday, May 23rd, following his surgery on Thursday. Ruth and Dick and Bob and Ginnie had arrived there on Friday evening and Floyd and I had planned to leave Terre Haute for Flint as soon as Floyd got home from Evansville. However, before Floyd got home, Evah called and said Dad was gone. So we never made the trip.

Dale, Ruth and Bob spent the time making arrangements for Dad's funeral and Evah stayed home to get a bit of much needed rest and fix food for the whole family. A funeral service was held at the Flushing United Methodist Church before he was driven to Newkirk's Funeral Home in Dugger.

His visitation and funeral for other family members and old friends at Newkirk's funeral home in Dugger was followed by a luncheon prepared by members of the WSCS at Hickory. We were all pleased to see so many of Dad's, as well as our friends, show up for the funeral. It was as if we had never moved away.

Dad was buried in the family plot in Hickory Cemetery beside Ann, his beloved wife of 58 years who had died 12 years earlier, and his young son, George Edward (Brother), who died of scarlet fever in 1918.

Chapter 22

Birth Of A Cookbook

Our family has always been a family of good cooks and of course at family reunions food is usually a topic for discussion. "Oh, wow, did you taste Aunt Dulsee's Dutch apple pie." "That must be Jenny's cherry cobbler." "I'd love to have the recipe for that chocolate cheese cake." etc. etc., etc.

This had gone on for close to 20 years at the annual Wolfe family reunion when someone said, "We need to write a cookbook." Everyone thought it would be a good idea but how do we go about it. Our daughter, Susan, volunteered to head it up.

Since the McMurrays had a cottage at Chippewa Lake in Michigan just two doors from Evah and Bill's cottage, Evah volunteered to help Susan since they would both be at the lake a lot during the summer. A call went out for recipes. In fact before there were enough recipes for a book, several calls went out for more recipes. Most of us are prone to think – yes, I have lots of recipes to send and I'll get them together tomorrow – or next week, it is so easy to put it off.

Susan and Evah started right away collecting "best" recipes from everyone in the family and they both worked hard at it. Most of the recipes that came in were hand written and Rhonda, Tim's secretary in his business at that time, volunteered to type them all up and get them ready for printing (for some extra money).

By mid-summer of 1986, Susan and Evah had collected about 600 recipes and decided it was time to stop since we really wanted to have the cookbooks at the reunion on Labor Day weekend. Susan and Evah separated and categorized the recipes under the usual sections of a cookbook, Appetizers, Soups and Sauces; Breads, Pancakes and Waffles; Cakes, Cookies and Pies, etc., before they sent them to Rhonda to be typed. We know that recipes are not easy to type from plainly written copy and the majority of these were handwritten and mailed out before everyone had computers. I'm sure it was no easy job to type from handwritten recipes.

A cute Preface was written by Pat Wolfe, Jim's wife in California. It was this short paragraph:

"There is a saying that has hung in our kitchen for more years than I can remember. Lord, warm all the kitchen with Thy love and right it with Thy peace. Forgive me all my worry and make my grumbling cease."

The book has a nice slick, heavy, plasticized paper back and on the back of the front cover is printed: "Ora's grandchildren have requested this table grace be included in the cookbook. One of their fondest memories of Grandad is him praying this prayer before every meal, even if he ate alone."

"Our Gracious Heavenly Father, we thank Thee for this another day and for life, health and strength. As we now surround these table comforts of Life, bless a portion of this food to its intended use, bless the hands that prepared it. Lead, guide and direct us and we'll give Thee the praise forever. Amen".

Most of Ora's grandchildren heard this table grace so often they committed it to memory. It is said often as the opening grace for the first meal at our Annual Family Reunion.

The first leaf in the cookbook gives a brief history of the Wolfe family written by my brother Bob that covers the front and the back of the page. It follows here:

The Birth of a Cookbook

Good cooks bring their best foods to a family reunion. Only those recipes that are favorites of individual families are served to the extended family.

What young bride is not awed by the enormous variety of flawlessly seasoned and prepared dishes that seem to flow so effortlessly from the kitchens of the more experienced cooks. As their own needs grow, they realize what a wealth of knowledge is available. How often have we heard the casual comment, "We should put these recipes in a book!"

One perceptive third generation gal took up the cause seriously with an aunt, and zingo, the book was born – no, it was conceived. All have been surprised at the length and complexity of the gestation period.

This cookbook is the product of one Hoosier farm family of seven children and more than 100 descendants. It is intended as a practical memento of a highly diverse and strongly bonded family.

The fact that this family has been widely separated geographically for the past 40 years gives this book an interesting flavor. Contributions to the recipe request were gleaned from three states bordering the Pacific Ocean, four bordering the Atlantic and four in the vast heartland of our country.

If you are interested in this only as a useful cookbook, feel free to turn to the "meat and bread" of the text. You will find a broad mixture of well tested recipes. Try the Kale Torte from Connecticut; the Baked Fish from California; Bea's Pound Cake from North Georgia, and Marinated Zucchini Salad and Prune Cake from the Midwest.

Also included are some unusual recipes that are a tribute to the wit and style of this large family. Don't miss the Walleye Grill recipe that starts with a trip to the Maumee River or one for Maple Syrup that takes you from "11 maple trees and 22 spiles" to enough maple syrup for family use plus Christmas gifts.

However, if you share our interest in the drama of family interaction, we are pleased to share with you the following paragraphs. We of the second generation feel unusually blessed with the example and value system that grew from that small farm in southern Indiana. We feel a strong desire to pass this "torch" to succeeding generations of the Wolfe family.

In the sparsely settled country 10 miles southeast of Sullivan, Indiana, September 1910 saw an event important only to those affected by it. Ora C. Wolfe, a 22 year old coalminer, married 19 year old Susie Ann Deckard, daughter of a farmer. They "took up" housekeeping in a tiny home "nearly half way to Sullivan, north of State Road 54." About three years and one child later, they bought four acres with a three-room wood frame home on land bordering Ann's father's property, just a long stone's throw from where she was born and reared.

This home, later enlarged to six rooms, is still maintained and used occasionally by most family members, has become known to the second, third and fourth generation simply as "The Farm".

To this central couple were born eight children. The second child died of scarlet fever at the age of five in 1918. The remaining seven and the additional members of the extended family continue to be influenced by a lifestyle that is unusual only in retrospect. It was a product of the dire economic need, the culture of the day, the firm belief that hard work and initiative would accomplish much and the certain knowledge that an all wise God ruled the affairs of mankind.

Ora worked in underground coal mines with three to four feet of head room. He was paid piece rate of 15 to 20 cents per ton of coal with gob loaded free. Later while working "on top" he fired the boiler and learned the electrical trade and other mechanical skills. He constantly needed to supplement this intermittent work with other income, and while the farm provided food, trapping fur and extra jobs provided additional cash.

Ann was a lifetime example of the magic of a farm wife. She was able to rear a family, manage the chickens, tend the garden, can fruits and vegetables, make virtually all the clothing, sell cream, butter and eggs and much more. Besides all this, she was still able to demonstrate to the family that the Christian faith, nurtured by the nearby one-room church, was the most important influence in her vitally lived value system.

From the earliest age, each child was taught, and accepted responsibility for some work to be done for family needs. There were farm animals to feed, eggs to gather, and kindling, wood and coal to carry in for both cooking and heating stoves. Also, food preparation such as wild blackberries to pick and can, peaches, apples, cherries and vegetable grown from seed to put up only scratched the surface. Standard basic needs included 30 gallons each of blackberries and peaches with somewhat lesser quantities of green beans, corn, tomatoes, pickles and other garden vegetables all preserved in half gallon glass jars. Apples, potatoes, turnips and other root crops were stored in the cellar. While certain jobs generally fell to boys or girls, no one was exempt from helping where needed.

Even the recreation of hunting and fishing and a "rabbit trap line" of the boys had a serious aspect. At a time when meat was either raised on the farm, bartered from neighbors or omitted from the diet, wild game was an important addition to the regular menu. The courage it took for parents to face providing for nine hungry mouths at the table three times a day is awesome.

In spite of the pressure the parents must have felt under this workload, the children were never expected nor permitted to stay home from school to help. An exception was occasionally made for butchering day when from one to three hogs would be killed and a winter meat supply laid in. Education was seen as the way "you kids can be better off than we have been." Each child graduated from Union High School in Dugger, Indiana, and each received the gold watch he had been promised, along with a Bible. Some went on to college and others to jobs but all appreciated the skills and judgment that came from the emphasis placed on education.

The umbrella covering all was an active Christian faith. It was learned at Old Hickory Methodist Church and lived daily to demonstrate its value in each endeavor. Ann was the strong consistent one in this phase of life, and continues to be remembered for her ready acceptance of all by her children, grandchildren, in-laws and friends and neighbors alike. All attended Sunday services, weekly prayer meetings, and special dramas at Children's Day and Christmas, youth meetings, etc. Through this, the Christian faith has become an important ingredient to nearly all descendants.

As the young adults left the nest one by one, home comings became highlights while life went on much as before. The weekly letters Ann wrote to each child was an invaluable point of contact. They lent stability to the young lives, solidifying their own private value systems.

With three sons and one son-in-law in service during World War II, Ora continued farming and coal mining. Each person did his job, marking time until the war was over. Through the unrelenting prayers of a devout family and the unmerited blessings of the Lord, all returned home to pick up their lives again. For several years the children and their families continued to return to the farm at vacation time to bask in the warmth of love and fellowship and to enjoy the seasonal harvest bounty of that remarkably fertile soil

The years slipped by with families growing and the inevitable restrictions of busy lives being accepted. In 1954, a major gathering at the farm brought three families from Michigan, two from Indiana and one from California and New Jersey each.

In 1960, the 50th wedding anniversary was observed with a week-long celebration and a Sunday afternoon open house. Five identical travel trailer were parked in the then unused calf lot with two second generation families staying at the farm house. With a 16 x 20 foot cook shack as the central pavilion, the fun and fellowship renewed the spirits of all. The 16 third generation members attending were introduced to the love and warmth of the entire family.

By 1967, the family had become aware that gatherings of this type were no accident and Ora's 80th birthday in September was cause to plan a weekend gathering at Pokagon State Park near Angola, Indiana. Again, the value of the renewal of spirit was encouraging. Although Ann passed away in March of the following year, all knew she, most of all, would want these bonds to continue – and so they have! In 1980, Ora died at the age of 92 after being the center of 12 of these celebrations.

This September, 1986, 64 members are scheduled to attend the clan gathering representing two Pacific states, three Atlantic states and four in the heartland.

Activities have always been geared around the interest of the changing group. As third generation members married, spouses were welcomed and fourth generation members were born and gathered in. Their interests and desires have been given attention, and of course food has been an important part of these gatherings. This cookbook represents the wide diversity and quality of that interest.

It is widely recognized however, that the main attraction is an ingredient generally not mentioned. The unconditional love of the extended family that encompasses all gives each one input into the activities and gives all the freedom to be themselves. This love is the ingredient that brings the younger generation back to the Midwest each year from such faraway places as Texas, Oregon, New Jersey and California. The interaction of the group with support where needed is clear evidence of why God ordained the family as the world's most basic and important institution.

The fervent wish of the whole Wolfe "Pack" for all who use this cookbook is that each family unit will be as truly blessed by this same loving God as this family has been!

Susan's brother, Mike Tryon, came up with the name "Hungry Like A Wolfe" for this cookbook and Susan and Evah thought that was a perfect name. Mike also knew a woman he had worked with previously who was a graphic artist. He approached her about designing a cover using the name as a theme. This artist's church was sponsoring a fund raising dinner for a special project and she bartered with Mike, a design for the book cover for two tickets to her fundraiser. The barter turned out to be a good deal. Mike and Cathy had a good dinner and we got a cute design for the cover. The artist drew a cute wolf in a top hat and overcoat peeking over the top of his turned up collar. The wolf was leaning against a tablet that bore the name "Hungry Like A Wolfe" with smaller print near the bottom of the tablet "A Family Cookbook".

A flyleaf before each section bearing the title of the section was decorated with a creative caricature-type drawing of something like a wolf in an apron flipping pancakes, a small elephant seated reading a book, etc., and a page for notes in the back added to the usefulness of the book.

A few weeks before the reunion Susan said the typing was coming along great and everything was under control. But as time went on she began to worry about getting it done in time for the reunion. About the middle of August, Rhonda told Susan the typing was all done and had been proofread, but Susan was afraid they couldn't get it printed on time. I talked to the printer we used for our business and he agreed to work with me if I could get it to him right away. I called Susan and she sent the typed copy along with the original recipes by Federal Express to our office.

When the boxes arrived at our office, the copy looked ready, but there was no index. Since being a food editor was part of my job before I retired from the Terre Haute Star Newspaper, I had dealt with many cookbooks and knew an index was an important part of any book. As pressed as I was for time, I had to make an index. Then I had to get "The Birth of a Cookbook" story from Bob before I could take it to the printer. Finally all was ready just a week before the reunion. We rushed the copy to the printer and Floyd picked up the 250 completed cookbooks on Friday morning just before we left for Pokagon.

After looking through a few of the books, I was very pleased. They were beautiful, slick and shiny off white front and back with a dark brown plastic spiral binding and off white paper pages with sepia printing. It was a lovely cookbook and just in the nick of time!

On Saturday morning at the reunion, we brought the cookbooks out and everyone thought they were beautiful. Naturally we were all interested to see the recipes and we were all going through them. Soon I heard Ginnie say, "There are no lentils in my lentil stew." I felt sick! That started everyone checking their own recipes and almost everyone found a recipe with an error in it.

Talk about disappointment! We were all disappointed but I, probably most of all. Not only had Floyd and I paid for 250 cookbooks at $5.10 each, but I had been a food editor and I knew how important good editing was. I should never have taken someone else's word for it – I should have checked them myself to be sure they were proofread. But I hadn't!

Now what do we do! As Mom used to say, "There's no use to cry over spilt milk!" James was here from California for the reunion that year and he said he would go home with me and help me correct them, then I could send the corrections to each one and they would correct them before they sold or gave them to anyone. So Jim and I spent several nights finding errors and listing them. One of us would read the original recipe and the other one would mark it and put the page number, recipe and the corrections on the list. I don't remember how many evenings we worked on that book, but I do remember one night when Jim said, "Nita, I have to quit for tonight – I feel like my eyes are spinning in my head."

We all bought sepia colored pens and used my list of corrections. They still didn't look very nice so my daughter-in-law, Cathy, came to the rescue. She took my list of corrections and a cookbook and typed the corrections on typing paper that had a peel off backing so we could use an Exacto knife to cut the correction and stick it in the book. If I live long enough, I hope to get all the books I have left corrected to be passed down to future generations.

That is the story of the "Hungry Like A Wolfe" cookbook. A few years ago, in 2014, the Wolfe family published a second cookbook. It was talked about for a couple of years at the Annual Family Reunion and Cathy Porter, Jim and Pat's daughter in California, volunteered to collect the recipes and get the printing done. Getting recipes, articles for "The Wolfe Call" or anything like that is not an easy task in this family, or in any family, I suspect. This second cookbook is called "Hungrier Than Hungry Like a Wolfe". It is a beautiful book – hard back with a three ring binder and much sturdier than the original cookbook.

Cathy has included the story from the original book "The Birth of a Cookbook" by Uncle Bob and Grandpa's table grace so future generations will have them too.

Another nice thing about the "Hungrier than Hungry Like A Wolfe" book is that the section dividers are not only full of helpful information but each of them has family pictures on it. Pictures are also scattered elsewhere in the book and will be of special interest to family members we don't know as yet.

A few recipes from the original book found their way into the new book. As Cathy said, they are "too classic not to include". Several new vegan recipes show up in the new cookbook since many of our older clan members, as well as younger members just getting heavy into food preparation are moving toward a healthy diet. Between the new and the older cookbooks there is such a variety of delicious recipes almost any category of food can be found.

Chapter 23

Annual Family Reunions

I believe I have mentioned somewhere else in these writings that we are a family that grew up going to family reunions, so family reunions have always been an important and enjoyable part of our lives. However, none have been so important or brought so much pleasure to so many people as this long lasting annual Wolfe Family Reunion.

Again, and I have said this before also, much of the credit for the annual reunion belongs to my brother Bob. He not only took the lead in getting the family together, he planned and chaired the first few reunions. However, he met no resistance from any member of this family. Everyone was agreeable and willing helpers.

Bob and Ginnie had each lived in only one home all during their childhood years which gave them a feeling of stability. Due to Bob's job with Union Carbide moving them to different states on a regular basis, albeit each move was an advancement, it added to their ambivalent feelings of uncertainty and uneasiness about "home". They were concerned especially for their children. They worried that they would not feel like they had "roots" anywhere.

Bob had planned Dad's 80th Birthday Party in 1967 at Pokagon State Park near Fort Wayne, Indiana, and it had satisfactory accommodations and was centrally located. Pat and Jim were the only family in California who was too far away for Pokagon to be an easy drive. But the central location had much in its favor and there was some talk that weekend of the 80th birthday celebration about coming back again the next year.

After Mom's death in March of 1968, it seemed more important than ever that we all get together as often as possible and we all felt that an annual reunion would be the best way to get all seven of us together. Pokagon had some grand plans for expansions in place. Already in 1967 two or three rooms in the new Hoosier Wing, the first straight extension of Potawatomi Inn were completed. Mom and Dad had one of those rooms, Pokagon's finest at the time, the weekend of

Dad's 80th Birthday Party. We all knew that Mom, most of all, would be happy if this reunion became an annual affair so we could all stay close together. That was the legacy she left us.

All seven siblings liked camping and cooking out – we all loved the outdoors. For the first few years Bob was in Ottawa, Illinois, then later in Bay Village, Ohio for three years. He had a lot of camping equipment and had built a rack for the top of his car to carry bicycles for the family. The bicycles stood straight up and all the kids would watch for Uncle Bob's car with the bicycles. They knew Linda and Karen and Kenny would be inside.

Bill and Evah were also campers and Bill had a trailer they loaded with camping equipment so it was not a hard chore to get it set up with a camp stove and other cooking equipment. In a short time camp could be set up and with food from the trunks of at least six or seven cars, a meal could be on the picnic table in short order. Hot dogs and hamburgers were often grilled and a plethora of salads, garden produce, pies, cakes, cookies, etc., made their way to the table. There was always enough food for one or two more meals.

Although in 1967, Dad's 80th Birthday Party was not planned as a family reunion it was talked about then and by the next year with Mom gone, all seven siblings were in favor of making it an annual event. It is now counted as the first annual reunion and not a year has been missed.

Bob planned the 1968 reunion, maybe even the next one, but soon the idea of a different chair family each year took hold and seemed the best arrangement for all. It was decided the best way to keep track of whose year it was would be to rotate in birth order but practicality was used also. One year when it was Bob's family's year, he was involved with a move and the Phillips family traded years with them. The following year they went back to birth order.

When any large problem came up it was that easy to change years, but by and large, each family was willing, even anxious, to get its year over with. The chair family has complete control of all activities in its year, within reason of course. If anyone in our family was disappointed or unhappy with the way something was done, I was always quick to tell them, "Just wait – your year is coming and you can change that if you decide to."

In 1976 we joined our nations request for all families in our nation to recognize in some special way the 200th Anniversary of the founding of our country. Each family planned a commemorative display of some kind and each member made a presentation entitled, "What I Want Our Family to Remember About Me at the 300th Anniversary". Those presentations were reviewed at the 35th year and have been preserved for review in the year 2076 for the 300th Anniversary of our country. These notes will be of much interest in the years to come for they show clearly the values of the founders.

As the years went by, more of our children were married and grandchildren were arriving – great grandchildren for Dad. On the 10th anniversary of our reunion, 1977, was Dad's 90th birthday and it was also the year Linda, Bob's oldest child, decided to get married at the reunion. The 57 people attending the reunion that year included 16 great grandchildren of Ora, five of them were babies still. Bill and Evah were the chair family and as usual they had everything well planned and under control.

Linda Wolfe and Del Shannon were united in marriage at 4:30 p.m. on Saturday, September 3, 1977, at the Congregational Church in Angola, Indiana, and the reception followed at the Redwood Lodge in Angola. After the dinner and reception we all went back to the Inn where one of the party rooms had been set up for the square dance. Linda and Del stayed for a part of the square dance because that was a tradition. The wedding couple left for their honeymoon and the square dance continued.

Sunday evening was devoted to celebrating the 90th birthday of the patriarch of the family. Balloons had been hung from the ceiling of the Wigwam Room, a birthday cake had been baked by Sue Phillips of the host family and Mr. Meyers of Potawatomi Inn had given Ora an Indian head dress. He enjoyed being the "Big Chief" for the evening.

That was a special year and Dad was there for two more birthday parties.

In 1981, when it was the Tryon Family's year to chair, Floyd wanted to have the reunion at The Farm. We talked about it, checked out hotel locations in Linton, Sullivan and Dugger. We found an old hotel in Linton that had been remodeled and was as clean as a pin. The rooms were comparable to what we were used to and the prices were about half the cost at any other hotel we had used. So the year before – in 1980 – we wrote up an invitation – two pages worth – outlining our plans with a very tentative, very flexible schedule from Friday evening through Monday morning.

Floyd had built a screen room for the 50th Wedding Anniversary Party of Ora and Ann in 1960, but it had been taken down after everyone left. This time the farm was empty and was just being used occasionally by family and he had plans for a larger, more permanent screened structure that could be used by the family for years.

Floyd and a couple of his buddies had bought a screened room complete with a used six burner restaurant stove, a stainless steel serving counter for hot and cold foods, two old refrigerators and a three compartment restaurant type sink when they decided to try the Vigo County Fair as a new moneymaking project. When working the fair didn't prove to be very successful, the equipment, complete with its screened sides, were stored at The Farm in the large semi-truck trailer they came in.

A tear off strip at the bottom of the invitation with a yes, no, maybe, undecided, need more time to think and other suggestions was handed out and collected at the end of the 1980 reunion. The Tryon family was somewhat surprised, but overjoyed that the answer was an overwhelming yes.

This gave us a year to prepare for the 1981 reunion. There was little we could do in the winter except complete our plans on paper. By spring we went to The Farm on the weekends we could get away and Floyd laid the forms for a concrete floor in the outdoor kitchen and dining area he had planned. By the time the forms were ready for the concrete the weather was hot and the sand to pour the concrete on had been put down the week before. In the blazing sun, the sand was so hot you couldn't hold your hand on it. But the wet concrete had been ordered and the truck came, twisting and turning and growling away. That was our first lesson in concrete and we learned more than we wanted to know.

After pouring the wet concrete, the truck driver stopped in the lane on his way out and rinsed out his truck with water he had stored somewhere that would have been a great help to us if we had just known. We later learned he was a new driver so he maybe knew little more than we did about pouring concrete and we knew nothing.

We worked and worked and worked and worked and finally got the concrete all spread. By the time it was dry it was barely usable, but it lasted as long as we had The Farm and was much easier than dealing with grass and muck.

It was now time to put the screened sides on. Floyd had measured the forms for them and they were set up and bolted together. The north wall of the shelter was the south end of the garage and that worked well. Max and Marie came down from Michigan and Max ran the electricity to the shelter, helped put the roof on and a myriad of other jobs.

While Max and Marie were there, Marie pulled the bed in the boy's bedroom out to clean behind it and one foot broke through the floor to the ground. Fortunately it was less than a foot to the ground but she had to yell for Max to come and help her out of the hole. A four foot by eight foot piece of plywood was placed over the hole to reinforce the floor but it was hidden by the bed so the damage did not show.

We had had an outdoor shower at The Farm for several years. Bob, with all his Boy Scouting experiences, had built a nice shower stall out of some rigid green plastic, put a shower head in the bottom of a five gallon white plastic bucket which was attached to an overhead pulley that could be pulled up to the correct height with the correct loop in the rope which made the bucket your height, was looped over a one and one-half-inch tree limb which had been cut short and trimmed for that purpose.

When the big, old Catalpa tree the shower was built under was in bloom and the floor of the shower was covered with spent blossoms, it only added to the delight of the cool air mixed with the warm water from the overhead bucket. What a pleasure it was!! One bucket of water was plenty for one person's shower and if you were careful and had the bucket full, there would be enough water for two.

I also had a shelf a little lower than waist high put up in the smokehouse and had a line of six wash basins and a two gallon thermos of warm water so five or six people could wash up or shave at the same time.

A square dance was planned for Saturday evening, church Sunday morning at Hickory Church, workshops on Saturday morning and yard games such as croquet and badminton for

Saturday afternoon. There was a special little screened addition for the children with tree stumps for chairs and the little kitchen cabinet Dad had built for Susan and Janice in 1954. We had Play Dough and a few other things suitable for the little ones. There was fishing and swimming for adults only in the "Bath Tub" (the big deep stripper pit with clear water that Max named The Texas Bath Tub). It was always called "The Bath Tub".

Meals were all planned ahead of time and most of the food was bought locally as opposed to being brought by the people attending because the cooking facilities were all on site.

A few of the young couples did come for the week before. The worst part of that week was that it rained one day and night and it rained so hard the water ran through the shelter where families were that it made a trench. I had not thought of anything like that and for some stupid, unknown reason, I had not told or even urged them to use the house if they needed or wanted to for any reason. I have thought of that over and over and over and wished I could do it again. But as always, hindsight is 20/20.

At any rate, it was a wonderful reunion. Floyd wanted to continue having it at The Farm, but in all honesty, it was not as comfortable as we wanted. It was not the work involved - it was just not the facilities we needed.

After 15 years or so of reunions, around the early 1980's, several of the young adults had married and had children. With somewhere around 20 young children or so, we felt the management at Pokagon was not very cooperative. If children walked in the dining room, we were asked to see that they held the hand of an adult and we were reminded often to keep them quiet in the hallways. As you can imagine, it was hard to keep two or three (or more) children from breaking into a run when they saw a cousin they hadn't seen since last year!

About 1983 or 1984, I think it was Evah and Bill's year to chair the reunion, they found Camp Calvary, a religious summer camp just at the entrance to Pokagon, across Interstate 69 and thought it might be suitable for our group. The camp counselors were mostly college students and by Labor Day they needed to get back home. The Board of Directors of Camp Calvary held its annual meeting starting with lunch on Labor Day, so they were happy to rent the cabins we needed when they would otherwise be closed. The cooking staff needed to be held over for the Directors annual meeting so we decided to try it.

In some respects the facilities at the Camp were ideal and in other respects they were barely acceptable. Our family enjoyed the dining facilities, especially the willingness of the staff to cook the things we wanted them to. They still allowed us to bring fresh produce from our own gardens, home baked cobblers, cakes and desserts. We had the whole facility to ourselves at a fair price – cheaper by far than rooms and facilities at Pokagon. The downside to this arrangement was, we had to take our own linens for beds and baths and there was much to be desired in cleanliness. A cleaning staff was practically nonexistent. Games and outdoor facilities at Camp

Calvary were good and our group enjoyed boat rowing contests, nature hikes and go carts among other games.

Our food being prepared by staff at Camp Calvary was a nice change from the rush of preparation and clean up that is inevitable when you provide your own meals. It also provided a time for reflection and a brief business meeting to help keep everything flowing smoothly.

However, the lake at Camp Calvary was not clean and suitable for swimming and the younger members missed being able to swim. A few of them tried swimming, but ear infections were not worth it.

After a few years at Camp Calvary, the adults especially, were missing the comforts and amenities at Pokagon. We were aware of the expansions that had been made there and we knew it had become a first rate hotel and conference center. It was becoming more popular and we wondered if we could reestablish our position there.

In 1990 Ruth and Dick, as chairman, moved the reunion to Amish Acres at Nappanee, Indiana. It was a good location for one season and everyone enjoyed it, but lack of a headquarters location and lack of variety brought us back to Camp Calvary.

When it was next the Tryon family turn to chair the reunion, we decided to attempt to return to Pokagon. As the head of the Indiana Department of Natural Resources, Pat Ralston was in charge of all state parks. Our daughter, Janice, had gone all through high school and graduated with Pat. They had been best friends all those years. Janice called Pat and explained our position to Pat, who made an advance call to Mr. Starling, the manager at Pokagon, and when our family went there to see what reservations were available, the reunion weekend was again established. Potawatomi Inn and Pokagon have become so popular it is now necessary to make reservations two years in advance.

The Christian faith dimension was always an important part in the lives of the seven siblings of this family. We had lived through some hard times during the Great Depression and had been the recipients of some very real support provided during these times. We found the very first year we were there that the park held an outdoor church service early on Sunday mornings. We attended these. However, in keeping with our do it yourself style we soon chose to have our own service and have done so since then.

Several early programs were built around the life of Ora and Ann with hands on demonstrations. Activities such as churning butter, making soap, making bread, making noodles from scratch, growing broom corn, riving white oak shingles, coal mining and similar skills were illustrated.

Sharing has been an important and enjoyable part of all our reunions and each family has been assigned a time to share following meals. Since the time when so many of the children became old enough to speak, the Sunday evening dinner has always been saved as a time for the children all to share. Each child (that chooses to) gives a brief talk about what the past year held for them and their plans for the future. For some of the adults (such as me) it is one of the most enjoyable events of the weekend. It is also a good experience for the children in public speaking.

We have worked our way through one generation of children – my generation's grandchildren – Ora and Ann's great grandchildren – who have "graduated" from the Sunday evening talks into being included with their families. Their children – my generation's great grandchildren – Ora and Ann's great, great grandchildren – now take center stage on Sunday evenings. Although all were not present, they numbered more than 30 last year at my count. There is still room for more and new babies are arriving every year. Sunday evening will soon be teeming with little people again.

In the beginning, there seemed to be no other reunions on our weekend. Much of our family used the motel, Potawatomi Inn. Some of our families tried the cabins near the lakefront. The cabins did not prove to be very satisfactory. Some had wet carpets, none were very clean and those families had to bring their own linens for beds and bathrooms. We still used the park shelters for preparing all of our meals except the Sunday evening "dress up" dinner. It was always saved as a tribute to Dad's birthday. Although Mom was gone, Dad was there for 12 more years.

In 1981, when Janice's second child, Katie, was a baby, and we were the chair family, she got the idea of making a favor for each family. The reunion was to be at The Farm and she thought it would be nice for each family to have as a keepsake to remember the reunion. She made wreaths out of bread dough and fashioned them with leaves and pieces of dough fruit – apples, oranges, pears, etc. When they fruit and leaves were wet on the back with water and left to sit a while before they were put into the hot oven, they melded together and made a pretty and lasting favor. Everyone liked them so well the tradition of giving a favor still continues today.

Much effort has been put into making different favors and many of them are still, loved and prized by the recipients. I can look around my house today and see a quart home canning jar filled with beautiful small green beans planted, grown, picked and canned by the Ruth Johnson family, a vinegar bottle with a colorful handmade label bearing the name "Family Harvest", :Mixed Herb Vinegar and the date 1988" made and presented by the Dale Wolfe Family, a mobile made from pieces of driftwood and sea shells picked up when the Bob Wolfe Family was on vacation, a four- inch clear plastic cube with five family pictures – one on each side of the cube – given by the Evah Phillips family. I can see several more as I walk through my rooms and many more in my mind's eye. They cost only pennies to make but the time and love that went into them gives me joy every time I look at them or pick them up to dust. No matter how insignificant they seem to others, they are among my prized possessions.

A few years into the reunion, a small, handmade directory was started mostly to be sure each family had the correct addresses and telephone numbers of all members but as time went on and the numbers increased, it has developed into a much larger professional looking (easier with today's technology) book that has a wealth of information, updated each year with new births, weddings, and useful information.

As the chair family plans the weekend, menus are prepared and a list of food assignments for each meal is made and sent out a few weeks in advance. This has proven over the years to work well so that a good assortment of food fills the serving tables for each meal and the cost of the food is distributed in a more even manner relieving the chair family of much of the hardship of preparation. The main dish for Saturday and Sunday noon meals are chosen and prepared by the family in charge and that cost, along with the tableware for all meals and the rentals for the Wigwam Room, the Warming Hut, the Sunday evening banquet room and dinner are shared equally by each family. Often pizzas, fried chicken or some other "delivery food" is brought in for the Sunday lunch and with left over salads and desserts there is ample food and the burden is lessened.

Sunday afternoon has always been the designated time for family games all these years. They are also planned at the discretion of the chair family. Several of the same games are played and looked forward to each year and a few new ones appear often for variety. One that has lasted all through the years is the "egg toss". Two long lines are drawn with distance between them. Partners – father and son, father and daughter, brothers, cousins, etc. – each face one another, each holding a fresh, raw egg. The leader yells, "toss". All eggs are tossed at the same time. The leader then says, "Step back", and each player takes one step backward. If someone misses the egg and it breaks, those partners are "out". If the egg does not break, the partners can pick it up and continue to play. "Toss" and "step back" are continued until all eggs except one have broken – sometimes by hitting the ground or sometimes when caught in the hand. (A bucket of clean water and a towel are kept nearby.)

Another favorite game that has stood the test of time is "bubble blowing". All contestants use the same amount of bubble gum which is passed out by the leader, are given time to get it chewed properly, then all contestants blow when the leader says "blow". Age has no limits here. From the youngest to the oldest, when the leader says "blow", all contestants blow and the audience decides who the winner is. Several rounds are given and one young woman who blew from a very young girl still wins in her 50's. Sack races, balloon stomp, and apple peeling are other contests that have been enjoyed year after year.

Ora's birthday dinner on Sunday evening is the last formal event of the reunion. After the dinner and a very brief business meeting, the "torch" is passed to next year's chair family. Many goodbyes are said. A few families need to leave before morning. Bob and his family, who now live in Connecticut, wait until morning but leave long before anyone else is stirring.

Of those families who stay the night, most of them meet in the Potawatomi Inn's restaurant where a large table is set up for 20 or so people. As some arise and come down to the dining room the early risers are finished and some may leave. More goodbyes are said and all go home feeling refreshed and loved.

A lot has been written about family reunions in a book entitled "Secrets of Successful Family Reunions" by our brother, Robert Wolfe, Bob to us. Many ideas learned from experience are written about. For a reunion to last more than 50 years – and to grow every year – is amazing to me. Bob wrote this book a few years ago and it is still available at Amazon.com.

Next year, 2017, will be our 50th reunion with Ruth's family as chair family. The attendance is expected to surpass the 106 Wolfes at the 2015 reunion.

Chapter 24

"Wolfe Call" Newsletter

By 1980 the Wolfe family was growing and new extended family arrivals were becoming commonplace. Usually news of a pregnancy was discussed throughout the year at various family functions, and almost always everyone knew who was expecting and what the due date was.

It was that year at the family reunion that Mike saw Sara Ann Reichel, Dale and Jeanette's daughter, with a newborn and said to me, "Mom, I just saw Sara with a new baby and I didn't even know she was expecting. How could you not have told me." Frankly I couldn't believe I hadn't told him and felt certain he must have been mistaken, but eventually I had to admit it was my mistake.

Later at the reunion, Mike cornered Uncle Bob and had a conversation with him to see how this sort of thing could be avoided in the future. They decided that a better way of communication was needed and maybe a newsletter would be the solution.

Immediately Bob assumed the position of publisher and Mike and Cathy became the reporters, typesetters, and production managers. Bob's responsibility was to call and prod family members when it was time to get articles in for the newsletter. Mike and Cathy took the responsibility of all the typewriting, the titles and filling in the odd spaces with short news articles of interest to the family.

Mike had named the newsletter "The Wolfe Call" and it was published twice a year. Publication of The Wolfe Call began in 1984. The first edition was in December of that year and continued until the late 1990s. It was a big hit with everyone and was such fun to read. Every time I found a copy in my mail, I immediately stopped what I was doing until I had read every word of it.

By about the late 1990's, children were growing up and everyone was so busy it was hard to get the articles in and get the newsletter published, so publication ceased.

Mike and Cathy revived the "Wolfe Call" in 2010 when the Tryon family chaired the reunion. Since the family had grown so much larger, it seemed too much time was being spent after family meals sharing each person's events of the past year, as well as speaking to the annual "ticket". There was hardly any time left for fellowship and for individual pursuits for parents and their young children.

The Tryon clan discussed this and decided that in the interest of shortening the speeches at the reunion, each branch of the family would be asked to submit its news and events for the prior year to be published in a Reunion Edition of the "Wolfe Call". Also, by reading ahead of time of others' vacations and activities, specific topics could be focused on in sharing with each other. The thought was that we would again have time for more fellowship and for the family activities everyone had enjoyed so much in previous years.

Additionally, the Reunion Edition of the "Wolfe Call" provides a written documentation of important family events and reunion topics for the generations yet to come.

Chapter 25

Goodbye To The Wolfe Family Home

In the year 2004, the year I moved from Evansville to Crown Point, the Tryon family was chair family of our annual reunion on Labor Day weekend at Pokagon State Park. After having a problem with my back in April of that year that was still on going, my children and I decided the time had come for me to move.

It had been a hard decision to make, for Floyd and I had lived in Evansville since 1980. Floyd died March 3, 1999, but we had been happy in our home there and I was reluctant to give it up. In this 10 room house, I had room to have all the children at once and besides I felt close to Floyd there. However, the house in Evansville had a big yard with lots of trees and there was much grass to cut all summer and lots of leaves to deal with in the fall.

For the first time that spring, I felt overwhelmed by the yard work I had to do. The kids had said to me occasionally, "Mom, don't you think it is time to move?" I had always said, "No, not really. I think I will know when the time comes."

Now, I felt like the time had come and together we all agreed that Crown Point, Indiana, where our younger daughter, Janice, lived with her family would be the best place for me. Mike's Cathy had her own mother who was a year older than I was living near her and Texas, where our older daughter, Susan, lived didn't seem to be a good option. It seemed too far away from my other children and all of my brothers and sisters and their families.

I put our house on the market the first of May in 2004 and I talked to the strip mine people at Peabody Coal Company in Sullivan about leaving The Farm. For thirty seven years, since Dad had moved to Michigan from The Farm, we had kept the grass mowed and trimmed as if we were living there. We did have to hire some help to keep it up, especially after Floyd was gone, and Billy Cook whose mother I had gone all through school with, was willing to drive out from Sullivan, even if neither Floyd nor I could get there, to cut grass.

Peabody was okay with me leaving because they had someone who wanted to buy 300 acres of their land that included the property that was The Farm. We agreed to have the buildings removed because I could no longer keep them up either.

My house in Evansville sold in about two months on July 1, 2004, and I had about a month to prepare for the move. We had had lots of use of The Farm over the years and in all the years we had it, there was never a summer we were not able to keep the grass cut, until now. The whole family, at least all the ones still here, felt like we had made the right decision.

The annual visit of Juanita and Bob and Ginnie to Ruth's home in Florida was changed in 2014 to Ruth's homes in Columbus and Nashville, Indiana. The Nashville house now belongs to Ruth's daughter Jenny and most of our time was spent there.

During our visit, we took one day and Jenny drove us back to The Farm. We had not been back since the house and out buildings had been destroyed and we were all anxious as well as a little fearful, to see the place again. No buildings were left standing and it was not easy in some instances to tell where they had been.

The acreage where the house and buildings had stood had been cleared and a variety of grasses had been planted there. Bob believed they were grasses planted to bring birds to the area and suggested that it was probably used for bird hunting. Around the cleared areas, trees had been left to grow up and there was lots of underbrush that would render those acres useful for hunting animals such as deer, rabbits, etc.

Jenny is the only one who did any "roaming" around. The rest of us stood under a huge oak tree at the edge of the meadow of grasses. We talked and tried to determine where the buildings had stood while waiting for Jenny. We then walked back to the car in the lane. By the time we got back to the highway Jenny was feeling as if bugs were crawling on her and she found a small deer tick on her leg. By the time we arrived at home, we discovered we all had deer ticks. After a change of clothing, a hot shower and careful inspection of our bodies we found we were all rid of the deer ticks. We realized then what a mistake we had made by standing under the big oak tree, while Jenny roamed in the fields.

I think I can speak for all three of us, four if I include Jenny, when I say we were not disappointed. Sad, yes, we felt sad to see so many changes, but we were not disappointed. To know someone is still enjoying using the property could not be a disappointment.

Following is the story I wrote for our reunion booklet that year in 2004 and it now seems to be an appropriate ending to this family history.

I can only say I hope Ora and Ann (Mom and Dad) would be pleased with the way we, who loved The Farm so much, used it through the years and the way in which we laid it to rest (gave it up) in the end.

GOODBYE TO THE WOLFE FAMILY HOME

Here on this hallowed ground in this humble farmhouse lie the roots to this quite large contingency of the Ora and Ann Deckard Wolfe family.

Ora and Ann were married September 18, 1910, at the home of Ann's parents, George and Nancy Robertson Deckard. They "took up" housekeeping in a small rental home north of State Road 54, but about three years and one child later they bought this house – then a three room farmhouse on four acres of land adjoining Ann's Father's property. He later deeded this 30 acre plot to Ann as one-half of her inheritance. He gave each of his six living children 60 acres of land and Ann's other 30 acres were a bit north and west of this plot.

In this house seven of Ora and Ann's eight children were born. Dale was born June 21, 1911, in the first little house and the others were born here. George Edward was born in 1913; Evah, October 22, 1916; James, October 5, 1918; Juanita, August 20, 1920; Max, April 25, 1923; Robert, December 30, 1925 and seven years later Ruth came along on January 23, 1933.

George Edward died of scarlet fever in 1918 at the tender age of five. Dale and Evah both contracted the fever but James, only about two months old and nursing, escaped it. Dale was left with a heart murmur but Evah at only two years of age had a much more severe case. She recovered completely but lost all her hair and had to learn to walk again. The only bright spot in this difficult time was that her hair came back curly!

The six older children were reared in these three rooms until 1932 when the house was enlarged to six rooms. Ora and Ann bought a three room house that sat on a small acreage adjoining their property to the south and tore it down to use for the remodeling – except for one room that was kept intact and moved. This room became the "smokehouse" and was placed over the cellar that was dug and lined with brick to accommodate the size of the room. All milk from the cows was strained into gallon crocks and carried down the six or eight steps into the cellar each morning and evening, only to be carried up again as it was used. Canned garden produce and canned fruits filled the shelves that lined the walls, and other produce such as apples, potatoes, pumpkins, turnips, etc. were stored in baskets and boxes on the cellar floor.

For Ora and Ann's 50th wedding anniversary in September, 1960, the six rooms were refurbished and a construction company was hired to remodel and enlarge the living room. With much help from Floyd and Juanita, Ruth and others as they could, floors were sanded and finished and every room was repapered and painted and new carpet was laid in the living room. That paper and carpet was never replaced.

All seven children and their young families came home to The Farm for the celebration. Five small house trailers were rented and placed in a semi-circle in a small sassafras grove to the west of the house (Ora ran electricity to each of them), and Ruth with her husband and one baby and Max stayed in the house with Ora and Ann. Floyd and his friends erected a cook shack in the vicinity of the trailers large enough for cooking and eating for the 30 people in attendance.

Ann died March 23, 1968, at age 78 and Ora moved to Flushing, Michigan in August of that same year to be near three of his seven children. A few years earlier, Peabody Coal Company had bought the 64 acres from Ora and Ann with the stipulation that they could live there as long as they wanted to. At the time of Ora's move, Juanita bought the buildings back from the coal company to be used by the family for as long as they wanted them. In May of 1980 Ora died at the age of 92.

With Ora and Ann both gone, the 13th Family Reunion brought most of the family together again on Labor Day Weekend, 1981, at The Farm. With Juanita and Floyd's family in charge and with the help of their children and other family members and friends, a large screened shelter was built adjoining the back of the garage. It was furnished with two refrigerators, a six-burner restaurant stove, a large deep triple-sectioned restaurant sink, stainless steel steam table and enough tables and chairs for everyone. All used equipment of course. A large brick fireplace on the south side of the shelter provided warmth when the weather was cool and a place to roast marshmallows in the evenings.

On Saturday afternoon the family hosted an open house for all relatives and long-time friends and that same evening a square dance was held on the lawn in front of the shelter. As a family, the large group attended services at Old Hickory Church on Sunday morning. On Sunday evening a few families who had driven many miles to attend took their leave and by noon on Monday the remaining families had dispersed to their homes in various states leaving Juanita and Floyd sad to have them gone, but happy to have been able to help provide the place for this wonderful get together.

During the years from Ora's move in 1968 through 2004 this old home place was used for many Deckard cousins and Wolfe reunions and for a multitude of family gatherings enjoyed by young and old alike.

By the end of 2004, Dale, Evah, James and Max had all passed away and on August 15, 2004, Juanita (I) (having lost Floyd in March of 1999) moved from Evansville to Crown Point, Indiana, to be near two of her three children.

Also in the summer of 2004, the land the house and out buildings were on was sold to Jon Bobbitt of Sullivan, Indiana, who graciously gave consent for the family to continue to use the property. Since Juanita's (my) move from southern Indiana she was no longer close enough to help care for the place or to host reunions there. So the summer of 2005 was the first time in the 37 years since Ora's move to Michigan that the grass around all the buildings had not been kept cut and trimmed. Hence "the vultures" had come in and much damage had been done to the house and buildings.

In July 2005 Mr. Bobbitt sold 150 acres of his tract, including the parcel our buildings were on to Darin Cissell of rural Sullivan. Mr. Cissell was concerned about the vacant building being used by riff-raff since a bag of marijuana had been found in the lane. So in lieu of the farmhouse being used by tramps and druggies, permission was granted by the Wolfe family for the buildings to be destroyed. That was accomplished by the end of September, 2005.

So, as we say goodbye to the old Wolfe Family Homestead, this is a brief history of this beloved farmhouse, so loved and revered by the entire Ora and Ann Wolfe Family."

This is our final goodbye to The Wolfe Family Farm

In Conclusion

With this family history we have found that our ancestors were a hardworking, determined people who had faith in God and maintained strong family values. Although we have not concentrated on the generations before us, we have learned some interesting things about them.

Instead, since we personally (Ruth, Bob and Nita) go back almost one hundred years, we have concentrated more on our own lives as children and the years we know about first hand.

It does not matter what I have done – nor what Ruth has done – nor what anyone else has done - on this project. Bob has been the driving force behind this family history, always, long before any of it became a reality. Bob has been the push behind me when I became weary or bogged down by the many interruptions that kept taking precedence along the way.

Each year since the early 1950's when he wrote the outline for this book, Bob added more information to the box that has become my constant companion for inspiration and for information. (The fact that that big box and its contents have kept my kitchen messy looking all this time is really not important.)

In closing I want the entire Ora and Ann Deckard Wolfe Family to know – if nothing else – the writing and putting together of this family history has been a labor of love. I myself at 96 years of age, think it is remarkable that it is really finished. On my part there were many interruptions - a heart attack, a bout with pneumonia, a tiny stroke (the doctor's words) - but I need to tell you that even then, I really never doubted that it would be finished.

On our annual trek to Florida in February of 2013 when Ruth, Jenny, Bob, Ginnie and I were gathered around Ruth's dining table, where we had long talk's daily and drank endless cups of hot tea after we finished Jenny's delicious meals (she was always our chief cook), the subject of the family history came up. Ruth made the remark that she, for one, was ready to get serious about it, and she thought it should be my "job" to write it. I quickly said, "Oh my goodness no, I couldn't do that."

Everyone else seemed to be in agreement with Ruth, and the more I thought about it and mulled it over in my mind, the more I began to think – well maybe I could do it. One thing for sure, I would never know if I didn't try. So, before the week was over, I finally said, "Okay, I'll do it."

Bob had already put together a veritable "mountain" of material over the years. He had written the outline in 1957 and that was the outline I used. All of this information was at my disposal.

Bob brought the large box packed with somewhere between 150 and 200 manila file folders of information to the Annual Family Reunion that Labor Day weekend, and Janice and Jim brought it from the reunion to my kitchen, plus a few extra boxes of old letters and other information. That big box still sits under the small desk in my kitchen so I can get to it easily. I expect even my Kinship Group, who meets often around my big kitchen table, will be glad to see the folders all put back in proper order and sent back to their rightful owner.

I spent several days pouring over the boxes of information including letters, newspaper clippings, copies, articles about family members – pulling out things I could use. I kept my head buried in my boxes of pictures for a few days, pulling out pictures to be checked through.

I owe so many thanks to so many people who helped me along the way and whom this book would have been impossible without.

First – thanks to my brother Bob for all the information he collected over the years – information that would have been impossible to gather - or even to remember - at this time. Also for all the "short stories", vignettes, he wrote through the years while the ideas were still fresh in his mind and for his writings of some of his knowledge and memories of things that were so much better than mine. Thanks to Bob for the hours he spent talking to me when I called, even though he didn't feel like talking and for urging me onward, ever onward, when I didn't feel like writing.

I also need to thank Bob's wife, Ginnie, for her incredible patience with my handwritten pages that needed to be deciphered and typed. She did the lion's share of the typing and to my sister, Ruth, and her helper Nancy who had a lot of my handwriting to unscramble too. Thanks to Ruth for her encouragement and her help in so many other ways.

Thank you to my favorite (only) daughter-in-law Cathy for her knowledge and especially for her patience with me as she transcribed and tried to teach me about files, folders, about "save" and "save as" and lots of other terms I was not familiar with – and really didn't want to know about – but needed to know. She was always there and incredibly patient when I called from home for help and thanks again to Cathy for never seeming to get upset about how messy I kept her kitchen table when I was at their home.

Most of my family was in Colorado for Timmy and Emily's wedding celebration when I had the heart attack and they all helped me through that. We arrived in Boulder on Thursday evening and the heart attack happened promptly on Friday afternoon, so I missed all the festivities. However, thanks to Timmy and Emily for filming all the events and bringing them to the hospital so I could see what fun they all had. That was almost as good as being there, maybe even better, for I could just lie quietly in my hospital bed and enjoy their parties.

Kris and Ava, Kim and Erin and little Van Mac, Ryan and Jenn, and Greg all had to leave before I was out of the hospital, but I did so enjoy having them close at hand at that time. Thanks to Katie Mac for coming by every evening after work and sitting with me in the warm sunshine while I recouped. And thanks to Lauriebelle (Lauren) who was close enough in Boulder to be my own personal nurse (and hair dresser) all the while I was in Colorado. Thanks to Lindsay, Kyle and Jared for your many phone calls – and to Katie K who said through her squishy tears, "Now Grandma, don't you go and die on me out there.", and I promised I wouldn't.

Thank you to Susan, Janice and Mike for renting a second house so that we could all stay together when I left the hospital until I was able to fly home, for the wonderful food you all prepared that tasted so good to me after the hospital food and for all the time you willingly spent with me when there were other places you needed to be. Thank you Timmy and Emily for the delicious food you brought by that house and shared with all of us.

Last, but not least, thanks to all my nieces and nephews who were so helpful by sending me bits and pieces of information about their parents that I didn't have access to for this book when I needed it. Your attitudes and your willingness to help brought joy to my heart. Thanks Stephen for continuing the search until you found Evah's handwritten notes for me.

As we close this part of the family story, I hope that we have accomplished - at least in part - what we set out to do. We hoped to provide an understanding of the family heritage, to describe the lifestyle and challenges of the first generation (Ora and Ann), to document the strong bonds and the love that united the seven children of the second generation throughout life's pursuits, and to provide a family resource for the generations yet to come.

I take great solace in my beliefs that divine guidance, hard work and unconditional love give this family the strength to face life's most challenging moments with the same determination and perseverance that Ora and Ann did on that small family farm in southern Indiana. Theirs was a courage that created the certainty that God's blessings are large enough and strong enough to encompass all, if we but follow His precepts.

Addendum

Robert W. Wolfe
1925-2016

My Adventure by Uncle Bob Wolfe
For Family Reunion 2016

Due to the return of his prostate cancer, Bob was not able to attend the Annual Family Reunion in September of 2016. This was the first reunion in 49 years that he had not attended. His family was the chair family in 2016 and the "ticket" they chose was "A Great Adventure". Bob wrote a bit about his great adventures with his family then told of his greatest adventure that started as a dream many years before.

This dream which he lived to see to fruition was the family story which he had never stopped collecting information for. The book had not gone to press at the time of his death, but the manuscript was finished and he was able to hold a completed manuscript in his hands, read it and comment on it. For that, his whole family is thankful.

This addendum has been added as a tribute to him after his death. He may not have been the author, but he was certainly the driving force behind it through most of the years of his adult life.

It would never have happened without Bob!

Following is the adventure "ticket" he wrote for the 49th Wolfe Family Reunion in 2016.

Bob's Ticket:

Such an opportunity to think about the adventures we have had: Boundary Water Canoe Country with three children 5, 7 ½ and 10 with two 85 pound canoes, four portages for one week, one week on bicycles in Lancaster County, Pennsylvania; two weeks hiking and canoeing on Isle Royale; Camp LaConte in Great Smokies National Park all with family and so many others, all of which were with family and great fun.

However, all these are overshadowed by one that started as a dream 35 or 40 years ago and has required effort of several the last three years. That is the writing of "The Life Story of Ora and Ann Wolfe". Make no mistake Aunt Nita is the author. It is a much better, longer, more complete and more accurate book than I envisioned 35 or 40 years ago. Aunt Nita did the difficult work of an author of arranging and pulling details together. Both Aunt Ruth and I were privileged to serve as her research assistants. I'm not sure I would rate it as fun – more like joy, complete satisfaction. To sit with siblings and remember life – not always good but how it shaped us – and to record how we as a family seemed to cope provides real pleasure.

For us, we miss the other four. As a reward, the idea was resurrected in the Johnsons' condominium in Florida, brought to fruition in the next two years at Jenny's comfortable home in Brown County, Indiana, and in celebration at our humble apartment at CVOC. All of this made better by Jennifer's TLC. It truly has been a great and moving adventure for me.

You will soon have a copy of the book in hand. As you read it, I want you to think of two things.

1. How did these strange happenings to one large, rowdy family in southern Indiana cause the bonding that has resulted in 49 annual reunions?

2. If you enjoy this story, think of how you and the next generation can make this happen for your grandchildren and other progeny.

I recognize that our present family narrative is not necessarily the one that fits the needs of the younger generations. Each generation has its own challenges to face.

Sorry not to give this message in person. By the blessings of the Lord I have attended 48 of these reunions; Ginnie and I have had 67 years of marriage and are both 90 years of age. We pray that you all are as blessed as we have been.

"Uncle Bob Wolfe"

Robert W. Wolfe's Final Illness and Death

Shortly after the manuscript for this book was completed but before it went to press, Robert W. Wolfe (Bob), Ruth's and my only living sibling, succumbed to cancer and went to spend his eternal life in heaven.

Bob was diagnosed with prostate cancer in 2009 and decided against most of the usual and conventional treatments for cancer. He did consent to the doctor's recommendation of a hormone shot every three months for about a year.

He changed his diet to what he had read and believed to be a better course of treatment. This diet consisted of about 80 or 85% raw foods, 15% to 20% cooked foods, and no meat, cheese or eggs.

Since Ginnie, his wife, decided to go on the diet with him, it was not particularly hard and fortunately they could choose foods they both liked. It amounted to lots of salads, lots of greens, a baked potato or other hot cooked vegetables a day and before a year was up, the cancer was in remission.

This of course was good news, but Bob relaxed only slightly on his diet. He added some fish occasionally. Bob was again diagnosed with cancer a second time in 2016. Of course Bob went back to the original plan, but not with the same success this time. By now, he was nearly 90 years old and his body did not respond in the same way.

This new cancer was in an inoperable location in his body, so removing it was out of the question. When it refused to respond to his natural treatments, he relented toward a few of the more conventional ones. They prescribed a very powerful drug and a round of 25 treatments of radiation which he chose to do in order to help curtail the growth.

Bob and Ginnie had moved in 2013 to a retirement village in Connecticut, Covenant Village of Cromwell (CVOC) that offered around-the-clock medical care in an area known as Pilgrim Manor. When Bob's condition worsened, after five days in the hospital, he was moved into The Manor since Ginnie felt she could no longer give him the full time care he needed. The Manor was a six minute walk from their living area and Ginnie was able to visit daily, as often as she could and keep tabs on Bob.

One of the activities at CVOC that Bob and Ginnie had enjoyed so much was the big garden that was divided into small plots and gardeners were allotted two or more spots if they felt they could take care of them. Linda and Ken, two of Bob's children who both live about 45 minutes from Cromwell, made a habit of visiting as often as they could, helping with the garden. Linda, who did not work outside the home, could come about once a week and she said it was one of her most enjoyable activities. Karen, who lives in Hawaii, could only help at vacation time.

The spring of 2014, Bob was given four plots that one of the other gardeners had had to give up, so he and his little crew of wife, daughter and son kept it up beautifully. They enjoyed much produce from it and were able to provide fresh vegetables for the neighbor who had given him his plots.

Bob had planted a Canadice grapevine the spring of 2015 that had about 35 beautiful large bunches of grapes that were about half grown when Ruth and Jenny invited me to go to Connecticut to see Bob and Ginnie in July, after Bob had made the decision not to go to the 49th Wolfe Family Reunion. He was not able to visit for long periods of time, so we kept our visits short and enjoyed them immensely.

Bob walked through the garden with his cane and I walked dragging an old chair behind me (so I could sit if I needed to,) as we talked about the garden and it's one plot of Ginnie's flowers. Bob enjoyed explaining about the grapes. What a delightful time it was and what a beautiful and delicious luncheon Ginnie and Linda served us – almost totally from the garden. However a big disappointment for Bob and everyone involved was that just when Bob deemed them ready to pick, the squirrels and/or other foragers, (they didn't see it happen), moved in and in one evening, cleaned the vines. They got every grape! Imagine the shock!!

How Bob loved that garden! As Ken told us in his beautiful remarks and memories at Bob's funeral, he was still teaching about these grapes just three weeks before. Ken said in his remarks: "Three weeks ago we were discussing how to start grapes from "slips" (small sections of grape vines) and I asked a question Dad thought I should know. Lying there in his hospital bed, he threw up his hands and said, "HEAVEN SAKES FELLA I am glad you asked"…and then proceeded to draw a picture of how to cut a vine for replanting." I'll just bet Ken will never in his life time forget that! – and will plant a slip from that grapevine in Bob's CVOC garden in both his and Linda's gardens in the spring of 2017.

Bob's family planned a beautiful funeral service for him at Union Congregational Church, the church he and Ginnie had belonged to and attended for so many years in Ellington before making their move to smaller quarters. The visitation the evening before the funeral service was attended by many of the friends they had made throughout the years and the funeral was attended by many old friends who spoke of their memories of Bob and his devotion to God and the church.

During the service each of Bob's three children spoke of their remembrance of a wonderful father and each of Bob's siblings was represented by a family member who spoke memories of their uncle. Linda, the oldest of the three children, remembered her father as a great man and an amazing father. She spoke briefly of the many trips he planned for the family when they were children and into their teens. They tent camped, they canoed, they biked, they hiked, and they back packed and slept under the stars, she said.

Linda told how her father used these trips as teaching lessons, as well as his lessons in the garden. She remembered even as a young child, dragging the watering can behind her as she walked down the rows helping him plant and listening to him talk – many hours of talking and planting. She made a sign for his garden that read:

> *The kiss of the sun for pardon,*
> *The song of the bird for mirth,*
> *One is nearer to heaven in a garden,*
> *Than anywhere else on earth.*

Going on to mention her father's strong faith in God and his faithfulness and work in his church over the years. Linda spoke of Bob and Ginnie's 67 years of marriage and their strong commitment to each other and the great role model they were – not only for their children but for many other people also. She closed her remarks with Bob's great love of poetry and told how many of the gifts such as graduation, birthdays, weddings, etc. from their mother and father were accompanied by poems Bob wrote for the occasion.

Following Linda's remarks was Ken, offering heartfelt thanks from the family to the audience for attending Bob's services. He then spoke of wrestling with his thoughts, wondering what of them to share and how to share them. As he read a blog he and Bob both enjoyed reading, he finds it is a review of the book, "The Road" by Cormac McCarthy. It is a story of a father and son in an apocalyptic world with the father teaching the son to know right from wrong and how to "carry the fire", to survive and still live a good life. They "carry the fire" as a light for them and to pass it on to others.

Ken realized as he read, that this is exactly who his father was and how he lived his life. Ken explained how his father "carried the fire of Faith" by living it in his family, by personal prayers and study and by service to his fellow man. Bob "carried the fire of health" by exercise and eating the best diet he knew how. He "carried the fire" for a robust outdoor life by fishing, hunting, hiking, canoeing, scouting and gardening. Ken remembered his dad "carrying the fire" of poetry and literature memorizing and reciting and teaching his children and grandchildren to do the same – Ken said Bob "carried the fire" of business and entrepreneurship by holding down a long career with a large corporation and when that ended and he retired, he started a machinery business which he invited Ken and his wife Barbara to join him in.

Ken ended his remarks by explaining how his father "carried the fire" of family - his immediate family as well as his extended family. Bob was responsible for the beginning of the Wolfe Family Reunion that met for the 49th annual reunion on Labor Day weekend of 2016.

Ken ended his remarks by saying, "It did not matter if we were walking side by side in the stripper hills of Southern Indiana watching his dog lock up on a point, fishing for bluegill off the spawning beds or with our fly rods or eating popcorn on a Sunday evening before his fireplace, Dad was always the same. He wanted the best for his family in every way and he usually had some good ideas he was willing to share – always trying to help us "carry the fire" in our own lives and to pass it on to others. In my heart of hearts, the strongest memory of him is walking with him – in the fields – by the streams or pushing a wheelbarrow for him in the garden."

Ken said, "Thank you Dad, for "carrying the fire" of a faithful, strenuous and balanced life and for teaching me that I could do the same – thank you Mom for being such a good partner for Dad."

Several members of Bob and Ginnie's church family spoke of Bob's work in the church and his leadership qualities, as well as his capacity for friendship and helping others. All of Bob's nieces and nephews waited at the microphone to speak of how Uncle Bob had affected their lives in special ways and how much they appreciated having him in their lives.

Bob was truly a special person. He had a wonderful capacity to remember back into our childhood and to bring those memories forward. As I wrote in my brief remark, "Bob was a wonderful brother and one of the best friends I ever had."

His funeral service was brought to an end by his daughter, Karen, who remarked that her father got his insight from many places. She emphasized that by reading one of his favorite poems entitled:

"Abou Ben Adhem"

Abou Ben Adhem (may his tribe increase!)
Awoke one night from a deep dream of peace,

And saw, within the moonlight in his room,
Making it rich, and like a lily in bloom,
An Angel writing in a book of gold:
Exceeding peace had made Ben Adhem bold,
And to the Presence in the room he said,
"What writest thou?" The Vision raised its head
And with a look made of all sweet accord
Answered, "The names of those who love the Lord."
"And is mine one?" said Abou. "Nay, not so,"
Replied the Angel. Abou spoke more low,
But cheerily still; and said, "I pray thee, then,
Write me as one that loves his fellow-men."

The Angel wrote, and vanished. The next night
It came again with a great wakening light,
And showed the names whom love of God had blessed,
And, lo! Ben Adhem's name led all the rest!

Karen sent me a few of her beautiful thoughts to share: *"Here is the "share" I would have liked to say; it really wasn't formed until after the service:*

Parenting is an interesting undertaking, we say what we do is for our children. However, whatever we give, whatever we teach, comes back into our own lives. Dad and I didn't see eye to eye for many years. Not because we didn't love each other, maybe because of those parts of ourselves that were similar, maybe because we both have a hard time opening up. However Dad never gave up on me, and I never gave up on him.

Over the last year, we had an opportunity not just to make amends, but to form an understanding and to give each other the love and blessings that I wish could have been achieved earlier. The weekly support Mom and Dad gave me while I was in Korea was a steady guide and pleasure to share as adults. I felt I received his blessing before he passed and it is the greatest gift a parent can bestow.

Thanks for listening – Kare"

When the funeral service was over, a beautiful luncheon was served in the church Fellowship Hall for friends and family. After the luncheon the immediate family and other family members who had not yet left for home attended the interment service at the cemetery in Middlebury where Bob's ashes were laid to rest.

Gallery

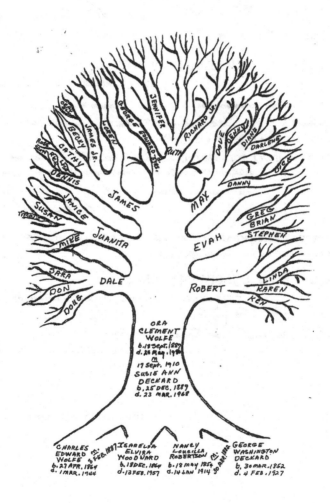

This family tree was made by Juanita as a Christmas present for her siblings.

Ora Clement Wolfe

To

Susie Ann Deckard } ss:

BE IT REMEMBERED, That on this ....17.... day

of ..*September*.., 19*0*0., the following

Marriage License was issued, to wit:

INDIANA, TO WIT: SULLIVAN COUNTY, ss:

TO ALL WHO SHALL SEE THESE PRESENTS—GREETING:

KNOW YE, That any person empowered by law to solemnize Marriages, is hereby authorized to join together as Husband and Wife, *Ora Clement Wolfe* and *Susie Ann Deckard* *and for so doing this shall be his sufficient authority.*

IN TESTIMONY WHEREOF, I, *Arthur E. DeBaun*, *Clerk of the Sullivan Circuit Court, hereunto subscribe my name, and affix the seal of*

(L. S.)   *said Court, at Sullivan, this* 17 *day of* *September* 1900.

Arthur E. DeBaun

Clerk.

BE IT FURTHER REMEMBERED, That on this 24" *day of* *Sept.* 190*0. *the following certificate was filed in my office, to wit:*

INDIANA, TO WIT: SULLIVAN COUNTY.

THIS CERTIFIES, That I joined in marriage, as Husband and Wife,

Ora Clement Wolfe and *Susie Ann Deckard*

on the 18 *day of* *September* 190*0*

Rev. C. O. Johnson

Marriage license of Ora Clement Wolfe and Susie Ann Deckard

George W. Deckard
—TO—
Nancy L. Robertson

Be it Remembered, That on this 28 day of March, 1882 the following Marriage License was issued, to-wit:

INDIANA, TO-WIT: SULLIVAN COUNTY, SS.

TO ALL WHO SHALL SEE THESE PRESENTS, GREETING:

Know Ye, That any person empowered by law to solemnize Marriages, is hereby authorized to join together as Husband and Wife, *George W. Deckard* and *Nancy L. Robertson* and for so doing, this shall be his sufficient authority.

In Testimony Whereof, I, *Thomas J. Mann*, Clerk of the Sullivan Circuit Court, hereunto subscribe my name and affix the seal of said Court. at Sullivan, this 28 day of March, 1882

Thomas J. Mann clk

Be it Further Remembered, That on this 30 day of March, 1882, the following certificate was filed in my office, to-wit:

INDIANA, TO-WIT: SULLIVAN COUNTY.

This Certifies, That I joined in Marriage as Husband and Wife, *George W Deckard* and *Nancy L. Robertson*; on the 30 day of March, 1882

Thomas Burton

Marriage license of George Washington Deckard and Nancy Lucilla Robertson

SULLIVAN COUNTY, INDIANA

RECORD OF BIRTH

𝕿𝖍𝖎𝖘 𝕮𝖊𝖗𝖙𝖎𝖋𝖎𝖊𝖘,   that a record of birth is on file,

Bearing the name of .... --------Deckard ....

Child of .... George Deckard and ---------Robertson ....

Born in .....Cass Township................................on ....December 25,........ year 1889

            Joseph E. Weeks M.D.

_ - SEAL _   County Health Comm.

                    Dugger, Ind.   Date ....July 7,.............. 19..76
Date recorded   January 15, 1890

Book.....H-2.....Page........31.....

Ann Deckard's birth certificate before she was named

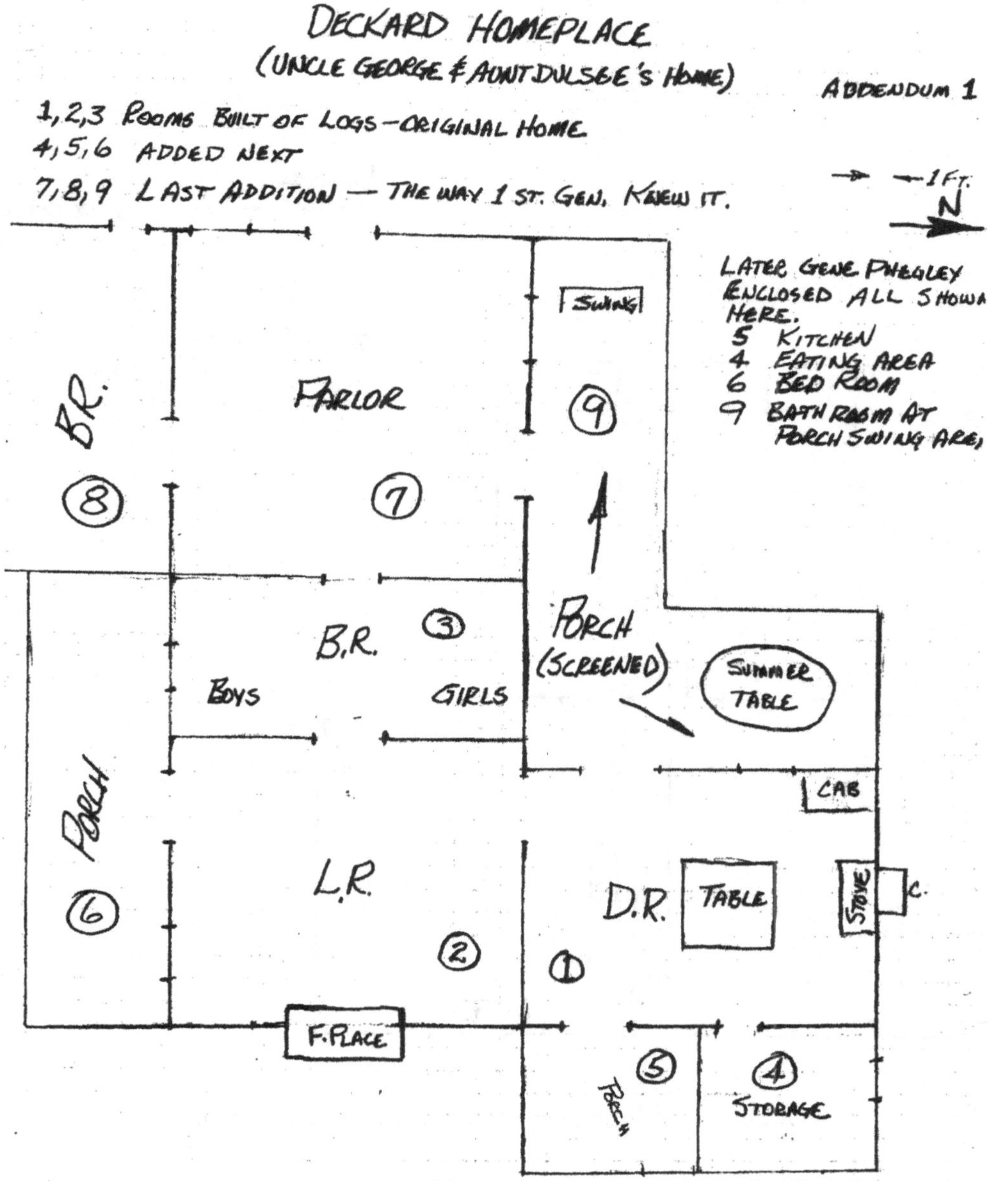

Outline of Deckard homeplace

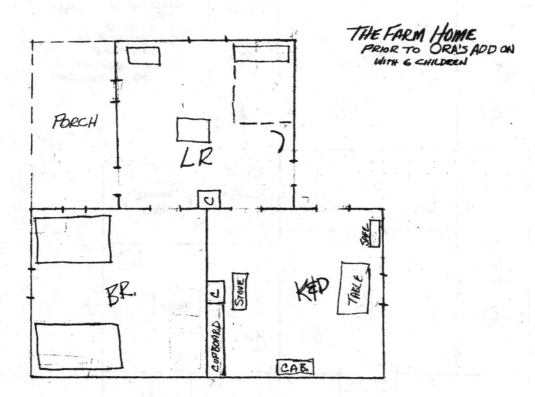

N. ← → 1 FT. ADDENDUM 2

THE FARM HOME
PRIOR TO ORA'S ADD ON
WITH 6 CHILDREN

Drawing of Wolfe farm floor plan when three rooms

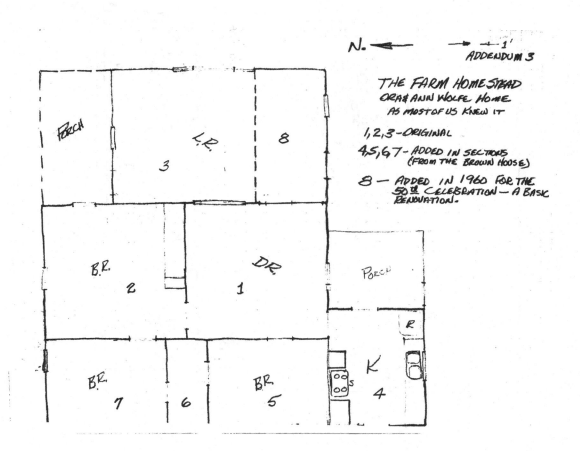

N. ← → 1'
ADDENDUM 3

THE FARM HOMESTEAD
ORA & ANN WOLFE HOME
AS MOST OF US KNEW IT

1, 2, 3 – ORIGINAL
4, 5, 6, 7 – ADDED IN SECTIONS
(FROM THE BROWN HOUSE)

8 – ADDED IN 1960 FOR THE
50th CELEBRATION – A BASIC
RENOVATION.

PORCH

L.R.
3

8

B.R.
2

D.R.
1

PORCH

R

B.R.
7

6

B.R.
5

S

K
4

Drawing of Wolfe farm floor plan after three more rooms were added

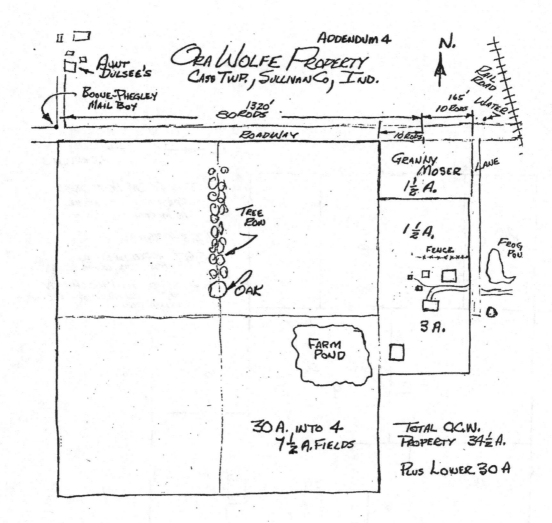

ADDENDUM 4

Ora Wolfe Property
Cass Twp., Sullivan Co., Ind.

N.

RAIL ROAD

Aunt Dulsee's

Boone-Phegley Mail Box

1320'
80 RODS

165' WATER
10 RODS

ROADWAY

10 RODS

GRANNY MOSER
1½ A.

LANE

1½ A.

FENCE

TREE ROW

FROG POND

OAK

FARM POND

3 A.

30 A. INTO 4
7½ A. FIELDS

TOTAL O.C.W.
PROPERTY 34½ A.

PLUS LOWER 30 A

FOR LOWER 30 A.: CONTINUE W. PAST BOONE-PHEGLEY MAIL BOX ON R. & STYLE ON L. FIRST DIP WAS BOTTOM OF HOLLOWAY HILL WHICH MARKED THE S.E. CORNER OF PROPERTY.

General overview of Wolfe Property from county road down our lane

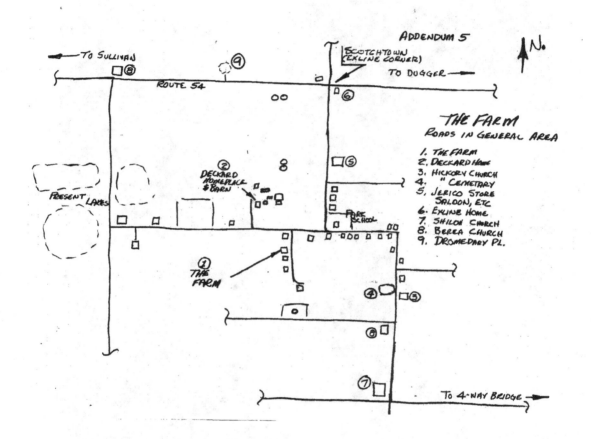

A drawing showing the location of many of the places mentioned
in this story and their relationship to the farm property

Portrait of Ed and Elvira Wolfe

Portrait of George and Nancy Deckard

Ed and Elvira's house on the hill with barn at base of hill

Wolfe Family Portrait. Back row: Ernie, Ora, Walter. Front row: May, Ed, Elvira.

George Edward, Dale and Evah

Ora Wolfe Family about 1936. Back row: Juanita, Jim, Dale
Evah. Front row: Bob, Ora, Ruth, Ann, Max.

Family picture taken at the 50ᵗʰ Wedding Anniversary with
everyone assuming the same spots as in the 1936 photo.

Spouses Picture taken at the 50th Anniversary. Back row: Floyd Tryon, Patricia Demaree Wolfe, Jeanette Macauley Wolfe, William Phillips. Front row: Virginia Whitsell Wolfe, Ora, Richard Johnson, Ann.

Ora and Ann outside the farm house with the kitchen window in the background.

Family picture taken during World War II. Back row: Bob, Jim, Dale, Max. Front row: Ora, Evah, Ruth, Juanita, Ann.

Ann's sisters with their husbands. Left to right: Cornie and Tilda Willis, Frank and Ina Creager, George and Dulsee Boone, Ora and Ann Wolfe.

Persons attending a Robertson Reunion held at the Sullivan City Park. Ruth is fourth from
left in first row and Ora on the end of first row. Uncle Bob and Aunt Eva Robertson are
in middle row, fourth and fifth from left and Ann is third from the right in middle row.

Picture of Farm home about the time of the 50th Anniversary

Gravestone of George Washington and Nancy Lucilla Deckard in Hickory Cemetery

About the Author

Juanita Tryon was born into a rural farming family in Southern Indiana in 1920. Her parents, Ora and Ann Wolfe, were of scant modest means, raising a family through the most difficult of economic times known as The Great Depression.

The fifth child in a family of eight children, she was educated in a two room school house not far from her homestead. She was an exemplary student and enjoyed reading literature, poetry and creative writing. In 1938 she graduated from Union High School located in Dugger, Indiana. When she was 18 years old, she moved to Terre Haute, Indiana, and met her husband Floyd Tryon. They married two and one half years later and together they had three children.

While raising their children, she became active in her church and in numerous community service organizations. She served as President of the W.S. Rea Elementary School PTA, Secretary of the Women's Society of Christian Service in her church and served in leadership positions of nearly every service organization she belonged to. In 1967, she was recruited to join the staff of the Terre Haute Tribune Star newspaper as the assistant society page editor of the Terre Haute Star and later became the editor of both the Food Page and the Women's Page, covering all social events, women issues, and lifestyle events in the Terre Haute area. She served in that position until her retirement in 1980.

Her strong Christian faith, dedicated work ethics and devotion to family has given inspiration to her family members and the many friends she has known. Inspired by her brother, Robert Wolfe and her sister, Ruth Johnson and with their love and support she authored "A Legacy of Love", the story of the Ora and Ann Wolfe Family.